Praise for *Her Last Death*

"A brave account of growing up with a glamorous, charismatic, compulsively lying and drug-addicted mother . . . [narrated] with an unflinching eye and a winning dispassion."
—Pam Houston, O, *The Oprah Magazine*

"A bracing memoir about growing up rich and glamorous with a savagely inappropriate mother . . . For every breathless tale of outrageousness, Sonnenberg simultaneously struggles, with cool gravity, to grapple with what it means to be the daughter of a liar."
—Karen Valby, *Entertainment Weekly*

"Compulsively readable . . . Sonnenberg demonstrates a hard-won self-awareness. . . . This scrupulously unsentimental writer saves her keenest narrative powers for conveying her mother's increasingly erratic behavior and the heartbreak of a young girl's innocence eclipsed."
—Megan O'Grady, *Vogue*

"Painful in its truth, searing in its candor, [*Her Last Death*] makes for compelling if oftentimes disturbing reading."
—June Sawyers, *San Francisco Chronicle*

"[A] beautifully observed memoir."
—Kim Hubbard, *People* (Critic's Choice)

"The wonder of this memoir is that the author survived her traumatic childhood and found a way of turning her memories into a fiercely observed, fluently written book. . . . Ms. Sonnenberg . . . [is] immensely gifted."

—Michiko Kakutani, *The New York Times*

"Powerful . . . searing."

—John Marshall, *Seattle Post-Intelligencer*

"A mesmerizing new memoir."

—Alexandra Jacobs, *The New York Observer*

"Raw and searing . . . an indelible memoir."

—*Elle*

"Enthralling."

—*OK! Weekly*

"Gorgeously written, Sonnenberg's transcendent book isn't just a gripping read—it's profound art."

—Caroline Leavitt, *Dame* magazine

"Provocative . . . Elegantly structured, compellingly rendered . . . Sonnenberg's story . . . tantalizes."

—*Missoula Independent*

"One of the best memoirs to come on the scene since Jeannette Walls's *The Glass Castle* . . . Precise, unsparing and luminous prose. Heartbreaking yet wickedly entertaining . . . Highly recommended."

—*Library Journal* (starred review)

"A deeply personal account . . . Tragic but arresting—a worthy companion to Simone de Beauvoir's and Vivian Gornick's explorations of the complicated mother-daughter dynamic."

—*Kirkus Reviews*

"Moving . . . a testament to . . . resilience."

—*Booklist*

"Riveting, honest, sexy, smart."

—Rosie O'Donnell

"All mothers are con artists on occasion. But what if yours is a compulsive liar and a serial charmer who accuses you of seducing her boyfriend and who seduces you with cocaine—when you're twelve? Susanna Sonnenberg's was a booby-trapped childhood, of which she writes unnervingly and with crisp control. Her pages are remarkable as much for their style as for their intelligence; the portrait is indelible."

—Stacy Schiff, author of *Véra (Mrs. Vladimir Nabokov)*

"*Her Last Death* is an emotional thriller. It is a manual for men and smart, searching individuals of any age or economic level. It is a disturbing story, yet at the end you might feel like cheering. It is a beautiful, beautiful book and I plan to give it to my nearest and dearest."

—Frank McCourt, author of *Angela's Ashes* and *Teacher Man*

"An irresistible book that is shimmering with life and the portrait of a glorious, frenzied, seductive woman who of necessity has been left, along with Susanna Sonnenberg's young womanhood, behind. Her mother."

—James Salter, author of *Last Night* and *Burning the Days*

"Riveting, sexy, smart and brazenly honest, *Her Last Death* is a memoir that demands and rewards total immersion. I couldn't put it down, didn't want to, and was sorry when it was over. Susanna Sonnenberg is a wonderful writer, and this is a marvelous debut."

—John Burnham Schwartz, author of *Reservation Road*

HER LAST DEATH

A Memoir

Susanna Sonnenberg

SCRIBNER

New York   London   Toronto   Sydney

SCRIBNER

A Division of Simon & Schuster, Inc.
1230 Avenue of the Americas
New York, NY 10020

Some material in this book originally appeared, in slightly different
form, in *Elle* and *Self* magazines and in the essay "Twins" in *About What Was Lost*.

First Scribner trade paperback edition October 2008

SCRIBNER and design are registered trademarks of
The Gale Group, Inc., used under license
by Simon & Schuster, Inc., the publisher of this work.

For information about special discounts for bulk purchases,
please contact Simon & Schuster Special Sales:
1-800-456-6798 or business@simonandschuster.com

DESIGNED BY KYOKO WATANABE

Manufactured in the United States of America

1   3   5   7   9   10   8   6   4   2

Library of Congress Control Number: 2007003515

ISBN-13: 978-0-7432-9108-8
ISBN-10: 0-7432-9108-5
ISBN-13: 978-0-7432-9109-5 (pbk)
ISBN-10: 0-7432-9109-3 (pbk)

Author's Note: This is a work of memoir and subject to the imperfections of memory. I have been faithful to what I remember, and people in my family may remember shared experiences differently. In the interests of the narrative, I have conflated or changed some events and dialogue, and created occasional composites. I have changed some identifying characteristics and have reconstructed some conversations and early experiences based on family lore. I have changed all names but my own to emphasize that this story could only be mine.

For E. & O.
For A.

HER LAST DEATH

Her Last Death

The phone shouldn't ring this early. When I answer, my aunt Irene rushes into the news. "Your mother's been in an accident. She's been in surgery all night. She's probably going to die."

This can't be true, of course. I'm waiting for the story. Irene will laugh her exasperated laugh and say my mother used to date the surgeon. Or she's already secured a better hospital room. But Irene says my mother's in a coma, and when she finishes that sentence, I stop moving around the kitchen and sit. She usually calls her sister Daphne, but she keeps saying "your mother." My mother had a head-on collision after a dinner party. I want to ask if she was sober. Irene probably asked the same question of the person who called to tell her.

"The police have a record this time," she says. "The hospital has a chart."

The adrenaline of true emergency goes through me, and I

draw a blank. I keep thinking, "My mother had an accident," but the thought has nowhere to settle and stick.

"Susy?" my aunt says. She's worried for me.

If I speak, I'll say, "Do I have to go?" So I mustn't open my mouth. I try to think what other people say in this situation.

I'm afraid my mother will die. I'm afraid she won't.

In a house in Montana thousands of miles from my mother, I am thirty-seven, leading an unremarkable life. My mother lives in Barbados, where she stayed after her third husband died. I've never seen her house. She plays tennis and has houseguests, I hear, but we don't speak. Instead, I concentrate on the organic granola my two boys like, the seascape mural I'm about to paint on their bedroom wall. I preside over their school board and review movies for the paper. I send the photos of Halloween costumes and birthday parties to my father and stepmother. Last night, like most nights, my husband and I read books to each of the boys, crossing back and forth between their beds with kisses for them and patient hugs for their stuffed animals. This morning my husband will pack the lunch for our six-year-old, and I'll play with the two-year-old until his nap. We've just purchased this hundred-year-old house. On moving day I realized we would never invite my mother to see it. We live in sunny rooms messy with socks and books, a bathroom scattered with tub toys that are always drying, never dry. Christopher and I wonder before sleep at our boys' happiness and their invisible trust. Sometimes I'm jealous of them.

Over the years my aunt Irene and I have wearied together of the stories that start "Guess what Daphne did?" I tell a couple of them myself, rarely now but sometimes at a dinner party. My mother gave me cocaine! You wouldn't believe what she said to my new boyfriend! She had an affair with a mobster! These aren't stories I tell my children.

The boys' voices topple down the stairs before they come into the kitchen. I'll need to hang up when they start to tug at me with their small demands. Irene says my grandmother, also in Barbados, has not gone yet to the hospital. "She's hopeless. A complete wreck." I should ask for the hospital's number but say, "Let's talk later," and hang up the phone. I tell Christopher enough to give him a sense of the news and go to another room to call my sister. What she knows will be different from our aunt's story. This is how we move forward in my family, calling one another in almost every configuration five people can make. One woman gets a call, puts down the phone, picks it up again, repeats the story, hears another version. We fold in the new details that are not yet our own and patch together pieces until a certain sense emerges. My younger sister and I have an uneasy truce on the subject of our mother. We don't want to fight, so we don't mention her.

When Penelope answers she sounds like she's drowning. "Oh, sweetie," I say until she can stop sobbing and tell me what she's heard. Newly married, lucky with fun jobs that flame out fast, Penelope lives in the New York apartment where we grew up, subletting from our mother. She doesn't seem to mind being buoyed by the swells of Daphne's manic behavior. When our mother comes to the city, Penelope gives her pink sheets in the room that used to be ours and carries the paper in to her in the mornings.

Penelope's report matches Irene's.

"I've got the first flight out in the morning. What about you," she says, inflection absent.

"I've got to figure out the kids," I say. I'll call her back.

Christopher's mother could stay with the boys. He says, "Just let me know what you need, I'll do it." I'll need him to come with me, but what else? What else do I need? I go on-line, look into fares. All the flights are full, the cost enormous. "I'm not sure I can do anything," my travel agent warns. I'm off the hook, relieved, but there's also the part of me that longs for my mother in moments like these, her gall and grandeur. In the airports of my childhood she'd say, "Girls, you sit down over there," and she'd straighten her fitted suede jacket, align the silk scarf at her throat and ease her way to the front of the first-class line for an over-booked flight. "Don't worry," I'd tell Penelope, holding her hand. "She'll get us on." I could pick out our mother's laugh above the other voices, then her confidential murmur as she made a gift of her attention to the clerk behind the counter. People, men especially, liked doing things she wanted, couldn't help themselves. She made them feel they'd be important to her. Her well-cut hair flowed past her shoulders, and she lined her eyes with kohl. She had elegant arched eyebrows. She wore platform heels, even with her bad back, and sheer blouses fastened in a V between her breasts. Sometimes people thought she was our babysitter, a sophisticated, pretty teenager. She'd brandish her knockout smile and say, "No, I'm the mummy." She knew wit made her sharp features softer, and she was funny, agile with an anecdote or a naughty observation. When she beckoned we got up and went over, and the clerk would say, "I'm sorry about your grandmother" or "I hope your daddy will be okay." We knew to fall into the act long enough to make it to those first-class seats.

When we went out together, my mother made us the stars and the champions. She tossed off rapid, irreverent remarks, urged indulgence out of the most recalcitrant of salesgirls, seduced the most unhaveable of men. She spent money with fuck-you abandon. To walk into a deli with her and order a sandwich was a particular commitment, a willingness to let her own the day.

I've lived apart from my mother since I left for boarding school at fourteen. I called home often then, pressing her voice to my ear, our mutual interest insatiable. She called me from restaurant cloakrooms and lovers' beds, ready to start new rumors. She called from hospitals after back surgery. She phoned from airports, dinner parties and the lobbies of movie theaters in which she stood weeping over a love story. She needed me, she said, to calm her down.

Her sexual allure extended from bartenders and cabdrivers to rock stars, football heroes and anchormen. "He calls me whenever he's in town," she told me of an actor whose name was bigger than any movie he'd starred in. I was eleven, precocious with contempt, and said, "That's too much, I don't believe you." She had him call me that afternoon from his hotel suite while she was there. "Your mother says you don't believe her, Susy." It was obviously him, his famous seduction in each slow syllable. "Susy? You should always believe your mother." I had to admit that now I believed her.

One night the following year, touring boarding schools, we took a *Cosmo* quiz together. We traded the magazine between the motel beds, circling multiple-choice answers on pleasure and technique. She used a pen and I used a pencil so we could tell our answers apart. As I tallied our scores she was restless, up and down, over to the dresser where she had cocaine set out. That admissions guy was cute, didn't I think? She wiped at her gums in the mirror.

"This is weird," I said, nervous. I tried to ignore the tiny smug feeling.

"How'd I do?" She bounced onto her bed.

It was there in the numbers. Her score meant she was a "Shrinking Violet," but I'd aced the test. The magazine called me—the eighth-grader, desperate for a first French kiss—"High-Powered Lover."

"I guessed," I said.

"Miss Know-Everything," she said and shut the bathroom door on me. I wanted to erase the pencil marks and give her my answers. I knew she seduced movie stars, even if *Cosmo* didn't believe her.

*   *   *

While I was pregnant with my first child a friend told me, "Having the baby brought me and my mother a lot closer together. You'll see." This made me uneasy, not just because I was dubious about that intimacy, its conditions; I couldn't explain to my friend that my relationship with my mother had never adhered to predictable guidelines, social models. I didn't have a language for the tangle of being with her. In the insomniac hours near my due date, I phoned Daphne a lot. It was true, pregnancy gave me permission to accept her attention, and we could make each other laugh so easily if I let go. She'd repeat the adventures of young marriage, of having me at nineteen, and I listened with new interest. She seemed to remember everything and told on herself so well. I'd quiet my laugh in the living room, away from my sleeping husband.

After Daniel was born, though, I began to inch off further. I needed my energy for my child. My mother hadn't given me a useful example, although she insisted she had. "I know I fucked up quite a lot," she'd say, merry. "But you always knew you were loved. You always felt loved."

I didn't want her around the baby, couldn't imagine leaving him in a room with her, and she knew it although we didn't mention it, real hurt on both sides, real loss. I just stopped inviting her, and I scheduled my visits to New York between hers. For a few calm years I only talked to her now and then. It seemed like that would work. At the birthday parties of friends' babies I watched grandparents help with the candles or the camera. I went into the bathroom and cried, jealous and ripped off. Why didn't we get to have that? At the time my answer, my comfort, was that no one was responsible for the rupture but stubborn me.

*   *   *

The morning I delivered my second son I called her from the hospital bed. We still shared the rare news in brief, formal calls. Daniel was four then, wearing the baseball caps she would send him. She sent more presents for the baby. Then she got cancer.

My sister called to tell me, weeping. "And it's such a *painful* kind," she said. "Oh, *God*."

"What stage is it in?" This was a question you asked about cancer.

"I don't know," she said.

I thought of my boys, whether I'd made a mistake keeping their grandmother from them, how there'd be no chance unless I hurried. After Penelope hung up, I called Barbados. Daphne answered quickly. I told her what Penelope had said.

"I've already started treatment," my mother said. "I'll probably have to leave the island to get better care."

"Is Penelope going to come down? Should I come?"

"It's too far," she said. "You have a newborn." She was vague on the progress of the disease and wouldn't let me talk to her doctor. "He's been absolutely wonderful, though," and in a faultless Bajan accent she gave me a few details about him.

We started flirting.

"Tell me about Jack. Has he smiled yet?"

I wanted to tell her. His noises, the way he watched his brother.

"And his little tiny toes?" she said, as I knew she would. "Are they tiny and perfect? Oh, *toes*!"

Even though this talk sort of revolted me, it was our way, a sumptuous code. As I held the baby, I wanted it obvious I understood that cancer took priority. And I wanted to share other news, too, sort through all our gossip together.

She said she was dying but brightened. "At least it's brought us back together."

"Yes," I said, careful, feeling an ominous weight. I had dropped my grievances too fast, drunk on the old intimacy.

"I'm glad we're back, darling," she said.

She called many times then, called lonely and looking for reassurance, called wistful and tired and sweet and sad. I took the calls, though I had to manage them amid breast-pump instructions and Daniel's meltdowns and supper prepared one-handed. In a quick few days this was too much.

"Can I call you back?" I said one morning, the baby at me, my sleepless temper frayed.

"You probably won't hear from me for a while," she said. "I'll be incommunicado during chemo."

She was suddenly better. She was cured. She didn't want to talk about any of it. She felt good now, she said. Could she visit, see the baby? My sister and I matched up our pieces of her recovery. We were used to checking with each other ("—and *please* don't tell your sister"), fitting together a complete story from the fragments she discarded. But we couldn't get these details to align. The discrepancies were too great, and we didn't want to notice this together. Then a family friend told me Daphne hadn't been "incommunicado" for six weeks of radiation. She'd been at a spa in France or at a diet clinic. There was no doctor. It was an invented doctor.

Usually I ignored the discovered lies until they mattered to me less. But that day I phoned.

"So you didn't have cancer." I made sure we both understood the topic.

"I can hardly move," she said. Her voice perked up. "How's the baby and his tiny perfect toes?"

"Can we talk about you?"

She sighed and referred to the emergency room. "I was in agony. It could have been cancer."

"I need to have a relationship with you in which you don't lie to me."

8

"What?" She slapped the word. "Don't *you* lie? Haven't you *ever* lied? How dare you?"

"Mum, you lied to us about having cancer. About dying." I would slow this down, go carefully. I didn't know how my sister had handled it, her reaction. "Lying makes farce between two people. It makes me stupid, and we can't have a real relationship if I—"

She pounced. "You're being melodramatic. And you can cut the formality with me, miss. You sound like your father."

I had expected an assault, then my habitual resolute surrender; it was easier to let her say what she wanted. In a few months or weeks, she'd be telling the man beside her on an airplane about the nausea of chemotherapy and the doom of medical bills. She told things compulsively until she believed herself. By next year she would be a real cancer survivor, and I wouldn't be able to recall why the episode confused me. I'd be the daughter of a cancer survivor. In the kitchen Daniel played at the table as Christopher unloaded the dishwasher. While my mother listed her accusations, I could hear my son's placid chirping and the radio turned low, a habit ingrained by years of napping babies. My mother, entrenched in her fictions, wasn't real life anymore. I thought: This is our last conversation.

Now my aunt says she's really going to die. My sister says she's going to die. After those calls, I cancel things. Around me, friends gather close, the network of concern immediate and effective. Someone drops off food and takes the boys to school. My Montana friends haven't heard much of Daphne, her absence in my life so thoroughly settled. This morning I have to say, "My mother's been in a bad accident." Because it's her it doesn't sound like the truth. "She's in a coma," I'm telling them, and resent the soap opera.

"I'm so sorry. How awful. When will you go?" They assume

that I'll leave quickly, that a daughter far away wouldn't stand around wondering about anything.

I go to bed and wake the next day, still not knowing whether to stay or go. My mother-in-law arrives. When the travel agent calls with a hard-won itinerary, I jot down notes about the connections. "Let me check with Christopher," I tell her. My mother-in-law sits me at the kitchen table and starts a list. Passport, sunscreen, a hat. She is grave but untroubled: disaster has its own rules, you just go. She pats the top of my hand and says, "You have to do it. It's not a choice." She's almost happy for me. I feel strengthened by this woman's moral compass, her certainty and sense of duty, and I leave the table to check the closet for my carry-on, then pick up the phone to confirm the flights.

"It's not a choice," I tell Christopher later. I'll believe it tomorrow on the plane. Today I'm relieved to have instructions.

"Why isn't it a choice?" he asks.

"Because she's my mother." I've started to stack folded clothes on the bed. I wonder if I should pack a bathing suit. "She couldn't help it this time. I have to go."

He gives me a tender look. For nine years he has watched me try to get the stories straight, or try to rebuild in the wake of her devastations and reversals. He knows the energy I've lost, the order I attempted to restore after each incoherent phone message, seething letter or abrupt departure. I tried to make each time the fresh start.

"You don't *have to*. You still can make a choice," he says. "It'll be hard, but you have the right to do that. *You* have a right."

I don't want the right. Of course I should go. Of course it'll be hard. Irene is going, my grandmother's there. My sister is waiting for me to arrive in a taxi from the airport. She's been on the island for two days already, grappling alone with news of nothing, while I, surrounded by my husband, my sons, my friends, have waited for paralysis to wear off.

* * *

This is the moment in the story when the facts converge: the estranged daughter, the threat of death and the one last chance. All the tellings should coalesce into a mutual truth. I overcame trepidation and did the right thing, my mother woke from her coma erased of her vulgar impulses and unable to lie, and my children admired my generosity and forbearance. Tragedy transformed us.

But that's not me. In my story I do not go. No one in the family disputes that.

I'm alone at the kitchen table, and I call my sister in Barbados, embarrassed I'm still at home. Right away she starts reporting. After three surgeries in thirty-six hours, the doctors are coping with our mother's shattered shins and pelvis. Her front teeth are gone; her organs won't reveal their damage for a few days. The details stagger me. Penelope knows too much and too little. Where's the relief of the con unveiled, the act resolved? But there's only my sister in dry tears and our mother, who won't wake up.

"Penelope." I stop her. For two days I've tasted nothing but contradiction. Should, can't, will, mustn't. I look around—coffee at the bottom of the French press, the balled-up sweat jackets on the floor by the back door, the dog's empty water dish. I fix the vision of us in my mother's hospital room, and I become a character who hardly matters, picked clean, used well. "I love you more than anything," my mother used to whisper, italics in every word, pinning herself against me in an embrace. My sister needs her sister; we both do. I imagine being on the flight, and I can't breathe. To go I'll have to shut myself down, put myself away. I've done it before.

I inhale exhale choose—

"I'm not coming."

I'm a person who isn't going to her mother's deathbed. What will people think of me? I'm so distracted by relief, by the surprise of what I've given myself, that I forget my sister for a second.

"Is it money?" Penelope says.

"Yes. Well, no." I don't blame her for the focus on practicality. She doesn't see what I see, and I can't infuse her with my history. My sister, having lived the same years in the same rooms, lived them differently. She thinks I don't love our mother. I've never told her that at thirty-seven, sick with flu or after too much wine with a rich dinner, I kneel in the bathroom, heaving into the toilet, and that's where I wish for my mother. When I needed to throw up, Mummy came and sat on the edge of the tub. She put her arm around my shoulders and swept hair off my forehead. I was afraid, but she made it safe. She kept my nightgown out of the way, and I retched. She soothed me and said, "Almost done." When I throw up now, waiting for the next heave, I want her to lift the toilet seat for me, wipe my mouth, steady me against my own contractions. That's when I had her.

"I can't go to her anymore."

"You think this is about you?" Her voice is cold and so tired. She takes a breath. "Have you thought about how you'll feel if you don't say good-bye?"

"I can't go."

"You're not coming?"

"I love you," I say, and I'm the one who's crying. I mean these three words, the whole "I," the fervent intricacies of love, the scope of Penelope. I don't want to lose my sister, but I must wrap my arms around myself. With my mother I had nothing left to lose, the last of a daughter scattered as ashy silt, the orphan collapse. "I have to stay here," I say. "I have to, and I love you. You believe me?" But she's not listening anymore.

I'm not going. The words are out, and they make it true.

The New Parents

I came to New York on a ship.

My parents boarded the *Queen Mary* in Southampton with their five-month-old daughter, two chows, a Norland nanny and a lot of antique furniture. It was 1966. We sailed to America. "You were on its very last crossing," my mother always told me.

We lived in a town house with a red door on Sullivan Street. My father's parents gave him money for the rent. My mother was nineteen and homesick. She cried and missed her mother, with whom she fought. Her in-laws on Gramercy Park adored her, but she didn't know anyone else. Every morning her husband left for a rented office he wouldn't permit her to visit. He was writing. Alone with me, she talked to people in the park. I was cheerful and would reach for strangers from my pram. "Everyone loved you," she said.

My parents brought me into their bed when it was morning and warmed me between their chests. They sang. I was in the high chair for supper, my mother spooning some orange sweet from a bowl, and the noise at the front door made us look. My father opened the door and the spoon reached my lips.

The nanny went away, and I cried, but my mother said a big girl didn't need a baby nurse. She got skinnier and drank Tab from pink cans. When I was two she went to New York Hospital to have a baby. "That's where Daddy was born, too." A different baby nurse came to live with us. She wore a uniform and a white cap. "Penelope was born starving," my mother said. My little sister howled except when I carried her around. "Imagine a two-year-old carrying a baby!" my mother would say. "But you did it." When Penelope could stay upright, I sat her in the dirt of our communal back garden and played with her. I gathered her up when our nurse called us in.

"Isn't Susy good with her?" said my mother. "Susy's so good."

In summer we drove to Provincetown, a big, big house, a big, big lawn, sand in plastic pails and hot pavement underfoot as we crossed to the beach. The chows left paw prints in the sand. My mother had a bikini and brown skin and white lines when she took it off.

I was three. Bob Dylan lived next door. That meant something. I heard my mother tell people. "We live next door to Bob Dylan," I told the children in my nursery class. Once he wiped my nose.

My father walked me the long way to my school. No, we must have taken the bus, but I remember a vast concrete plaza, his hand wrapped around my curled fingers, then walking up a busy avenue. At windy intersections I stood against his leg. "Here, cry here," he would say if I fell. He knelt and pulled my head against the soft place beneath his shoulder. "You are the only one allowed to cry on my shirt."

After school I ran up the stairs to Penelope's room. I could hear the crib rails shaking with her fists. She saw me and crowed, "Suzzy! Suzzy!" It made me feel huge and happy.

One day when I was three and a half my parents called me to the living room. I climbed into the butterfly chair. I liked to scratch my fingernail over the rough red canvas. They spread out Polaroids on the table. "This is our new house," my mother said. Her voice was sparkly. She was happy. "We're moving to Millbrook," my father said, also happy. White house, dark trees, gray stream. In black-and-white it looked like a page of a book, not a real place. We drove into the forested reaches beyond the city. The drive went on and on until we came to a stop by a bright green slope. Before Mummy was out of the car I ran up to the house, my shoes disappearing in the sloppy grass. The sun lit up the white house, hurting my eyes. I raced around and around the porch. Through the windows the rooms were magic. My parents stood arm in arm, smiling.

I said, "There aren't any beds."

"We're going to buy some," they said, and they told me they had started shopping for furniture. Antique shops in the city would deliver things here. They were excited, and I was too, and my mother hugged my father, setting her head against his chest.

Millbrook. Storage. Separation. These were the words. My parents weren't happy anymore. The baby was always crying and crying. The boxes, the bookshelves that had been cleared and the rolled-up rugs went away, to storage. Storage. Separation. Our rooms emptied as men came and went. From upstairs I looked down on the roof of their truck. The walls bare, my mother's voice called, my father's voice called back from another room. They didn't call to each other much. "Daddy and I are going to live in different houses now," my mother said, kneeling in front of me, "I love you and your sister more than anything else in the world." I wanted the house in Millbrook. I don't remember what they said about the dogs, who went away. My mother took me, Penelope and our suitcases and left.

We moved to a residential hotel on East Eighty-sixth Street. She said, "We're going to have an adventure." She slept a lot, and we watched television. I turned four. My sister waited for me to climb into her crib and snap up the straps of her blue-and-white striped overalls. I worried: Where would we get groceries now that we had said good-bye to the Grand Union on LaGuardia Place? Would the hotel be mad about the lamp my sister pulled over by its cord? I unwrapped the paper packages from the Chinese laundry and put our clothes away in the dresser. Just like Mummy, I sniffed the milk in the fridge to see if it was bad.

The Croyden Hotel was like a dollhouse we could live in. The elevator and the doormen belonged to us. We stopped for mail at a wall of brass doors, surprises in the tiny windows. Cabs came to our curb when our mother put up her hand. We knew the name of the woman who stood behind the rows of Wrigley's gum and Life Savers in the lobby coffee shop. I forgot about my father between his visits, but when he came we got delirious. Sometimes he took us on a long taxi ride to Gramercy Park, straight down Lexington Avenue until we saw the wrought-iron fence around the little park and, beyond that, the deep red hue of his parents' grand house. Or he took me and Penelope to a luncheonette a block away from the Croyden, and we sat on orange vinyl seats.

"I don't like being called Daddy anymore. It's babyish," he said. I had a cream cheese and jelly sandwich. Penelope just had jelly. Purple was smearing her plate. "Call me Nat."

I told our mother there was no more daddy.

"How pretentious," she said. "Typical."

Eventually we settled on Papa, pronounced the English way.

My mother started to have fun. "I deserve it," she said. "He wouldn't allow me to be a teenager." The phone rang, and she messed up her date book with scrawled numbers and doodles. She talked and laughed, and then she clicked at the phone button to get a dial tone and start another call. I listened to the up and down in her laugh as I turned the pages of her book, examining her mysterious, opulent scribbles. She hired a mother's helper. We played with jewelry on her bed, watching her at the mirror. "How do you like this skirt?" The mother's helper answered. Mummy gave her clothes. She tipped the open perfume bottle to her wrist. "You can get arrested if you wear patchouli," she said. "Police think you've been smoking marijuana." I didn't want her to go out. I didn't know how young she was, what twenty-three meant. The purple suede boots hurt her back, she said, but fuck it.

In the mornings she put Penelope in a stroller and walked me to my new school. We crossed to the sunny side of the avenue. She had to find a job, she said. "Your father doesn't give us enough." One day she came home really happy.

"I'm going to drive a taxi!"

She drove at night, so the baby-sitter slept over sometimes. Occasionally we went to our father's on Mulberry Street or, after he moved, to the Chelsea Hotel. Sometimes my mother double-parked her yellow car in front of the Croyden and dashed upstairs to get us. We sat on the front seat and slid under the glove box (her British word) if she stopped for a fare. After the car was back in traffic we'd pop up to say hi. This earned us bigger tips, she said. She drove Penelope to Montessori, then we went to my school. "Tell them, what does Mummy do?" The kids didn't care. At home she explained that they were confused because usually men drove taxis.

"But now *you* have a mummy who drives a taxi! I'm the only woman in New York. I know all the men at the garage, and I'll take you there one night. They're dying to meet you." I imagined the avenues filled with taxis, all the men, all the men, and her.

I heard her on the phone or in her room with the babysitter, telling about creeps who got into the cab and wouldn't get out when she asked them to, the fares she shouldn't pick up but did. She was robbed. She could just see the gun out of the corner of her eye. How *pet*rifying, she said, not meaning me to hear. But I heard. I heard the clatter of her hanger replaced in the coat closet, the pause of her finger between numbers on the phone dial. I could hear her turn over in her sleep. I didn't understand every noise but heard enough to wonder when I woke if she had come home.

Every day our mother had something to tell. She'd made a new best friend. She'd found the best dry cleaner's. She'd met very important writers from *The New Yorker*. She got a part in a movie and took us to the first shoot. In a cavernous freight elevator she whispered, "You're my protection in case he's weird." My sister and I sat on the studio floor, which was painted black and scuffed with shoe prints, and I held on to the strand of our mother's voice coming from over there.

"Come on, children, quickly!" she called, and we trotted over to the lights. "This scene needs two little girls in it, and *guess who* gets to be the two little girls?" On the way home she told the taxi driver we were actresses.

She took us to see the movie when it came out, but she wasn't in it. "I ended up on the cutting room floor," she said. "As it were." We weren't in it either.

She came through the front door one afternoon and said, "Children, I found us an apartment." That was the end of our hotel. We moved to East Eighty-first Street. "Henry Fonda lives next door," she told the baby-sitter. "Lillian Hellman is across the street." Penelope and I galloped in the living room, hysterical with space. Our mother leaned in the doorway, laughing. "This will all end in tears." She liked to say that. She made friends in the elevator with a divorced woman from upstairs. "Amanda's *super*. She's my best friend." Our apartment had three bedrooms. "It's expensive," she said. "We're poor now." That's why we were sleeping on mattresses on the floor. Her mother sent parcels from England, sheets she didn't use anymore.

I turned five. We had a live-in babysitter. We had white ice skates. Our father's parents paid for the pediatrician and private school. We went with our mother to the hairdresser, waiting for our turns after hers. The fridge held smoked salmon and Perrier bottles. At suppertime the buzzer rang, and our mother clutched the phone between ear and shoulder as she angled money from her bag. My sister and I paid the delivery boy and took the sandwiches to the kitchen. Our mother liked prosciutto, watercress and butter on black bread, and we arranged it on a plate. We carried the plates to her and ate on her bed.

The pink hat was in her closet. When she got it down for us she'd tell about her wedding. It wasn't a wedding like everybody else had. She eloped. She was proud of her pink suit, how it made her look old when she was sixteen. She said, "I had to forge my parents' signatures," and explained what "forge" meant. She said she'd show me one day how easy it was. Her sister's telegram had arrived too late: "Whatever you do, don't marry this man, I beg you." The warning note tolled early. Our aunt Irene was the authority because she'd had a love affair with Nat when our mother was still a little girl. "I thought he was just like Heathcliff," my mother said, saying her sister's affair lasted for five years, enough time for her to grow up. "Then," she said, "he made me fall in love with him." Nat, ten years older than my teenage mother, sent an enormous box of chocolates to her boarding school, where she'd lived since she was eight. "How big?" we asked. "Like this, like *this*," and she widened her arms. She stayed up half the night, treating the other girls. "I wanted them to like me," she said. For that night she was the star. The box came with its own map and a set of gold tongs, which I could feel between my fingers as she described using it to pick up each wonderful chocolate.

She was a bad girl at school, always trying to run away, dropping bedsheets out the dormitory window. One day Nat came, pretended to be family, and they left. They didn't have a first date, she told me. He took her to his flat in London, where they necked on the couch. He put his hand under her skirt and pulled her underpants down and left them on the floor.

She wanted to go, but he said, "Don't you know, Daphne?" She imitated his sternest voice. "You must never let a man remove your knickers unless you intend to sleep with him."

"So I did," she said. "You see how naive I was?"

"You see how naive she was?" I told my classmates. They didn't tell the stories of how their mothers lost their virginities. I knew how to make them listen.

As Sullivan Street dropped away from our real life my mother told me my father had had affairs. "He left me alone with a brand-new baby, and I was terrified." We looked in the first album, and she pointed to photos of her with a baby propped up in a wash-tub. She said, "I thought you would break."

Two Beds

I sat on the classroom reading rug with the list:

cap
map
nap
snap

Each letter lay in a white sea. Suddenly, they startled me, melted together and stood up as words. They were like open windows. I was elated. I could read anything! Then the jolt of my mother's voice made me look up. She was standing at the door with my teacher, wearing a coat I'd never seen.

She waved, which made my heart leap, and my teacher beckoned me over. My mother knelt and hugged me hard. My teacher stuffed paper into a folder and wrote my name on the front in red pen.

"I want you to practice on your trip," she said. "Will you do that for me?" I loved connecting the segmented lines, making the same S, the same U.

"Can I have some more word lists, too?" I said. She gave me a phonics book and said I could keep it.

Outside the school my mother walked us to a station wagon.

"Is this ours?" I said.

"I rented it. Let's get your sister."

"Where are we going?"

"On an adventure."

"Are we going home first?" I looked in the back, which was piled with sleeping bags and new winter coats.

"No, I've got everything we need. I'm taking you to see the Grand Canyon."

"What is that?"

"It's America's most magnificent natural wonder."

We picked Penelope up at her school and crossed the George Washington Bridge and kept going. I sat in the front. My mother wanted to sing Carly Simon songs. I knew the words too, but Penelope got mad and frustrated and tried to make us stop singing; my mother and I looked at each other so she wouldn't see. We went into one state and then out and then into another, over and over. My legs got hot under the windshield, and I climbed over the seat into the back. My mother said restaurants would be too expensive. She stopped to buy bread and peanut butter and jelly from a service station, and while she drove I made a sandwich with a plastic knife and gave it to my sister. Penelope threw it on the floor and wanted the peanut brittle she'd seen our mother slip into the glove compartment.

"No candy," my mother said, and Penelope screamed. "Stop it! You two are going to see your country."

In the dark, Penelope fell asleep.

"Is she sleeping? Do you want to come up by me?"

I eased out from under my sister and climbed into the front again.

My mother covered my lap with her new coat. It was heavy and soft. She called it a chocolate brown shearling, which sounded delicious.

"It's cold in the desert at night," she said. "That's why we needed new coats."

"But aren't we broke?" I said.

She flashed glee. "I stole them."

I said, "Wow," but I knew that wasn't a good idea. What if she went to jail?

"I just walked into Bloomingdale's and stole everything we needed—the coats, the sleeping bags, this—" She pulled a necklace from under her collar. "It's a fetish. The Indians use them for luck. And we're going to a reservation, so." She picked up my hand and started a new conversation in a different, slowed-down mood. "Garrett wanted to come, but I told him no." That was her boyfriend, an anchorman. "Do you know why we left? I just wanted to be with you. With my girls. You see, I'm very sick."

"What do you mean?"

She explained "leukemia." It was such a long word. I would never hear it again without feeling that someone had taken her property, like a label yanked from the back of her sweater.

"Just a few months left," she said. She started to cry. "Isn't it good we're taking this trip? You'll always remember it."

I made sure Penelope was sleeping. "Who will take care of us?"

"I haven't decided yet. Not your father. Maybe Irene?" The thought of her sister cheered her.

"But she lives in London." We'd been. It was far away.

"Where you were born." She squeezed my hand hard. "Let's think of things you could do if you found out you only had a month to live. Come on. You could charge lots of things and never see the bills. Or eat anything you wanted. Penelope could have all the peanut brittle in the world."

We slept in motels. I lost my tooth, the first one, and in the morning there was a quarter inside a pretty beaded purse. At a motel in Nevada dust, a helicopter arrived with the anchorman. He took us to a roadside restaurant, and they talked about people I didn't know. He didn't seem sad. I wondered if I should tell him this was probably his last time with her.

After bedtime I watched my mother and the anchorman talking through the motel-room door. They had set up plastic chairs beside our car. "Those fuckers," my mother said to him. Penelope was asleep, but I didn't like falling asleep. "They want to cut off their own grandchildren. The rich son of a bitch." She was talking about my father's father. "Would it be so hard for him to give me some money? I went to see him, and he wouldn't even talk to me. Fine, I thought, I'll go shoplifting in *Bloomingdale's,* and I'll get arrested. Then you'll have your goddamned name in the paper because you wouldn't even support your own daughter-in-law." The anchorman said something too low for me to hear. My mother said, "But, you know, I was so good at it, I couldn't get caught."

By the time I fell asleep she still hadn't told him about her leukemia.

In our next motel, she turned the television to his channel. He was talking about Cambodia. "And he was just here," she said. I sat close to the screen and searched his face. I was certain he was thinking about her.

We picked up her friend in New Mexico, her best friend from when they were teenagers in London, and they spoke in giggly voices and didn't finish their sentences. Our mother got a brown poncho with white llamas on it. For the rest of the way I sat in the back with Penelope, observing how hard they laughed. They cried, too. I couldn't always tell the difference.

The stretch of the Grand Canyon was too big to take in all at the same time, and when we got out of the car I wanted my mother to stay very close to us. "I had no idea!" she kept exclaiming. "What an extraordinary country!" She rented donkeys, and we rode them down, a single file, a slow, hobbled parade. I was terrified.

In Beverly Hills, my mother and her friend talked a guard into letting us through the gates of a fabled hotel, and we drove under palm trees and had drinks at a bar. Natalie Wood came in, and my mother almost went and talked to her. We drove to Malibu to stay with another best friend. She grew tomatoes on her patio, and she let me pick some. It was very sunny, and the hot leaves smelled better than anything I'd smelled before. Everyone was always happy around my mother, always doing the things she suggested.

When we got back to New York, my mother discovered the hospital had mixed up her chart. She didn't have leukemia! They'd been trying to contact her!

"But no one could find me because we were driving around the country," she said to me. "I pulled you out of school the day I got the letter." There had been an envelope with test results, she said, and she'd read the letter and thrown it away and rented the car. "I came straight to your school. I didn't know what I'd do if they didn't let me take you."

She told the miracle everywhere. "The *stupid* hospital's *stupid* mistake," she said to people on the phone. "I should sue them and make them pay for the trip. And some poor woman out there doesn't know what little time she has left. How horrible."

Soon after, our mother noticed the man across Lexington Avenue from her bedroom window. Each weekday morning he trotted down the steps of his brownstone, walked to the corner and hailed a cab. She figured out from watching that he was married. Getting ready for school in her room, one of us might look out and say, "There he is." She came to the window and stuck her tongue between her teeth. She called him "fetching."

One afternoon we came out of our room where we'd been playing, and our mother was handing the man a drink on the couch. He stood up.

"You must be *Susy*."

He had a British accent. He shook hands with Penelope. She looked funny, doing such a grown-up thing. My mother's child-hood accent was fluttering around. Later I imitated it for Penelope, which was like tickling her. I could make her laugh so hard she couldn't breathe.

Colin came over a lot. "Everyone thinks he's on a business trip in Egypt," my mother told me when he came to spend a whole weekend. That night in my constant insomnia I thought about the short distance between the bed he was sleeping in now and the bed he was supposed to sleep in.

My mother said Colin had to stay in New York and work. He had a very important job at Sotheby Parke Bernet. But the three of *us* were going on an exciting trip. I was six and Penelope four. In Tangier we arrived at a palace and forgot our jet lag. We couldn't believe we got to live here, like princesses. The hotel stood in a bright courtyard surrounded by short trees. "Olive trees," our mother said. She opened her arms. "This is all ours." A woman peeked from a doorway wearing a veil that covered everything except her eyes. We thought she was a princess. There were no other guests.

The first night, as our mother unpacked our things, she told us that the cook was named Fatima and spoke only Arabic, and that oranges grew here. We might see monkeys. She kissed us and went to her room down the hall. I stayed awake, feeling unsettled.

The next day Hugh arrived. Because Hugh was a friend of

Colin's we already knew him a little. She explained what "lover" meant. At lunch she said the spicy fish soup was absolutely divine.

"Can't you feel your lips tingle, girls?"

Mummy and Hugh took us to a crowded market in the city, and they bought us flat purses made of leather and stamped with gold. We filled them with the coins Hugh gave us.

In the afternoon they slept, and the next day Penelope and I wandered under the olive trees. It felt like the air had stopped breathing. There was a stilled fountain and tables without chairs. We found a shed for a hiding place. I worked the door open, Penelope behind me. Her palm was hot against my cotton shirt.

"What's in there?" she said. She was nervous. It smelled sour, but I couldn't see. The sun had made our eyes useless for the dark.

We heard whimpers, and I pushed with my shoulder until the door opened all the way. A dog looked at us, curled around a bunch of puppies. They were the size of eggs and covered in mucus.

"We have to tell Mummy!"

"It's puppies!" said Penelope.

"They just got born! Let's go tell her!"

Then a noise made us jump back. I thought we were in trouble for seeing the puppies, but it was a taxi pulling into the courtyard. As if in a magic trick its door opened to reveal Colin. He looked red in the heat but pleased, and he bent down and said he'd come as a surprise.

"Do you have any coins?" Penelope said, holding out her new wallet.

Our mother appeared in bare feet. She did look surprised. We had to wear our sandals all the time because the stones were burning hot, but she didn't notice as she walked toward us. She wore a long silk scarf crisscrossed over her breasts and a skirt that showed the shadow of her legs. She put her arms around Colin's neck, and they tilted their faces, kissing.

"Let's see if we can get you your own room," she said, and they went inside. She looked back and widened her eyes.

When she tucked us in that night she said the three of us were in charge of a big secret.

"I can trust you, right, darlings?" she said. "Colin mustn't ever know that Hugh's here."

We said yes. We wanted her to come see the puppies. She said she would tomorrow.

In the morning she called a taxi and took me and Penelope to an empty beach. We brought steak sandwiches packed by the princess in the kitchen, but the wind blew sand into them, and our hair into our mouths, and we couldn't eat. Tar flecked the beach, and during dinner that night with our mother and Colin, Penelope and I picked at the black glue on the soles of our feet. "Do stop it, you two," she said. "It's unattractive."

Our mother spent the rest of the week going back and forth between our room and the other two rooms. She took food into Hugh's room. We took milk and scraps of bread to the shed and left them on the floor for our secret puppies.

An Important Education

My parents got their divorce one day when I was in second grade. During journal time at school I drew a picture of a bench. My mother sat on one end, my father on the other. I drew tears falling out of their eyes and a cane for my father, who had started using one because he got multiple sclerosis. My mother kept books about it next to her bed and said we'd all have to learn about the disease, which made her cry. She said people got MS when they were in their late twenties, and he was thirty-six so he was luckier than some. She said they were still really good friends. On Fridays Penelope and I stayed the night with him at the Chelsea Hotel, swallowed into the big lobby and up the grand stairs. His rooms were crowded with books, and we unrolled our sleeping bags on the floor in the hallway. He wouldn't buy the toothpaste we liked and said baking soda was better, so we used that, but it tasted like dirt and salt. One night when Penelope was asleep he called me from bed. "Come, Sue," he said softly. "It's *The Phantom of the Opera*." He settled me in his arms in front of the small television. The movie was scary, and when I felt afraid he told me the names of the actors and said one of them was famous for his ways with makeup. "You see?" he said. "It's pretend." I wanted to watch to the end, see what would happen, but I was too scared, shaking. He let me hide my face against his shoulder until the movie was over.

He took me to see *Freaks,* then *Tommy.* "You should know about Ken Russell." He took me to double features in Chinatown, which made my mother nuts. When he dropped me off she yelled at him, "What kind of asshole takes a seven-year-old to movies in Chinese?" He said, "Susy will know the difference between Mandarin and Cantonese."

As he and I walked along the street, his pace keeping us slow, he pointed out architecture, prompting me to identify details. We rehearsed "vermiform rustification," and then he praised my clear pronunciation. He had a new girlfriend named Laura, and they moved into a loft on Great Jones Street. Laura's three-year-old son, Joe, had his own room, which my father called "the children's room," but Penelope and I didn't have any stuff there, except the sleeping bags. My mother and Laura became best friends. They started a jewelry business and had a counter in Bloomingdale's. *New York* magazine published a picture of my beautiful mother wearing one of the necklaces, big beads of amber and bone. She was looking off to the side in a way that was sad and romantic. "Laura's the creative one, and I can sell anything to anyone." Laura would come uptown, bringing Joe, her handbag filled with tiny plastic boxes and clear plastic bags. Exploding with laughter, they would talk about Nat back and forth as they sorted the pretty beads on my mother's quilt. Joe and Penelope and I played house, and Penelope screamed when he damaged our toys. "That's *mine!*"

Of the three children, I was the eldest, the one my father took to things. He took me to a rehearsal of *Enemies* at Lincoln Center. I didn't want to be bored, but the play was long and solemn. At a Japanese restaurant afterward he asked me to say something about the play, and fright at sounding stupid kept my mouth shut. "Never mind," he said, irritated. But then he taught me to hold chopsticks and was proud of me for getting it right away.

One afternoon we went to an Orson Welles double feature at the Thalia, *The Stranger* and *The Third Man*. Except for two or three heads visible in the front rows, the theater was empty.

"You're not to ask questions during the movie," he said. "You must save them until it's finished." I knew that, of course. We did not get up at the intermission.

During the second movie a man sat down next to me. My father stared ahead, his concentration absolute. The man cupped his hand over my knee, and I froze. I wanted to change seats. The hand moved up and squeezed my thigh. This made my leg warm, as if I'd spilled tea on myself. I edged across the velvet seat and leaned over the armrest my father and I shared, to get his attention. The stranger's fingers followed, and I didn't dare move to brush them away. I didn't dare disturb my father. I just wanted him to *know* to look over at me. I was sure I'd be sick.

"*Stop* fidgeting," my father whispered.

Eventually the man got up and left by the exit. As he opened the door, daylight sent the screen into pale shades, and my father gave an aggravated huff.

In the lobby, I started to cry.

"Now what's this, what's this?" My father pawed for his handkerchief. I felt embarrassed to explain it aloud, but I was relieved, too. The movies were over, and I could talk again, which was like letting air fill up my lungs. I told him about the man.

He smiled. "All right, listen to me carefully," he said. "The next time this happens, you are to say in an extremely loud voice, 'Take your hands off me!'" He was satisfied.

I could never do that. I wanted him to say he was going to find the man and yell at him. But he walked out of the lobby onto the street. He didn't like waiting for me when he wanted to go, and I tried to think up a comment about *The Third Man* as I followed.

My father married Laura in the summer. She wore a dress to her toes and had a pregnant belly like a large hard ball. They had moved to Woodstock and held the ceremony in their backyard. My mother arrived in an unfamiliar car driven by Hugh, the lover from Morocco. Penelope and I hadn't known she was coming, and she cried when she saw us but said that was because she was happy. It scared me, though, and I watched her carefully. She had presents for us and for Joe. She hugged other people there, other kids she didn't even know.

In November my father called to say, "You have a new sister." My sister, my baby. Hattie was mine. While my father bickered with my stepmother, while he shouted at my stepbrother to stop his mischief, I'd be good for her. As soon as Penelope and I arrived for the weekends in Woodstock (we came by bus, my mother seeing us off at Port Authority), I camped in the baby's room, worked the side of the crib up and down and sorted her clothes. My parents teased me about my somber maternity. I carried the baby from room to room. At her naptime I sent Penelope and Joe outside, and I stayed with her. When she started to stir, I went downstairs and told the children through the screen they could come in. I warmed her bottle in a pan of water and shook drops of milk onto my arm. My heart would leap as I went up the stairs because I was about to see her. I climbed into the crib and gave her the bottle, petting her hair as she drank. When she learned to crawl I held her tighter. I didn't like to watch her crawl away from me.

* * *

At home I moved into the wedge of the maid's room off the kitchen. My mother and sister had the bedrooms on one side of the living room, and I was on the other. It was bizarre to turn my back to them as I headed to bed, but I loved getting my own room and felt grown-up for eight. My window overlooked Lexington Avenue. I had a teeny bathroom with a miniature sink that couldn't support a glass or toothbrush, so I still used my old bathroom, where Penelope and I had matching Minnie Mouse electric toothbrushes standing in chargers.

One night, lying awake, I heard my mother's cry. I was always alert to her disasters. I heard trouble and her fear, her battering, I don't know what, but it was awful. My legs collided as I started up out of bed and raced the length of the apartment. I pushed at her partly open door, and she was gripped and flattened, Colin on top of her, her throat up to him, and the noises grating. It paralyzed me, and I knew it was sex without knowing that I knew it, and I was still scared she was hurt.

"Go back to your room, Sue," came her voice as she got control over it. "I'll be there in a minute."

Cross-legged on my bed, I rocked, my corduroy bear pressed against my stomach. My nausea was insistent but without a reason I could name.

In a minute she came in wrapped in a towel, a deft tuck above her breast to keep it up.

"Were you scared, darling? It's all right, everything's all right. I'm sorry you were awake. I thought you were asleep."

"Why were you making those noises?"

"I was making that noise because it was a good thing, really." She hugged me, her neck to my neck. My hands felt the terry cloth, her body under it, and I inhaled soiled perfume. "Orgasm's the best feeling in the world. You'll see."

* * *

My grandmother's deck jutted over the sand. At low tide in Provincetown a fishy smell rose from the dried seaweed. Joe, Penelope and I hopped around on the breaker rocks, scouting for periwinkles, and we called up, "Nana! Hi, Nana!" She waved from a white canvas chaise. She helped hose the sand from our feet. She kept ice cream sandwiches with silver wrapping, a brass dish filled with pinecones and little cat-shaped pillows stuffed with balsam. Everything stayed in the same place.

Across the street she had another house, and we called it "our house," because she got it so her children would visit in the summer. My father and his sister took turns, dividing the three months. The house was white and massive, shutters painted dark green. "Hold Susy's hand!" Nana said to the other children when we crossed. I was eldest, eight, and this was my eighth summer in Provincetown. Penelope and I slept in the room at the head of the stairs with the glossy red floor. Joe got his own room, and baby Hattie had a bassinet with Laura and our father. We woke when the gardener pulled the lawn mower cord in the garden. On rainy mornings Laura melted American cheese on hot dogs while we colored rocks at the kitchen table with markers. She taught us to bead and how to make patterns, and we made wide bracelets she would tie onto our wrists with leather string. Mostly, the grown-ups didn't pay much attention to us. We ate a lot of candy.

Each afternoon Penelope and I warmed the backs of our thighs on the painted front step, watching for the mailman. Our mother, at home in New York, or in England with her mother, or looking at antiquities in Beirut with Colin, wrote us almost every day, and we carried the envelopes upstairs to my father's study. If we heard the typewriter, we had to wait. Our father's windows opened over the garden, and his fitful typing drifted down to where we sat on the swings, kicking at the grass. I liked his big office, royal windows soaring up to the roofline. He and I would go in after dinner, and he'd shut the door on the younger children. We were reading *Jane Eyre* together, each of us holding a Penguin paperback. I had a pencil for underlining words I didn't understand: *novice, boudoir, tyrant, pungent, incredulous, wantonly, conjecture, agitation.* He'd explain them when he'd finished the chapter.

If all was quiet we could knock, and he picked apart our mother's handwriting. She made up stories that had us in them, which pleased me so much. She sent emphatic hellos to the gardener, to the neighbor family and to Norman Mailer, who lived across the street with his wife and beautiful sons and sometimes his pretty daughters, who babysat. I was shy around him. "When you were two years old," my mother had told me, "Norman said, 'Susy's got a great ass. It's going to get her into trouble one day.'"

My father typed our responses, setting our words on his yellow paper. "Papa is writing this with a typewriter. We played on the swings," Penelope dictated, and my father sighed. I told her about *Jane Eyre.*

Nat and Laura's friends visited from the city, painters and actors and writers and playwrights. Then my father would make the dinners of tomato salads with coarse salt, stuffed peppers, grilled cod, and the adults would fill up the living room after we went to bed. They played records and smoked.

My father liked to sit up in bed in the mornings and for us to come in. I brought him tea in a glass with an ornate silver holder, my step steady all the way from the kitchen. His robe flapped over his white shins, and he used a lot of pillows behind his head. He took the glass. I wasn't to disrupt the cribbage board on the bedside table. His hair was shiny with damp. I dropped on my knees at the foot of the bed and let my elbows dig in. It was nice to smell his tart cologne and the smell of the sea mixed together.

One morning he asked, "Do you masturbate?"

I didn't understand.

Impatient, he said, "Do you know how to give yourself an orgasm?"

"For Chrissakes, Nat," said Shelly, leaning in the doorway. She'd been visiting this week with her boyfriend. She was younger than the rest of the grown-ups and spent a lot of her time with us, showing off bracelets on her skinny wrists. "She's eight! Come on, Susy. Let's get out of here." She grabbed my hand and tugged me from the room. In the kitchen, she said, "Do you know what he was talking about?"

"I think so." My stomach didn't feel good.

"You know what masturbation is?" Shelly said she'd show me. "It's easy, and once you know how to do it, oh, man."

She took me to an upstairs bathroom and turned on the bath. "You get it to a good temperature, lukewarm." She ran her wrist under the water. "You lie down there." She pointed to the floor of the tub. "Scoot up close. Your legs go here." She pointed to the wall on either side of the faucet. "And you just wait."

"What are you waiting for?"

"Man, you'll know it when you feel it. Go on. Try it." She plucked a towel off the rack and set it on the toilet. She went out, pulling the door shut. "Take as long as you want," she called. "I won't let anyone come in."

I took off my pants and underpants and lay down in the tub. I waited. I thought, "Papa is finishing his tea, Laura's getting out of the shower, the other kids are waiting for me on the landing." Water rose up the sides of the tub, lapping against my hips. I waited and thought about the lawn mower mowing, my mother putting a stamp on a postcard, Shelly holding the door, and then my first orgasmic flush spread up my thighs, around my ass and into my tummy, which still felt queasy from my father's interest.

* * *

When I was ten my mother told us she and Colin were getting married. "He loves you both very much," she said.

I looked for proof. I would run into his arms when he came home, and he'd try to get it over with. I was confused. Once she made him take us to Radio City Music Hall, because her back hurt. She didn't want to see the movie anyway. Movie theaters hurt her back. Riding in taxis hurt her back, and stepping too hard off a curb hurt her back. As soon as we were in the taxi, Colin looked as remote as anyone on the passing sidewalks. I wondered what it felt like to be kidnapped, pretending I'd never see my mother again.

On the wedding morning, Penelope and I dressed in Mexican wedding dresses Colin had brought us from a business trip. My mother's many best friends filled our apartment, blocking doorways, lifting their glasses of champagne high up to avoid spilling on one another. The phone rang, corks popped from bottles and laughter spiked in my mother's room, where someone was taking pictures of her as she posed on her bed in flared jeans. She was going to wear a silk suit, cream colored. It was hanging in the bathroom. Penelope and I were special because we were hers, and the day was hers. At the reception, we made a forest of the guests and darted between people as they hung up their coats and stretched bangled arms toward passing trays. We collected the champagne corks, turning them into little people with bloated bellies and tin hats. "I'd watch Colin from my window!" I heard my mother shout. "What a dish!"

The next year my father got divorced and moved back into the city. My stepmother took Joe and Hattie and left for another state, which I couldn't do anything about. Hattie was three, and I didn't want to let her go. I cried and cried. "Sue's absolutely heartbroken," my mother would say into the phone, repeating "heartbroken" with emphasis, telling one person after another.

* * *

In a Judy Blume book, the girl went into the closet with her crush, and they sort of kissed. The character was twelve, only a little older than me, just two years away. I read the passage repeatedly, the tension delicious and almost unbearable. My father left R. Crumb comic books lying around, and I examined the drawings of hardened nipples under tight T-shirts. I found *Penthouse,* and the letters and stories gave me more of that feeling, the lush, unfurling excitement, all done with words. I bought a copy at the newsstand a block away, where the owner had known us since we were little.

"My mother would like a *Penthouse,*" I said.

"Really," he said. I ran home with my purchase, worried he'd telephone her.

I read it every night, couldn't stop, letting orgasm put me to sleep. We'd say good night, and I'd close my door and lie down and prop the heavy magazine on my chest. I hid issues under my mattress, confident they didn't show. But my mother knew. "I know everything about you," she told me with the look down deep into me so I didn't quarrel. "You were always very sexual. I used to find you masturbating when you were three." She told this to other people, too.

After that, if she passed my door after bedtime she'd call, "Are you *otherwise engaged*?" I could hear her setting wineglasses on the counter or pushing down the button of the toaster. She barged into my thoughts as I came.

I was home from school with a painful cough. My mother tore everything off her bed and remade it with clean sheets. She flicked the quilt in the air and let it settle. She slid fresh cases onto her pillows and plumped them. I longed for her cool bed when I didn't feel well.

"Here, this will be lovely." She held the sheet open. I could spend all day in her room. She had a lunch date and said I could watch the 10:30 movie. I hoped for something with Clark Gable or Bette Davis. She lowered the blinds so the sun didn't light up the dust on the TV screen. "Don't answer the doorbell or the phone," she said, and went down to D'Agostino to get me a can of soup. She came back and tossed me a paper bag from our news-stand. The top of the fat *Penthouse* edged out onto the quilt. I pushed the magazine back into the bag and examined a box of cherry cough drops.

"You don't have that issue yet, do you?" she said. I must have looked appalled. "Personally, I find it revolting, but if you want to look through it, you should."

I did want to. I wanted her to go to lunch. I wanted to take my magazine to my room.

"Go on, my little pervert. We have no secrets. I know every-thing about you, I always will. I'm your mother, and you're made of my spit." That refrain, repeated through years and years, made me and my sister squeal with feigned disgust. I thought of her collected saliva coating my skin like suntan lotion. "Don't you love the letters, Sue? You know they're all made up."

"They are?"

"The editors invent them. It's true with those question-and-answer things, too, the advice columns? Darling, you *couldn't* have believed that stuff really happens. And they put makeup on the models, on their . . . Well, look." She pulled the magazine from the bag and flipped to the centerfold. She put her finger down on the page. "You think it looks like that? That's practically fluores-cent pink. You *know*. You've looked at yourself, right? You're a dif-ferent color, a darker pink, like me." I had looked at myself, angling a hand mirror. She knew that, too?

She went into the bathroom and plugged in curlers. She took up a lip brush and leaned toward the mirror over the sink. "Read me a letter," she called. "Don't be a prude." Now that I held the magazine, I couldn't help reading it, drawn by that tug in my belly. She must be right: it's the best feeling in the world, and she's here, I don't need to be scared.

"'I never thought this would happen to me,'" I read. In another few sentences we were both laughing, me so convulsively I couldn't see. I got the joke—she showed me, and my sister was at school and too young. This was just us.

Later I took the magazine to my room ("I don't want your sister to see it") and read from the first page to the back cover, my methodical system: table of contents, masthead, ads for cognac and watches, "Call Me Madam," pictorials. Pages of women on the beach, on top of each other in the spray, or a woman naked on horseback, her blond hair skimming over her nipples. The special girl in the centerfold got to fill out the questionnaire. It was all there to be learned, I just had to study. Aroused, I missed nothing.

Famous Names

My mother married Colin as a last act, and soon after, he was gone. My father and stepmother had been happier before their wedding, and they hadn't taken long to break up either. Getting married seemed to me to be the end of a relationship, not its start. The start, the big push and impressing people, that was the best.

My mother could start things in an instant. Out of nothing. She could connect at a stoplight. After her first day of jury duty, the mob lawyer drove her home in his black car. "It's terribly dangerous for him. If he was seen with a juror!" Later she signed us up for summer camp where he sent his daughters. She referred to him forever as the mobster. One of the jurors, she said, was mad for her. He booked Madison Square Garden, and for a spring and summer we went to everything. She met Roger Daltrey backstage. "Do you want to come to Queen with us?" I said in school to my friends Marcy, Elise, to the boy I liked. Penelope and I had black T-shirts and glossy programs we didn't have to buy.

When my mother was born, her father was famous. They lived in Santa Monica, where he composed Hollywood film scores, had novelty cameos alongside George Burns, Vivien Leigh. He played the harmonica brilliantly. My grandmother Patsy gave soirees and sent her three children to the birthday parties of movie stars' children. She was a noted beauty, first as a model (of hats), then as a ringer for Carole Lombard. "After the plane crash Clark Gable stopped at her table at the Stork Club, mute with grief," my mother said. "Daddy had an affair with Ingrid Bergman!" she told us about him. "Imagine if *she'd* been your grandmother!"

Blacklisted, my grandfather moved the family to England, and his name was expunged from his Oscar-nominated credit. He achieved fresh fame, and my mother counted on the reaction when she mentioned him. She taught me to pick the people who would be impressed. "If they're American, they have to be over forty," she said. "Of course, in England, everyone has heard of him." I told some of my friends' parents, and she was right.

She grew up in London in the sixties, and her absolute best friend dated Paul McCartney. In restaurants, girls climbed crying and screaming through the windows to get to Paul and John, who always had to leave out the back way. I felt like she was there, it seemed like she was. At school I repeated for Marcy and Elise her story of warning John that "Strawberry Fields" would never be a hit. In high school, I told it less frequently because I began to recognize its unlikely quality. Not impossible, but unlikely.

When her father played concerts in New York, she took us to see him. "He's sold out Carnegie Hall. Isaac Stern is coming." She'd sit between us and squeeze my hand so I couldn't let go, tears on her face as he played "Rhapsody in Blue" and "Summertime." I watched her. Although she hardly mentioned him when he wasn't in town, she was overcome during the performances. "Isn't Daddy the most extraordinary musician in the world? Gershwin wrote for him, you know." Our grandfather still lived in London, married to a different wife. They had a daughter born in 1966, one year after me. This fascinated me, that I was older than my own aunt, although I only met her once or twice and don't remember visiting his flat. In New York, he didn't stay at our apartment, didn't take us out to dinner. Shyly we talked to him backstage and stood at attention for his renowned comic anecdotes. He gave me and Penelope tiny harmonicas, his autograph etched on the top. On the way home our mother told us he'd had them made for us.

Patsy lived in New York at the Osborne. She was also married again. "He's the love of her life," my mother said, though she didn't get on with her stepfather, who disapproved of her behavior. "Oh, *fuck* off!" she'd yell when they fought. Patsy took us to Bonwit's for velvet party dresses and Mary Janes, to Broadway musicals. She was proud of her own applause. "I can clap louder than anyone else!" I loved her fur coat. "I don't feel the wind at all," she'd say as we waited for her town car after the performance. "I could leave this to you in my will, if you like it. Although I think Penelope wants it." When she and her husband bought their flat in London, an entire floor of a former embassy, we went. Our mother bought us matching hats at Biba. The chauffeur took me and Penelope to Hyde Park. My grandmother and her husband bought an apartment in Monte Carlo. We went. "Stand on the balcony, darlings. You can look right down on the route of the Grand Prix." Patsy took us to the Ballets Russes and for dinner to the Hotel de Paris on the Place du Casino. "Won't they even try a taste of caviar?" she'd ask my mother fretfully.

* * *

My mother visited John Cheever where he was "drying out." We knew the family. My mother taught reading to inmates at Sing Sing, and she gave some of them our phone number "to cheer them up." When we went to the movies she always knew somebody in the credits, people she'd grown up with or known in England. As the movie started, she'd give a satisfied laugh and then say, "Old Jenny!" or "Caw! It's Richard!"

My mother said, "Children, this is a detective with the narcotics division of the New York Police Department. Remember yesterday, the brown paper bag from the Optimo, all those little blue pills that spilled out? I had to involve the police. Imagine what could have happened had Penelope eaten them—you thought they were candy, didn't you?—she'd have died! This man is going to help us arrest the drug dealers."

She dated a New York Giants quarterback. "You should see the way he's battered from the game," she told us. "Every inch of him." We asked him to show us scars, and he did. A director, a writer from *The New Yorker,* a big executive at the BBC, the head of a *Times* desk. A Broadway actor appeared from under her covers as we brought in coffee one morning. One of her men made documentaries, heir to the something fortune; another one ghostwrote political memoirs. "If anyone knew the truth about Kissinger!" At a party at our house, a TV actor wandered into my room and saw my prized photograph of Farrah Fawcett, black-and-white and unpublished, a present from the photographer boyfriend, the one who did the *top* magazine covers. The actor said, "I'm doing a movie with her. I could get you her autograph." When the oversized envelope came, I pulled out my picture. Farrah had written in immense ballpoint loops, "Susy, Can't wait to meet you!" I believed her.

My mother needed painkillers. It was because of that mean boy at her boarding school, she always said. He pulled the chair out from under her as she was sitting down, and she landed on her tailbone, and that was that, the reason she had slipped disks, the reason she had to have back surgeries. "Blame him," she said. "And that's why you must never play that joke, not ever. Look what can happen." She pointed out that I had the same tailbone as she did, an extra long one. "Your coccyx," she said. "Right here." I was at risk, too.

She lay in bed. "Don't bump the bed," she warned as we entered her room. Don't bump the bed. Don't bump the bed. While we told her about school, sometimes her face contorted, and we had to stop talking. Then she'd say, "I'm all right, just a spasm." I was shocked the first time I heard someone else use "spasm," her frequent word. She went to the hospital. She came back with narcotics. "If the pain weren't so bad I wouldn't have to take so much," she said. With a needle she sucked the clear liquid out of a glass vial into the body of the syringe and showed me how she'd been taught to give herself injections. "This way we don't need to hire an expensive nurse." She was proud she could do it. "In spite of my fear of needles," she said.

The household adapted. I was ten and got used to her bottomless sleeps, the uncapped needles in her washbag, the tiny bottles of Demerol lined up on the black glass shelf in her bathroom. I felt sort of friendly toward them, little soldiers helping her fight off pain.

One day from the kitchen I heard a faint, thin name, over and over. My name, or something like it. I went to her, and she lay naked on her side, her hips oddly raised, arms extended.

"Sh-shwip-sh-sh," she whispered.

I came nearer and saw the syringe planted in her thigh. "What? Can you say it again?"

With great effort she pointed to the needle. "I need—need—push it in." Her eyes rolled up. "You. Push." I couldn't. Then I grabbed the syringe and used my thumb to press down the plunger.

Her body didn't resist. Almost immediately she opened her eyes. "Thank you, darling."

One morning she wafted into the kitchen, the nightgown a sliver on her. Her hands reached for the table. I was deciding about breakfast in front of the open fridge.

"Hi," I said. It was a giddy surprise to see her upright, to have her come in, but I didn't want to make a fuss in case that sent her back to bed. I just wanted her to stay. I could feed her. "I told Penelope to get dressed," I said, school mornings my responsibility. My mother stood next to me, the fridge casting light on her nightgown. The two of us looked at the shelves, sharing a concern. We were out of milk.

"Well, there isn't much," I said. "There's Jell-O. I made it last night. You just pour boiling water in. The mandarin oranges sank to the bottom, though. How about Jell-O for breakfast?" I wanted to make her laugh. She made up voices for turned-down TV commercials, and I hoped never to be sent to bed, never to stop laughing like that. I wanted to be funny the way she was.

I pulled out the platter and started to jiggle the green mound. *"Jell-O for breakfast,"* I sang. I held the plate up to her face, making the Jell-O dance. Her eyes fixed on it. She started to quiver and jiggle, too. I thought she was playing, and I was still laughing when I realized something was not right. Her jiggling was not like the Jell-O's. Violent convulsions shot down her body, and as I watched her I couldn't stop shaking the Jell-O, unable to break the live current between me, her and the plate. She sputtered for a few steps until she seized. Then she dropped, and I let the plate drop, too.

Her tongue was swelling where her teeth had snapped together, and blood pooled in her mouth and ran down her chin. I wiped the floor with a paper towel and her chin with my hand, listening for my sister's approach. I didn't want her to see our mother with her face slack or smell the dead smell of her breath. This was our intimacy, me so necessary.

"Get up, get up, get up," I said, and forced her to answer me. I'd done that before, other times she'd passed out. She focused her eyes and gripped my arm as I stood her up. "Go get into bed," I said, and made sure she went. She limped across the living room.

"I'm sorry, Sue," she said.

"It's okay," I said, but I was afraid. Her pain ruled us. "Don't be scared," I told Penelope. "She'll be okay." We were late to school. My hand still vibrated. When I looked at it, the scene replayed. If only I hadn't. My teacher asked if I was okay, and I said no, my mummy's sick. I pictured a caricature of the plate, the frantic shoving, my grotesque hand, and I didn't say more. I didn't want to surrender my crucial knowledge of crisis, and I was on top of it.

Throughout the day, each time memory roused the image, the picture grew stranger and uglier. When school ended I hurried Penelope to the subway entrance. We'd be home soon. Our mother would be in her bed, safe under blankets. If she was awake I'd bring her coffee.

I listened for her voice as we unlocked our big door and swung it open. We left our coats on the antique chair in the hall. We wanted that sound, her voice like a bird caught in the apartment, bright, wings beating. She was on the phone, and we stood in her doorway and waved, and she waved and put her hand over the mouthpiece and said, "Your father," and kept chatting. Things were okay. She needed nothing from me. Penelope and I settled in the brown love seat with frozen yogurt bars and tried not to shed chocolate on our clothes as we watched *The Partridge Family*.

She could pull herself together. And she was very beautiful. Everyone said that.

In restaurants. In airports. On Madison Avenue. At Sotheby auctions. During her marriage to Colin she developed the habit of attending the big sales, and I went with her sometimes and sat straight and solemn on the chair, listening to the murmur of faintly English voices, to the approving hum as a painting or sculpture sold. She'd write the prices down feverishly in the catalog. Sotheby Parke Bernet. *The* auction house. We scoffed at Christie's. We often ate at Les Pleiades, where a lot of Sotheby's people went. She hugged and kissed the maître d' after we'd given our coats to the coat check girl.

Patsy and her husband had a house in Barbados, and we went several times a year. Everyone remembered Daphne. At Christmas, the boys from *Monty Python* were staying at the next beach. Mick was at a party, and I danced near him. "Star-fucker," my mother cooed in my ear. Claudette Colbert had us over "for luncheon." "I think the old dyke wants me," my mother said. Lauren Bacall came for dinner, and we called her Betty.

In Barbados my mother met the very famous lyricist. "*Everyone* has heard of him, and he isn't even *in* the band." He was English, agreeable and unkempt with denim sleeves too long over his hands and his jean cuffs frayed over pretty shoes. The famous lyricist came back with us to New York. His cigarettes smelled of fake mint. "They're mentholated," said my mother. "It hides the revolting odor." It didn't, but I liked it. The sickly smoke made its way across my face as the famous lyricist tucked me in at night, telling me about his mother tucking him in, about his nearly ex-wife. He kissed me on the forehead and went to my mother in the living room, leaving his smell behind.

The famous lyricist rented a house in Barbados and invited the three of us for Easter. Our mother said we weren't to tell our grandmother. "She'd be hurt if she knew we were on the island and didn't call."

"Here's your bedroom, girls, and he and I will sleep here." She lowered her voice. "Although no one actually sleeps except you two, ha ha."

We stayed ten days, and Penelope and I had new headbands and new bathing suits. We played backgammon, Penelope winning again and again. I was never certain of the houseguests. Band members wandered through. People appeared beside the pool. Someone might sit at the grand piano and plunge into an elaborate riff for a minute, then stop to sip his drink. The grand's glossy top was strewn with toffee wrappers, crumpled cigarette packets and the cellophane that my sister and I liked to peel off the Benson & Hedges boxes the way we peeled skin from our sunburned shoulders. Once, the lead singer dropped by, his rented house some distance away, and a couple of skinny women who'd been hanging out on the couch sat up taller, pulling at their macramé bikini tops. The adults were always quiet during the day. They were waiting for the coke to get there, wrapped in tiny packets called sno-seals, which were squares of slick paper cleverly folded to make a miniature envelope; or they were waiting for the hour when it would be time to leave for a party. Penelope and I stashed Cadbury Fruit and Nut bars, which got mealy in the heat. We collected the tortoiseshell guitar picks, scattered throughout the house, sorting them into who-gets-what on our twin beds. People left empty sno-seals in the pantry and the bathrooms, wings opened, on stucco ledges out by the cars. In the evening lots of formal settings appeared on the table, and the butler announced dinner. Penelope and I sat down amid empty water glasses and lined-up silver. My mother was so skinny and never ate but would sit with us sometimes. She wore halter dresses and Charles Jourdan high-heeled sandals with gold under the sole of her foot. She'd pluck a grilled cristofene from my plate, and the smell of her tea rose perfume overwhelmed the fragrance of the food.

One night my sister was whining for a present so the famous boyfriend unclasped his gold chain, slid off the chunky gold charm and handed it to her. He was wearing it in all the inner-sleeve photos. She closed her fingers so I couldn't see. "Can I have the chain, too?" she said. I wanted something but didn't want to ask. I wasn't a baby. He ruffled her hair and handed over the chain, and I fastened it around her neck.

Later she and I turned up in a song. My mother said, "There you are! In the song about me!" Our brief mention—"daughters"— came at the end, and we made our friends listen all the way through.

The affair ended after a few months. "We argued," my mother told us when we asked why she'd dumped him. They must have done it privately. I missed the famous lyricist hanging out in our bedroom when my mother's knees hurt or her back was out. He was calm, and he was generous. Right at the start of things, he had taken us to FAO Schwarz and said, "Anything, yes, anything," and we chose an immense stuffed animal each, near the entrance. We didn't even wander into the store, in case he revoked the offer. He bought Penelope a panther as long as her bed and a giant leopard for me. No one we knew had anything like that, and when our friends from school came over we said, "Guess who gave us these?"

Brunch

I turned twelve in Venice. My grandmother Patsy took us to the Hotel Regina on the Grand Canal. Hubert de Givenchy was staying there, too. My mother said, "He just got on that *vaporetto!*" She met a man with a teenage son, and we started spending days with them. We went to the Lido Beach to swim, and we went to Harry's Bar. I don't remember the museums. The son stood next to me at the glass factory, and our bare arms touched. My mother called him my boyfriend.

One afternoon my mother drew me off from the group—we'd all meet later for dinner—and took me to the Piazza San Marco. She picked a café table beneath the arcade, and we faced the square. "Look up, Sue. Look at the horses." The waiter came, and she ordered. "*Gelati, limone e cioccolato,* and two Bellinis, if the peach juice is fresh.

"I think that's him! That's Givenchy, over there." She pointed at a silver-haired, straight-backed man seated several tables away. "Givenchy is following you, Sue." I tasted the sweet drink and the crisp wafer in the ice cream and knew Givenchy was nearby and looked at the sky marked with birds. My mother said that I was drunk. "Oh, my little lush. You'll always remember this, you know—Venice, the piazza, getting drunk with me for your first time."

When we returned to New York I started seventh grade, got braces, taped up pictures of models from magazines, my scissors outlining their bodies. That's what all my friends did. I had a crush on almost every boy in the class, my diary a catalog of daily preferences. Over the summer my friend Elise had seen *The Rocky Horror Picture Show*. Marcy had grown breasts. On Saturday mornings my friends, girls and boys, met outside the Regency Theater. We saw double features of Hitchcock thrillers or Gene Kelly musicals, hands grazing hands in the refuge of the dark. Afterward we jammed the pizza parlor, shrieking about 45s and who was going to be boyfriend-and-girlfriend. I slept over at Marcy's a lot, her parents washing up after dinner together in their small kitchen. In the mornings her father, dressed in his undershirt, pushed open Marcy's door and said, "Girls? Time to get up." Elise taught me to lip-synch in front of the mirror, Tim Curry over and over on the record player as we flounced in my room. She wanted to take me to a midnight show of *Rocky Horror* in the Village, but my mother said, "Absolutely not." My class took a weeklong trip to the school's farm upstate, and we played Run, Catch & Kiss. At lights out the girls ran around and weren't supposed to be in the boys' rooms, but we went in anyway. The teacher on duty paused in the hall to listen for whispers, and we muffled our glee.

My mother wanted me to join Weight Watchers. "You're always going to have a big ass, Sue. Even Norman knew that." I didn't mind worrying over my weight, the way a grown woman would. Some girls in my class took gymnastics, and I started with them in a studio overlooking Broadway. When my father came to get me I met him on the street because he couldn't climb stairs anymore, the MS progressing. The instructor gave me exercises to straighten my spine. "She gets that from me," my mother told her, lifting the back of her shirt to show the teacher the scars from back surgery.

"I'm mad about that teacher," she said on the way home.

"Her husband pinched my bottom," I told her.

"Maybe he's part Italian."

A few weeks later, after school, she said the teacher's husband had come that morning to our apartment. "He wants to have an affair with me. But I sent him away. I told him no." I told my friends at gymnastics how the husband was in love with my mother.

One April Sunday Daphne took us out for brunch. We walked up Third Avenue, the day dazzling and fresh, my mother pausing at shop windows. "Isn't that color divine?" Penelope, who was ten, liked to skip ahead, singing to herself, and my mother and I held hands, enjoying her silliness.

The restaurant was popular and crowded. Our mother had had a few dates with the owner, but then he got married. "He's not happy, you know," she said. "He tells me everything." He wasn't there today, but she got the manager's eye, and he seated us ahead of other people. He walked us to a corner table, a good table. She asked for a mimosa, and he brought it back, saying it was on him. Penelope and I piled up the sugar packets and traded our ruffled toothpicks when our club sandwiches came. My mother ordered eggs Florentine but left them. She reached over to my plate and pulled the middle layer of bread out. "You don't need that," she said. The waiter brought another mimosa.

"Excuse me?" she called. I looked up, but she wasn't talking to anyone. Her eyes jumped around, her gaze everywhere. She zeroed in on the neighboring table and invited the four people to come and sit at ours. I thought she knew them, but they didn't move and looked back at each other, so she began to invite people from other tables.

I was annoyed. "Do we need more people?"

She grabbed my hand, which startled me and hurt. "This is an unforgettable lunch, unforgettable," she said. She was talking through her teeth.

"Why?" said Penelope.

"Why?" I said.

"It's an unforgettable lunch," she repeated, her voice pressing. "Don't you see? People have finally begun to realize that we have magic powers."

Penelope said, "We do?"

I thought we should leave.

Outside the restaurant my mother hailed a cab and told the driver to take us to Gramercy Park, where my father's parents lived. We hadn't planned that. She sat between us and gripped our hands. "You're special girls, you know that. You're so special to me. Do you have any idea how much I love you?" When we went over potholes she made terrible faces of pain, her grip tightening, and Penelope looked at me, worried. "It's just a spasm," my mother said. "You're so special. You're so special."

We pulled up in front of the house on Gramercy Park, and Grey the butler opened the immense black door with the brass lion's head on it. My mother hugged Grey and asked about his parakeet. I didn't know he had a parakeet. I couldn't remember ever being here with our mother, and with her I felt like an intruder, that we'd stepped into a mistake. I loved it there usually, the hush and order, glossy white banisters, red carpets, prisms of surprising light from the chandeliers. My sister and I sat on a couch in the little den with Nana, who held her arms around us, while my mother disappeared to talk to our grandfather. Nana asked Grey to bring us ginger ale, and he returned with two tall glasses, etched with the family initial. Soon my mother collected us, and we climbed into a taxi. She wouldn't stop crying. "My back," she cried. "Your grandparents hate me."

This scared Penelope, her eyes frantic from me to our mother. "No one hates *you*!"

I wanted my mother to calm down. "What's wrong?" I said.

"They despise me for leaving your father."

At our building, she dropped us off at our floor and took the elevator upstairs to Amanda, her best friend. We went into our apartment. The doorbell rang, and in came her friends Meg and Walt, invited but forgotten. The phone rang, and it was my mother. She asked me to put Meg on. Then Meg left and went upstairs. My mother phoned again and asked to speak to Walt. He said things like, "Now don't do that! That's just stupid!" I stood close to him, trying to figure this out. Amanda lived in the penthouse with an open terrace. I was scared my mother wanted to jump off the roof. She'd promised me once she wouldn't commit suicide. "For you two," she said. "I can endure the pain."

The grown-ups finally returned, my mother drooping in their midst. They put her in her bed. The doctor came, the father of a boy in my class. He and Meg got her out of bed to take her to the hospital. As they were leaving the doctor said to us, "Your mother has back pains. And she is very unhappy for no apparent reason." I didn't like the way he said that. I thought I knew the reason— my grandparents, wasn't it?—but he wouldn't understand. Walt stayed with us, and we sat in the living room while he talked on the phone about business and smoked, piling filters into a saucer from the kitchen. Meg came back and said, "For a psychiatric hospital, you know, it's not that bad."

They didn't say how long our mother would be gone. An hour? A day? "We can't stay all week," Meg said to Walt. Their drinks left marks on the tables. They slept over. I don't remember them calling my father (surely they must have?). I saw what was what and was afraid: my mother was really messed up, and no one wanted to take care of us.

The next day our grandmother Patsy arrived from London, a town car bringing her from the airport. Usually she would stay at the Carlyle, a suite, but this time she put her suitcases in my mother's empty room. Meg and Walt left.

Patsy took us to the Payne Whitney Psychiatric Clinic, an important name. "At least she's in a good hospital." Everything there was beige and pale green and ugly. My grandmother kept saying, "Oh, *Daphne,*" as if my mother needed to clean up her room. "This *can't* keep happening."

"Darling?" My mother reached her hand out, and I took it. It was clammy, and her face didn't look good, gray and spooky. "Will you bring your friends to see me? Bring Elise! I miss her craziness. Will you bring her on Wednesday?" I said okay just to answer her and dropped her hand and took Penelope out to the hallway. I didn't know how to stay in the room.

Back at our apartment, our grandmother said to us, "Daphne will be in hospital for two weeks." I wanted to call my friends, find somewhere to sleep over, but Patsy wouldn't let us make any calls. We were sequestered.

But then our mother came home, and she'd been in Payne Whitney only three days. Penelope and I were elated, but my grandmother said, "It's just for the night. Tomorrow she's going to another hospital." I heard her tell my mother she would cut her off without a penny if my mother didn't go into a five-month treatment program. This worried me, as I knew Patsy gave us money for rent and bills. While my grandmother made us scrambled eggs, the one thing the women of my family knew how to prepare, I sat with my mother on her bed. Would she really leave us for five months? I wanted to ask, but she started talking.

"What do you think, Sue? Do you think your gymnastics teacher's husband is attractive?"

I said no.

"Are you attracted to any boys in your class?" she asked. "That you haven't told me about yet?"

The next day she left again. My grandmother had gotten her a private room at New York Hospital. "And it wasn't easy," she said. After school, I took my sister to visit.

On the bus Penelope said, "What if we're late, and they don't let us in?"

"Don't worry." I'd memorized the visiting hours. Our mother had had several back surgeries, so many hospital stays that we didn't count them. We knew the routine. We behaved in the hallways, made our steps quiet, our walk calm. We knew what "ICU" meant and that the proper name for a shot was *injection*.

We passed shoe repairs, delis, cleaners and locksmiths on York Avenue, and then we got off the bus. We used the hospital's front entrance, its doors set back a long way from the sidewalk, the path covered by an awning. I followed signs to the elevator, Penelope's hand a constant in mine. I let her push "up."

"Have you been here before?" Penelope said.

"No, but you were born here. Papa, too."

When we came into the room, my mother was laughing with the nurse. She had set her hair, and it looked nice. "This one's smart," she said to us. "She's not like the other nurses, are you, Monica? You're not a bitch, are you?" The nurse laughed in spite of herself and shook her head. The time went slowly in the room, and I wanted the visit to be over. My mother used Monica's name in every sentence, and the nurse stayed. The ward smelled of food that had the opposite effect of making me hungry, and I bet my mother wouldn't eat it, that she'd order up from a deli or have Monica bring her things she wasn't supposed to get, that no one else got. Except for the moment of being excited and happy as we rounded her doorway, and the first look at her eyes, there was nothing good about being here.

The next day it rained, and there was a long rubber mat beneath the awning and by the elevators. I felt so angry about it, that things were different. After a few days the nurses recognized us, saying, "Hello, girls. Hello, hello. Won't Mommy be glad to see you?" Patients called our names as we passed their rooms.

"I tell everyone about you," my mother said to me. "I want them to be as impressed as I am."

Territory

I had two months left of seventh grade when everyone decided Daphne should leave New York. My aunt and grandmother and father thought it was a good idea. Her friends thought so. Obviously, she needed a break. She should get away from the hospitals, the memories of surgery, all those drugs. She needed a chance to get off Demerol, for good. That was the problem, she said, that day at Gramercy Park. "I should never have mixed Demerol and champagne. Now I know. And no more men, Sue. I promise."

She decided we'd move to New Mexico. "Remember how we loved it? How beautiful? Our trip across the country?" I asked to stay and finish the school year.

"Where will you live?" she said.

"With Marcy and her parents. They've said I could. They want me to." They also invited Penelope, but my mother was indignant.

"Who do they think they are? She's ten! Surely they realize a ten-year-old needs her mother."

I was a sleepover expert, polite to the parents, responsive at meals. At home I guided my sister from toothbrush to hairbrush, tugged her tights on, scheduled our dental checkups, thawed peas, scrambled eggs. I'd been doing these things since I was eight. I turned off the television when we'd watched enough. But at Marcy's, at any of my friends' houses, I didn't have to do anything but wash my hands before dinner. As 3:00 neared on school days, I'd look around. Who today? I'd call home from the school office, leaving a message with our service if my mother didn't pick up. The parents were happy to have me. One time Elise's father took me aside and said, "If you ever need anything, Susy, I want you to call me. Anything at all." I thought he was creepy.

My mother tried to talk me out of the Cohens, convince me of something sexier, like the house of the handsome headmaster and his wife. She liked to mock Marcy's mother: "Did Carla make you a *big* meal? Did she insist everyone have home*made* baked apples?" She said the Cohens were strange, but if they were, I liked it, and that's where I was going.

The last night we spent together in our apartment, my mother slipped a letter under my door as I was sleeping. She'd written it at dawn, noted at the top of the page. The morning was busy as she and Penelope got ready to fly to New Mexico, and we had our crying and hugs and long looks. I didn't read the letter until I was at school. She wanted to tell me she was sorry she had disappeared "down the tube into the terrifyingly dead world of drugs." But, she added, "I'm not sorry for anything that has happened to you if it took all this shit & pain to make a Susanna Sophia." She went on about magic, how we were all magic, etc. She urged me to send her all my "thoughts & feelings," and I stuck her pages in my diary and wrote "Ho hum" after them.

* * *

At school, my stomach was jittery, half afraid, half excited. One of the boys I liked sat beside me for lunch and made jokes. "There's a smile," he said. After school I'd be going home with Marcy, to live, for almost two months. My suitcase was already there, and my mother had sublet our apartment to some singers. "They'll be staying at our place while they're cutting the new album," she told people. I wouldn't continue at Weight Watchers because the Cohens lived out of the neighborhood, and my mother canceled my gymnastics lessons. "I don't want you there anymore," she said. "I heard the lechy old husband's making passes at the girls."

My mother called from Taos each night. Marcy's father would answer, laugh, enjoying something he wasn't used to, and then he'd call me from homework and hand over the phone. "Do you know what adobe is?" she'd say. "How would you like to be in a play this summer?" "You should see the sunsets." "Your sister's school is in a double-wide trailer in a field of sagebrush, and her teachers are hippies." "Groceries here cost nothing, just nothing."

She asked about the Cohens, their habits and friends, how Marcy and I were getting along. She asked about my schoolwork and teachers. Did I miss her? Did I miss Penelope? My mother reported Penelope hated Taos because everything was unpaved and people walked around in flip-flops. "But you will love it. I do." She said the cocaine was cleaner. "It's cut with better stuff." She said, "I met someone. A real cowboy. Well, he looks just like a real cowboy." He was divorced. "This move is so important for us," she said.

In the mornings, Marcy's mother lined us up before we left for school and hugged us in turn with hard, long hugs. Her hair was stiff from yesterday's hair spray, and she had the remote control in one hand, a cigarette in the other. She'd lower the volume on *Good Morning America* until we were out the door. Once, on my way to school with Marcy, someone on the bus lurched forward at us and said, "Hey, Susy! It's Barney!" His mouth opened really wide. "I was in Payne Whitney. With your mom! How is she?" I made Marcy get off before our stop.

One Saturday, I crept out of the Cohens' before anyone was awake and took a crosstown bus to my neighborhood. Besides the driver, I was the only one on the bus. I phoned the tenants from a pay phone to ask if I could pick up our mail.

"Sure, come up," said one of the singers, sleepy.

She let me in, then went back to bed, leaving me in the front hall. My apartment was in disarray. They'd moved our furniture around, and there were four or five mattresses on the living room floor. People were asleep. Bottles and ashtrays covered the mantel, and take-out containers and dirty napkins sat on the tables. I recognized the sound of my sister's door as it opened. A naked man started out of the bedroom hallway. Seeing me, he retreated.

I went to the kitchen to gather the stack of mail, and I phoned the Cohens. I wanted Marcy to meet me at the movies.

"Where are you?" said Marcy's dad. He sounded angry. "You cannot just leave and not tell us where you're going. We're responsible for you."

"I'm at my house."

"Come home at once!" He hung up. I started to cry and went into my old bathroom so no one would hear me. I missed my sister. The Cohens were responsible, but they never asked me the questions my mother did, looking for the heart of things, eager for all my "thoughts & feelings." No one else made me feel really interesting, different, magical. I just wanted to get to New Mexico.

Before my flight I spent the night at my father's. It was hard to be around him. I wasn't allowed to talk while he played classical records or had the news on. He moved slowly, yet he was impatient. He resented my phone calls to my friends. He didn't like my bus pass on the kitchen counter. When I talked in the aimless way of other seventh graders, he turned his face away.

I bore the hours on the plane, drinking black coffee, its bitterness something to do with being unsupervised. The man next to me said I was way too attractive for a twelve-year-old and gave me his card. At the gate my mother was transformed by a suntan and a pink satin baseball jacket, which made me reserved. "Oh, stop that, silly billy," she said and grabbed me up, and my lips met the skin of her warm neck. She was whispering into my ear, kissing it with nibbling kisses. She wiped mascara from under her eyes and pulled a man over by the arm. "*This* is Randall," she said. I shook his hand.

She sat between us in his pickup, legs around the tall stick shift, feet browned in sandals I'd never seen. "Tell us everything," she said and then interrupted, narrating context to Randall as I tried to report on the last days of school. I didn't mention the messy apartment. She'd start ranting. She stroked my hand. "Look at our little hands," she said, holding them up for Randall, evening up our palms and fingertips. "They're almost the same size." I pulled back, but she held on, so I curled my fingers in and tried to let her hand encase mine. They were almost the same. She could no sooner envelop mine than I could hers. Randall downshifted on the steep passes and said little. "He owns a movie theater," my mother said. "He can two-step. He has a little girl." She wanted me to know him all at once, and I wanted to be interested.

"What's playing?" I said.

"He's getting *The Turning Point* for me," she said. "I *have* to see it. Don't you think it'll be better than sex? And he's going to get Clark Gable movies for you, any one you want." Her finger cut across my line of vision. "The Rio Grande, Sue, look! What about that view? Better than sex!"

By the time we reached the house, her feet were coated in the reddish dust that seeped across everything in Taos, sky, dry ground, riverbed. Randall swung my case out of the truck's bed and carried it in. My mother gathered my arm and said so he wouldn't hear, "Just look at that ass." I had already looked. "Notice their bodies first," she used to say. "You can always tell if they're any good in bed." It was in the wrists, she said, the mouth, the laugh, the Adam's apple.

We came inside to the sudden cool of adobe walls.

"Have you ever seen a man look so fabulous in cowboy boots?"

"He seems nice," I said. "Where's Penelope?"

"She's at a sleepover. I wanted you to myself your first night. Oh! Penelope's got a little job! She's working in Randall's theater." She spoke fast. "It's so cute. Can you imagine our little Penny behind the concessions stand? Do you want a job? We'll get you a job. All the kids here work. Everything's so relaxed. The bars let kids in. And I've got both of you signed up for auditions—there's a play they do every summer—it's *Bye Bye Birdie* this year—have you seen it? You'll love it!—that's tomorrow—all the kids do it."

"Slow down," I said. "There's an audition tomorrow?"

"Need a nap," Randall said, stretching, and light landed on the flat snaps of his shirt. He grinned at my mother as if I wasn't there.

"I'll be along in a minute. I want to talk to Sue first." Randall left, his boot heels knocking against the tiled floor. *Now* she'd stretch across my bed, ask about everyone, postpone sex even. No one else could plumb so deep.

She yanked my wrist up. Her party was gone, her bright fizz gone out, and I felt the threat of oh no. Her lips whitened around the edges. "You *keep* your hands off my man. You want a man? Go find your own!" She released my arm, and the skin stung from her grip.

"I don't—"

"And don't sleep with anyone this summer."

My stomach flopped as if a boy was about to kiss me. The reality that sex was near. "Why would I want to sleep with someone?"

"Well, all the kids here are doing it." She walked away, and I heard her bedroom door shut. I took my diary out of my backpack and sat on my new bed against the uneven, chalky wall. "FUCK HER!" I wrote. "I have enough goddamned sense not to! How dare she?"

Randall gave me a job at his movie theater, and it was fun. In the daytime Penelope and I rehearsed the musical at the high school. She was in the chorus, and I had the role of a floozy secretary, which required I learn tap. Our lives were overtaken by the new friends forged in the heat of rehearsals. They were high schoolers, because, my mother explained, "You're more mature than they are." Randall picked us up in the high school parking lot and drove us to his theater, or one of the older kids gave us a ride into town. Randall let me work the box office, and Penelope stocked candy bars. New boys for new crushes came in every night—Bradley, Owen, Andy, etc., a lot to keep track of. We ate all the candy we wanted and carried around cups of Dr Pepper. If we forgot where we'd set them, we poured ourselves more. We stayed up late in Penelope's room, getting the names and gossip straight, who was whose brother, who used to go out with whom. Penelope had made lots of friends, and they absorbed me. Kids gave parties, and our mother always said we could go. She was happy and in love.

People around town knew me and Penelope because we were Daphne's daughters. Our mother of the pink satin and the lip gloss and the sometime-English accent. When we went into the bakery next to the post office people asked first thing where she was. When we showed up at the roller rink, kids asked.

She liked to have us come in her room and talk. Mostly about men and cocaine. The difference between the dealers you could trust and those who were just cokeheads. She gave me coke to try, holding out a tiny amount at first, offering tips for comfort as I inhaled. Eventually I was allowed to use the spoon myself. "A gram," she was always saying into the phone. She wrote large checks to the dealers and sweet-talked the landlord about overdue payments. Two rooms off, I knew the difference between the long sniff of inhalation and the swift sniff of cleanup, mucus sucked back in. She let me sift new coke through the little grinder. Sno-seals fluttered out of her bag on the post office counter, and I worried that she'd get caught, that she'd have a car accident. "You're so self-righteous," she teased me. "Melodramatic." Her fingers hovered at the inflamed edges of her nose, checking and wiping. She yanked the rearview mirror to view her face before driving. At home she had taken framed pictures off the walls, and they lay on the coffee table, the couch, her bed, kitchen table, skimmed with the translucent dust, tracks left by her razor blades, which were scattered in their paper sheaths. If you needed a razor blade, there it was. "I think we should put these away," I would say, and she would laugh. "Want a hit?" she'd ask me.

We dressed for men, putting on the pretty things my mother lavished on us—red tights flecked with silver thread, silk camisoles, new necklaces. She had a crush on this married guy, Michael; we weren't to breathe a word. I had a crush on one of Randall's friends, who was over forty. His laugh percolated with smoker's cough, and his breath smelled like Grand Marnier. My mother let him drive me into town in his pickup. She said yes when he offered to cook me dinner alone at his house, and my chest vibrated with what-if. *She said yes!* But I didn't get to go. She took it back, called him a pervert and forbade me to see him.

My mother welcomed my friends, demanded details in a raucous, friendly way when they picked us up for rehearsal in the mornings or brought me home after the movie theater closed. She invited them to stay and draped them all over the living room furniture. They loved her for her attentive ear, her famous generosity. "She's so cool." "I can't believe your mom." "She's awesome." She had rules: If you were too stoned or too drunk, you slept over. If you brought drugs or beer, you shared. Lincoln came over a lot, rolled joints at our coffee table. Lincoln, I could hardly speak in front of him. He was seventeen, five years out of my reach. I had a major crush on him, staring at his hands as he arranged the dope, but I wouldn't take more than a toke. Nor did I like the way beer made my head empty and made the boys shout over each other. I preferred cocaine, the wide-awake supervising energy. Kids brought hash and beer; kids brought peyote, but I was scared to try it. "Susy's our straight one!" my mother would laugh. Skinny Owen brought mushrooms and sat by himself fussing over the rancid little clump. One late night, my mother made me and Owen baked potatoes, and the three of us sprinkled mushrooms over the sour cream and ate them on the floor beside the fireplace. I wished Lincoln hadn't gone home. "It's Susy's first time," my mother said. "Look at her, looking at the flames! Are you hallucinating, are you hallucinating yet?" The three of us got into her bed to sleep, putting Owen in the middle. We traded innuendo and talked about his body to see how antsy we could make him, which was very.

We went to all the movies. Penelope and I watched *Grease* for days, acting it out at home. Randall got *An Unmarried Woman* because we wanted to see it. He gave me old posters, old stills from *Serpico* and *Annie Hall*. When *The Man Who Fell to Earth* came my mother asked me for a special date, just the two of us. First we went out for pizza and she told me how sexy David Bowie was.

Before the lights went down in the theater, two men came in with a girl. She was about five and filthy. They sat behind us, and my mother turned and started to ask where they were from, etc. The men had hippie beards, and probably she had meant to find out if they wanted to score coke. She said to one of them, "Is this your daughter?"

He said no, that they were hitchhiking across the country. He said, "We're kind of homeless."

"Oh no!" my mother said. She looked at the girl, at them, at me. "Well, I think she should live with me, until you can sort things out. Okay, Sue?"

"I don't know," I said. Please God no. The men ended up taking the girl. My mother leapt up, said, "I'll be right back," and followed them out. I watched the strange movie and found her in the lobby afterward. She was agitated.

"I'm so terribly worried about that little girl."

"I'm sure she'll be fine," I said. I wanted her focus to return to me.

"You can't turn your back on people in trouble, Sue. You have no idea what they could do to that little girl. Thank God you have no idea."

Randall and my mother broke up a lot. "He's so bloody jealous. Of everyone! Of Michael!" But we knew Michael had spent the night. He'd come over at one in the morning, and I could hear them making love in the room next to mine. I heard Randall yell at her about it. They'd get back together, and break up again, and so on. "It's animal," my mother said. "We can't keep away from each other." She said the same about Michael. She told us everything but then seemed to forget, each evening a fresh dance, a new script. Penelope started to stack up grudges against Randall for what he'd said, what he'd done, what he'd shouted at our mother. One night I ran into him in a bar in the plaza, and he sat me down and looked at me hard.

"Look," he said. "I may call your mother a bitch and a cunt, but I'd never do anything to hurt her."

"I know that," I said, but I was preoccupied with my own anger. She was driving me crazy, inviting strangers into the car, doing way too much coke, flirting with my friends. I knew how a person could want to hurt her.

One night when we were working my mother arrived at the theater. "I want to talk to you, miss," she said. She grabbed my arm and walked me through the lobby faster than I wanted to walk. She stopped by the bathrooms, where no one could see us.

"*Listen, you*," she said. "The theater is Penelope's territory. She staked it out and claimed it, and for once you aren't going to take it away from her!" She hit me in the stomach. *What?* Even though she'd done it before, each time was a shock. She gripped my chin, squeezing her fingertips into the bone. I was crying but I agreed—Penelope should have her own domain. She wasn't listening to me and went on. "When you were in New York, you called Penelope and said, 'Oh, I miss you, I love you, you mean so much to me . . . blah, blah, blah.' Then you get here and you don't spend *one* day with her. *You* are a phony, Susy, a phony, phony, phony!" Each time she said "phony" she punched my stomach. By the end of her sentence I felt used to it. But I had spent the first three days entirely with Penelope. We sat together at the auditions. We hung movie posters in her room. I'd give up the job, I didn't care.

My mother left, and I cooled my face with water in the bathroom, checking my expression in the mirror. My mind refused the hitting, turned my body off. I went back to my station by the soda machine. I couldn't tell if Penelope was mad at me. Soon my mother emerged from Randall's office. She had her body curved against him, her hand over his ass, and she was giggling into his ear. I hated her. She tried to hug me but I walked away.

Later, at home, she called me into her room.

"Don't you ever do all that dramatizing in front of Randall again."

"What do you mean?" I was trying to be stony, still unforgiving about earlier.

"Oh, you know: red-eyed, puffy-faced, et cetera. And stop flirting with my man!"

I don't *want a man,* I wanted to scream. I'm twelve.

I wanted to kiss. I watched movie kisses with acute attention and kept an index card tucked into my diary, titled BOYS I LIKE. When I wrote "Lincoln" my chest ached, and I often had to leave the theater during "Hopelessly Devoted to You," because I was crying so hard. He was every song on the radio, long jags of obsessive talk, lengthy journal entries. My mother would happily listen, explaining that I was attracted to his authority. She added how utterly not her type he was.

"He's so hilarious," I said. He wasn't all that funny, but he was cynical and theatrical, which compelled me. She talked tactics with me, cross-legged on her mattress as she stared down at the spoons and powdery piles, her underpants a visible triangle. Penelope was drawing. I tapped coke into new sno-seals. *The Rockford Files* was on.

"What if we invited Lincoln for a special dinner?" she said. "Or we could give him a lift to the airport." She speculated on his kisses. She wanted me to lose my virginity to him, "when you're old enough. Lincoln would be a good first lover. He'd know what he was doing."

"But I'll never see him again!"

"Of course you will. We're going back to New York in September so you can graduate from eighth grade with your friends, but then we're moving here for good. I'm going to buy a house." She looked up at James Garner on the television. "Now that man is divine. One day I *will* have him." Penelope and I smirked at each other.

At my mother's birthday party—her thirty-second—I stayed near the door, distracted and anxious for Lincoln to show up. She had invited everyone. Painters, drug dealers and musicians filled the kitchen, their toddlers against their legs. Teenagers huddled, older girls exiting the bathroom in trios. Lincoln drove a Chevy Nova, his car discernible to me at a distance, even in the dark, because I knew the height and spacing of his headlights. He arrived with a couple of other older kids from the play and smoked pot outside. I watched him leaning back against the door of his car, arms folded as he waited for the joint to come around. He was loud, being sarcastic, which I thought incredibly adult. I hated the mulchy smell of pot, but I wanted to be leaning next to him. He liked to tell me I really needed to get stoned, and I liked to tell him how much better life was without being high.

The night he left for college, I cried extravagantly, stirring up hysteria in my body. Such enormous proof of love. I wanted to soak my pillowcase so it would still be damp in the morning. My mother sat beside me, her hand rubbing the small of my back.

"Little one," she said. Her voice was gentle. "You really love him. Don't you?"

"Yes, yes. It hurts!"

"It won't hurt so much in a while."

"How do you know?"

"I know. You'll see. It will stop. What about, for your birthday present, if I bought Lincoln a ticket to come to New York? He could stay with us for a week. Would you like that?"

"Really, Mummy?" She could divine the best remedy, make me and everything special. She was going to fly him to New York for me.

We returned to New York a few weeks later. I had my thirteenth birthday and started eighth grade, reunited with my old friends. I told them Lincoln was coming, but he never did.

Why I Went to
Boarding School

Her bedroom in New York was painted chocolate. My mother was proud of her taste, her audacity. The velvety brown was set off against white trim and doors, and the corner room had fine-hotel dignity. The year before she'd had the living room painted a vibrant peach. She liked to point these things out because paint, or having something framed, or arranging a dinner party showed her to be organized. A good mother. She wanted to be and told us she was. I knew she didn't want the junkie's disarray, the lame excuses, and when she stayed up all night alphabetizing books in the living room she expected to be congratulated in the morning. She didn't see herself, the penetrating stare of mania gone soft, her jerky motions. She couldn't hear the random and incoherent lurch from phrase to phrase. If she had, I thought, she would have decided things differently. She would have said more than "I'm sorry, kids." She would have said, "Let me fix this." I cleaved to that fantasy, imagining that I'd be generous toward her, help her get well. Almost nothing can blast that sort of hope apart.

But I was also thirteen. I didn't really care what things were like for her. Her back pain was in my way. Her early-morning rants were distasteful. Her nights out meant extra TV. I badgered her for a Mason Pearson hairbrush and stole twenties from her bag while she slept because she'd said no. I talked for hours each evening on the swimming-pool-blue phone she had given me, with its own number to ensure her line stayed free. Eighth grade meant getting ready for high school. Suddenly—and it was very sudden—I could smell open air, a way out. Our possible separation a reality, it was harder to cope with my mother. I still woke each morning, however, ready to start again, all trust.

It was the night before the admissions exam for boarding school. I was at her door when the pain burst beneath my ribs. I sort of fell forward.

"My God, baby!" my mother said. She sat on the quilt surrounded by books and legal pads. She pushed some papers aside. She'd been writing a lot of poetry. I curled up in front of her. She pressed her fingers around my appendix, and I screamed, which I hated. I looked babyish and incompetent.

"Poor little tummy," she said, still pressing, the way a doctor would. "But you don't have a fever. It's not your appendix. It's nerves. I had the exact same thing happen to me before a test, too. Although I was a little younger. I was twelve."

Another shock, and I gripped her fingers together. I didn't want to hurt her, but I couldn't let go. With her free hand she picked up a paperback Emily Dickinson from the bedside table.

"'After great pain, a formal feeling comes,'" she said, and started to read the rest of the poem.

"Mummy! This isn't helping." I was twisting, as if I could roll out of the way of the pain. Her pages crinkled under me, but she didn't seem to mind.

"You have to calm down," she said. "Oh, darling, I never wanted you to know what agony was. But now you know."

I thought I'd throw up. She offered me a Valium.

"I don't want to take anything," I said. "I have the exam in the morning." I had to do well, had to get into boarding school.

"How are you going to sleep?" she said. "If you don't sleep, you won't be able to think, and you won't be able to pass the test." She split the blue pill in two. "Just take a half. This is psychosomatic. You need to relax." She gave me one half and popped the other into the pillbox that looked like an acorn carved of ivory. She had a lot of pillboxes.

The Valium helped me fall asleep against her, but pain woke me again.

"It's stabbing me, Mummy."

"It will stop," she said. "Trust me. This is one thing I really am an expert in. It seems like you were never not in pain, right? I know it seems like you'll never be free of pain again. I know. Then afterwards, it's hard to remember it."

I was a wreck in the morning. The pain had vanished. As she'd predicted, I couldn't remember it exactly, but its assault had left me limp.

"How's the attack? Better?" my mother said.

"I guess so."

"This is how I live, Sue, every day."

The exam was held in some gym I'd never been to. I joined the anxious sea of thirteen-year-olds on the sidewalk and then through the tall double doors into the brightly lit room. No one else from my school was there. During the test I could feel boredom, fear and feverish effort everywhere, my own feelings made huge, shared by the others.

Choose the synonym: Enervate

Weaken
Energize
Expel
Innovate
Initiate

Now and then a grown-up walked among the rows of us, and the restless kids would sit still and the concentrating kids would work faster. The sound of pencil tips in all the holes set off a nervous terror in me that I wasn't thinking hard enough. I got scared the stomach pain would come back. I felt the lump of the ivory acorn in my pocket. I had a headache. The math problems dissolved, senseless, in front of my eyes.

When I got back to the apartment my mother was waiting with pink roses, and she took me out to lunch.

"Tell me everything about the test."

"It was okay," I said. "What does 'enervate' mean?"

"'Enervate'? It means 'energize.' No, wait, or is it the opposite? Let's ask someone. Him, he looks smart." But the waiter passed.

"I had to find the synonym. I think I blew that one."

"I'm sure you did brilliantly. Okay, time to talk about the school tour. Oh—" She switched subjects, and I pushed away my exasperation. "As you know, your grandfather left you a great deal of money, and I've put it in the bank for you. You'll have a checking account, and you're going to have to be responsible. What would you say to a budget of a thousand a month?"

"A budget?" The sum was meaningless to me. I spent my money on movie stills and 45s, two dollars each, *People* magazine, movie tickets to the Regency, plastic belts at Fiorucci, but I was interested in this development. I didn't get to say more before she jumped to the next thing, pulling paper from her striped basket bag. One of her poems filled the page in her inky scrawl. She put the blank side up on the table, but I could see the press of her pen from the other side. She listed the schools, and we narrowed the choice to three to visit and had steak tartare for lunch.

"You'll knock 'em dead in the interviews, darling."

My mother and I took the train to Boston and rented a car. We drove around in the country, coming upon those New England schools. I strained my smiling muscles during the chatty tours and interviews. I noted the tartan skirts and ribbed navy blue knee socks. My mother kept saying to kids, "Are you a preppy?" Tall girls walked past us with lacrosse sticks.

We drove back to Boston.

"Let's see Harvard!" she said, parking. We wandered among the pretty buildings, and I had her to myself. Cambridge felt like our own, a playland put here for us.

The next day we woke up at the exact same moment in our king-sized bed, and she ordered room service. "Very softly scrambled," she told the kitchen, our favorite way to eat eggs. We walked through Boston Common, where she surprised me by identifying some of the trees, their names confirmed on discreet plaques as we came closer. We agreed: Of course I'd get into Andover (I didn't). She believed in my writing ("But you can't sing. Penelope's the singer"). Everything went slowly, and she listened to me, whatever I wanted to talk about, about kissing and about the boys I liked. We talked about her poems. She asked if I would edit one. Our friendship was different than any other daughter had with any other mother, richer, more candid, beyond school and poetry, far beyond the talk of sex, the crushes and relationships.

"You're so beautiful," she said. "Look at all the men looking at us." They were, and we drifted through the gardens. We took the train home to New York, and I gave Penelope a box of Red Hots from a dorm vending machine. She was amazed there was a place to live where you could get candy whenever you wanted it.

I just had to wait until April 15th, acceptance-letter day. I listened to eight-tracks of *A Chorus Line* and *Chicago,* and my mother clapped when Penelope and I performed in the living room. I spent Thursday nights at my father's, sometimes with Penelope, sometimes alone. You should be reading Chekhov and Cervantes, he said, not Judy Blume. I bleached my upper lip with Jolen Creme. My bedroom door shut, I studied the boarding school catalogs, which all had photographs of a chapel in the snow, the intent face in pottery class, the Frisbee games, the handsome boys in sports uniforms laughing in the dining hall.

My mother read her poems aloud to us. When my friends came over, she read to them. She was having an affair with a married playwright whom we weren't allowed to meet, to protect his privacy. He came over while we were at school, and they made love. Once she suggested I come home early, and we'd pretend to him that she was surprised. "That way you can meet him." She said she was going to marry some Italian guy "to help him out, so he can get his papers." He was nobility, she said. "We'll all be princesses."

"What about Randall?" said Penelope. Although he still lived in Taos, they were back together. In the summer, when we moved to Taos permanently Randall was going to teach me to drive.

"Don't worry, girls. Randall knows I love him. I'm just doing this to help." The Italian prince slept over two nights then disappeared, and she didn't get married.

*   *   *

We had to knock on her bedroom door, no matter what. She might be writing or making love. I knocked and heard a commotion. Then she opened the door. Michael, her other lover from Taos, was sitting in a chair in bare feet. He waved and went into the bathroom. My mother snorted a hit of coke through a rolled-up ten, her hair falling forward, hiding her expression.

"Right," I said. I was angry.

"You could say hello," she said, gesturing toward the bathroom.

"You're going out with Randall, and remember last summer when he found out about Michael?"

"You don't have to be rude, Susy."

"Okay. Hi. 'Bye," I said and went back to my room. "This is insane," I wrote in my diary. "It's insane that I'm used to cocaine and lovers and sex. I don't feel surprised when she opens her bedroom door, just disgusted." I thought of the previous summer: Randall had burst into our house and punched the adobe wall. We were scared, and my mother was furious, and he stood there, and she wouldn't talk to him. There was clay dust all over the floor.

I sat on my bed, fuming. She didn't remember anything. I wanted to get out of there so badly, and I would. I was going to boarding school. Please let me get in.

My mother shoved open my door, hurtled into my little room. She seized my arms.

"I came back to New York for you!" She yanked the lapels of my bathrobe, her hands up at my chin. She plowed a fist into my stomach. I looked down at her hands, unable to feel them. Her thin, tight skin was almost blue. I heard fabric tearing, and it sounded far away in another room and pleasing, something definitive in the sound. She held on and shook me, and my neck lurched back and forth. "I came back here, much against my will, *for you,* so you could go to your precious school! I won't have you judging me! Do you understand what you have cost me, simply the expense of all the plane tickets?" She launched me out of her grip onto the bed.

"I'll pay for it!" I screamed. "Give me my money. I'll pay for my own tickets. Just go back to Taos. I don't care."

"Your money. What money? Really!" She slammed my door on her way out.

"I hate you!" I screamed. The hatred raced in my body and wanted violence, but she was the one who got to be violent. She was always the one.

We went to Barbados for weeks, leaving before spring break, school unimportant. My mother pointed out that the boarding schools already had my transcripts, were sure to accept me, so eighth grade didn't matter much anymore. Late to JFK, we picked our way through slush and luggage to check in, but the flight was over-booked, and people stood around. Penelope fretted. We became weary of each public address. My mother marched off to find a manager and returned with a huge grin.

"He knows who he's dealing with now," she said.

"What'd you say?"

"Just that we were going down to collect Patsy and bring her back for open-heart surgery *and* that I just happened to be the editor of the travel section of *The New York Times* and if he didn't want the airline's name splashed across the front page on Sunday, he'd bloody well find me three seats."

"But you don't work at the *Times*," Penny said. I recognized the confusion. Of course our mother didn't work at the *Times*, but for one sparkling second we wondered—*did* she work there?

"Darlings, all you have to do is threaten. Most people don't have the guts."

Once we were arranged in our seats, the flight in the air, my mother handed me a few loose-leaf pages. She'd written "The

Story of How We Got On," and I read it, admiring the details, the comic asides. I thought this was funny. She knew how to live, I thought, to make life hers. What would I do without her unique instruction? In the hot, open-air Barbados airport we glided from baggage to customs to cab stand. New York didn't exist, our friends didn't exist, just this fairyland of teatimes and house parties. The first red hibiscus was always a shock. But then we were beyond tourist novelty; we belonged. The taxi turned in between the gates and progressed to the central courtyard, and the gardener stopped whisking at the dried leaves and waved. Patsy hurried from the front doors, past the urns bursting with flowers, money for the driver in one hand.

We hugged our grandmother, and Rodney the butler carried our bags to the blue room in the annex Penelope and I always shared. We were in time for tea, and Patsy summoned us to hurry. We raced after Rodney, opened our bags, stripped off our travel clothes and threw on airy dresses. We ran up to the main house, where our grandmother sat erect, teapot in hand. Little brown birds swooped in through the massive window, alighted on the window-seat cushion and hopped toward the tea tray. We loved dropping grains of brown sugar for the cheeky birds. "Shoo!" Patsy cried.

"Oh, let them," my mother told her.

After tea my mother sent us to unpack, but we returned to our room to find our clothes already set into the drawers, hung in the closets.

Our Barbados days were divided by clothes—long T-shirts at breakfast (a sarong for Aunt Irene), swimsuits all morning, cotton skirts at lunch and perfume and fancy dresses for dinner. I loved the sentence "Go and dress for dinner." I loved the old-movie glamour of this life. The estate was the one place my mother's family gathered, her older brother traveling from England, Aunt Irene arriving with her husband.

Fresh eggs got delivered to the kitchen. A waterskiing instructor brought the boat by in the mornings. Our mother would take me and Penelope out in the Mini Moke to the Coral Reef Hotel, where she would lie by the pool with a book (*Montgomery Clift* by Patricia Bosworth, *My Mother My Self* by Nancy Friday) as we did underwater handstands and investigated other children, who always seemed reticent in their French or German. Penelope and I begged maraschino cherries off the obliging bartenders and scored virgin piña coladas, for free. "Look what Winston gave us!" We'd come home for tea, the fresh slices of cake and thickly buttered cucumber sandwiches, and listen to our grandmother's frustrations with the telephone company or a guest list. We were the only children of the family, and at Christmas, which we always spent in Barbados, the presents under the tree were mostly for us. My mother told us we were lucky and not to forget it.

At night my sister and I woke up together, scared together in the dark. Penelope's hand crawled over the coverlets to grab at my hand. In the thick black silence, we had no hint of the grown-ups scattered around the estate—not our beautiful aunt Irene and her younger husband asleep in the Tea House, not my wild-haired uncle, who wore a turquoise wrist cuff and linen shirts, sleeves rolled up over tanned arms. Not the occasional houseguests—knighted British actors, gay fashion designers. Not my mother, back from the discotheque, in her deep, forgetful sleeps right next door, also locked in.

I tried to make Penelope go back to sleep. She was the little one, soft and slippery with sleep. She was the need and the famine. I was the reader of maps, the tidying, the tucking in.

When we went in to kiss Patsy good morning, we found her propped in bed against various pillows, expecting the maid with the breakfast tray. She'd raise her arms toward us, as if waiting to be picked up. She sent us to play when the cook came in to plan the menus.

* * *

My mother called me to her room. I was on my way to the sunny terrace built high over the sea. Penelope was already rattling the backgammon dice in their felt-lined cup. Rodney would make us planter's punch without the rum and bring it on a tray with coasters. He was a genius with a lime, I'd heard Patsy say. As I passed my mother's room, one panel of her French door ajar, her voice trickled out.

"Susy? Is that you, Sue?"

I found her lying on her stomach, the sheet pushed down to her knees. The naked rest of her filled the room. That and the smell.

"I can't do this myself, darling." Her hand flew back and fluttered over her spine and the open sore the size of a quarter. Pus seeped from it, dappled yellow stains on the sheet, some post-op infection she'd told me all about, but I'd forgotten the details. She beckoned with the silver tube wrapped in a prescription label. "Could you rub this salve into my hole?"

"I don't want to," I said. I really didn't want to inspect her. I wanted to be out in the sun.

"Come on. It'll just take a minute. Don't you have a minute?" She pushed the tube into my hand and tugged me closer by my wrist. With salve on my fingertips I dabbed the rim of the hole, the ointment the same color as the pus.

"Ow! Don't press too hard, and make sure it goes in." The spot was hotter and wetter than it looked, the rim puckered with wet scabs.

"It's totally gross, Mummy."

"Don't be rude. Stay with me while it dries."

"I was going to play backgammon with Penelope."

"Do you think you could possibly spend one single morning not being selfish?"

Her bedside phone rang, lunch announced. She straightened up, as if I'd fastened a necklace for her, and I waited on a wicker bench while she dressed. I didn't want to sit on the stained sheet. She laced her cool, thin fingers into mine as we made our way to the main house.

She looked glamorous and well put together to everyone, to her mother, to the staff we'd known intimately for years (without ever learning their last names), and to the diverting guests invited almost every evening. She was entertaining, leaping up to put a record on, saying the one thing you were instructed not to say to Lord So-and-So, who'd left England in disgrace. Often, Patsy broke down in the middle of scolding her for a vulgar joke or a late arrival and started laughing, annoyed at herself. Her fondness for my mother could not be contained.

Barbados
Sunday, February 18th, 1979
    I'm only scared for her! I don't give a SHIT how many of those fucking Percodan she shoves down her throat! I don't want her to turn into some goddamned junkie! I ask if she's taken some pills from Patsy's bathroom. Yes, she says. Oh, good, I say, that gives you just one more to take every day. Would you rather I was taking 12 a day as I used to? Or maybe 20? I'm trying damn it, she yells at me. And you make judgments! I began to cry because I wanted her to realize that I wasn't telling her what to do, I was only expressing fear. Go do your self-pitying crying somewhere else, she snaps.
    I love Mummy desperately. I don't want to see her in pain, but I don't want to see seizures and her in a coma. Not only Percodan either. There's the Valium, the soma comp., the sleeping pills. Yes, I'm glad she's off Demerol. She used to punch her thigh with so many

holes it looked like a pin cushion. My mother weighs
108 pounds.

New York
Thursday, April 5, 1979

I am very worried and very scared. Mummy seems
worse than she's ever been in terms of her back. For
simply walking she needs two canes to support herself
and ease the pain. She isn't taking Percodan anymore,
but a lot of Methadone, plus healthy doses of Valium and
substantial amounts of cocaine. I don't mind about the
drugs if it would do good, but her pain is so intense and
mostly psycho-somatic, that these pain killers usually
have little if any effect on her. I feel so helpless and
frightened. I want to help her but what is there for me
to do?

The boarding school letters arrived on the same day. I was sleeping over at Marcy's, and my mother phoned.

"They're here," she said. "Shall I open them?"

"I want to."

"Do you really think you can wait till tomorrow?"

I did want to know. "Okay, go ahead." I got ready.

In my mother's voice Andover turned me down. One school
put me on the waiting list, and I got into my second choice.

"I got in! I got in!" I danced with Marcy. "Praise Connecticut!" we shouted.

When Penelope and I came home after school, my mother was
blazing around the living room.

She grabbed me and hugged me. "An editor wants my poems!"

"What?" we said.

"I just spoke to the *president* of *Random* House!" The secret playwright had arranged a meeting, and the editor-president was interested in the whole manuscript. "He might give me a thou as an advance! I'm so nervous I don't know how I can let him read them. I just have to remember they're good."

"They're really good," Penelope said. "They're brilliant, Mummy."

"They are, aren't they?" she said.

Our mother would be published. For a few days we kept constant track of the subject. Then, on her way to the important editor, she was so agitated that she left her folder in the taxi, every poem she'd ever written, the only copies. She called the cab companies, but no one had turned in the fat folder. There was no meeting, no advance and no book. I remember the folder with mismatched pages sprouting from the top and bottom. She carried it everywhere, until she said she lost it.

My mother had to leave suddenly for Taos. I don't remember why. Some friend of hers we barely knew stayed with us, and Aunt Irene, who had divorced and moved to New York, took me shopping in the Village for my eighth-grade graduation dress.

Wednesday, May 9th, 1979
    Mummy came home. I was so happy she was back.
Suddenly she got angry and I ran to my room. I
slammed the door and cried. Not in self-pity but in
anger. How could she treat me that way after a full week
of not seeing either me or Penelope? Well, she came to
apologize as I knew she would. But she grabbed me and
shook me back and forth. She hit me across the face,
punched my stomach and banged my knee. I was
terrified. I had no idea what had gotten into her. She left
me telling me I was to come to her room before the

night was over to apologize. I was incredulous. How could she ever expect me to do that after that ordeal? Mummy came to me Monday morning and told me this: she had overdosed on one drug and then another drug that was almost lethal with the first one. She called the Poison Control Center when she started having difficulty breathing. They told her to go to Lenox Hill Hospital and get a teaspoon of some syrup to make her throw up. She apologized to me in the morning, claiming she didn't know what had gotten into her.

My orthodontist had promised, and I got my braces off in time for Thursday's graduation. The week was filled with appointments, assemblies and outings, class picnics in Central Park, feverish rehearsals for *The Skin of Our Teeth*. I had the lead role of Sabina. For my costume my mother lent me her red dress and heels, and I vamped it up.

During the final performance, the hour before we graduated, I could see my mother in the audience with Penelope beside her. (My father had attended the play the night before, uninterested in ritual good-byes.) She was in her seat during the diploma ceremony, but when we were dispersed, and my lifelong classmates spilled out into more rooms of the school, I couldn't find her. My adopted mothers scooped me up in excited rushes with their children. Marcy and Elise and I clutched each other, our arms tight, our shrieks of relief and invincibility filling the hallways. The teachers gave us cards, presents and hugs ending in tears.

Then my mother was whispering it was time to go. "Paul's coming," she said, as if confirming. He was out on the sidewalk, Elise's older brother. When Paul talked to me at Elise's, it felt embarrassing and weird, like looking at a movie of your future self without understanding it. My mother, dancing across the pavement, stuck two fingers in her mouth to whistle her sharp taxi whistle. A cab made a U-turn and pulled up. I couldn't think what to say: Paul was in college, and now he was in our taxi, crowding into the backseat, my mother's lips against his ear.

The next morning, I lay on the couch, halfway through *The Memoirs of Sarah Bernhardt* my teachers had given me. Paul walked shirtless out of my mother's room and said hi.

She came and slid her hand into the hair on his chest, gently pushing him away. "Finish dressing. You, too, Sue. My little graduate! We'll go out to breakfast." He left the room, and she bent over and whispered, "He's fabulous in bed, natch. He's nineteen."

We went down the block to the Skyline for French toast and fresh orange juice to celebrate me.

Assault

My mother flew east with me so she could take me to boarding school. Paul was going to drive us up in his VW bus.

"Isn't it sweet, on his way to Harvard, to give us a lift?" she said. "Otherwise we'd have had to rent a car."

Paul showed up at Eighty-first Street early. "Nervous?" he said to me.

"I'm excited." I was wearing a navy blue skirt, a white button-down shirt and a lavender-colored wool vest, all new. I felt very crisp, very orderly.

Paul carried out my bags and trunk and arranged them in the back of his van. My mother wanted to drive, and Paul hopped into the passenger seat. My father had given me a hi-fi, and its new boxes sat next to me on the backseat.

New York disappeared as we headed up unfamiliar highways. I only knew how to get out of the city by airplane. You took a taxi over the "Tri-bra" Bridge (her accent) and arrived at the airport. At the rest stop, my mother fished her little brown vial from her bag and reached down her blouse for the tiny spoon on a chain, scooping up hits of coke.

My mother said, "I'm dying to meet your roommate."

I said, "I wonder what kind of music she likes." I had spent a lot of time conjuring this certain friend. My mother told Paul her own boarding school stories.

In the New England town we turned onto the main route through the campus. I tried to spot anything I remembered from the tour. The campus looked much, much bigger. Cars drove slowly, left- or right-hand signals blinking. My mother had Paul read the directions.

"Now where's the admissions building?" she said. "Oh, there. Next left, then?"

As Paul unloaded the bags, my mother and I went up the steps of the dorm and found the dorm head's apartment, her door ajar.

"Come in! I'm Miss Peters." She wore khakis and a pink sweater, her hair in a short ponytail.

"I'm Daphne. And this is Susanna Sonnenberg."

Miss Peters checked her clipboard. "It looks like you have a single."

On the stairs my mother said to me, "You have no *idea* how lucky you are to get a single. My roommates were always complete cows."

"But you said you were dying to meet my roommate."

"I only said that to cheer you up."

The little room smelled of carpet cleaner, and my mother opened the window. We could hear shouts from some sort of game. A mattress on a metal frame, an industrial desk pushed into the corner, matching dresser.

"This isn't so bad," she said.

"Hi, are you Susanna?" A girl pointed down the hall. "Your brother's looking for you."

"She seemed nice," my mother said. She called out the door to Paul. He brought in my trunk. She lifted the lid, started to pull out towels and sheets. "Here, give me that pillow. And let's get something on the walls." Paul came back in with the stereo boxes. I watched my mother fix things up. She was showing off for Paul. I was curious about the voices in the hallways, the singing and shrieking.

My mother picked a leaflet off the desk. "Convocation at noon. Followed by a 'Welcome Third Formers Luncheon.' Parents are invited, too."

"Hi, I'm Beatrice. Are you from England?"

"Yes. I am," my mother said, extending her hand. "Although my daughter's from New York." She got more British. A blond girl with a cast on her foot came in, using a crutch.

"Hi! I'm Kelly. I'm the proctor."

"Oh, wonderful." My mother stepped close to her and took up the hand that was on the crutch. "Listen, love, will you keep your eye on Sue? Look out for her? Promise me?" The girl nodded, big smile. "And where's the loo?"

The girl shrugged.

"Oh, right, sorry. The bathroom." She trotted down the hall. I knew she needed a toot.

"Wow, your mom's gorgeous."

"Thanks."

"That's your mom? How old is she?"

"Thirty-three."

"Did Miss Peters say your brother could come in? Boys aren't allowed in the dorm."

"He's not my brother. He's my mother's boyfriend."

"*No* way!"

"How old was she when she had you?"

I was going to say seventeen, which my mother sometimes told people, sometimes told me, but these girls might add fourteen and seventeen, then see the math was wrong. I said, "Nineteen."

My mother held Paul's hand as they walked me to the arts center. We followed a winding path through stands of trees. Sunlight, then shadow, then sunlight. I worried I wouldn't remember how to find my dorm. People thronged in front of the theater.

"We'll wander about," my mother said. "And meet you back at your room before the lunch."

The ceremony was long, the dark auditorium packed. The headmaster listed the rules against drinking and smoking, about coed visiting and being on time for classes. He talked about the honor code. It was a big deal. "The foundation of a healthy community," he said. The hallmark of something-or-other. Teachers sat in folding chairs behind his dais. "Was that your *mother*?" someone whispered at me. I nodded. At the end, a brass march blared over speakers as we filed out according to our year.

The door to my room was open, and I started to walk in. Another mother was folding sweaters.

I checked the number on the door. "Sorry."

"You're probably in the next section over," she said. I had come in through the wrong entrance, and the common rooms, stairwells and hallways were identical.

I opened my door to see Paul and my mother seated on the bed, which was still bare, except for the pillowcase.

"Listen, love," she said, getting up. "We're not staying. Paul has to get to Boston." She said to him, "Will you wait for me outside?"

"Good luck, Susy." Paul cuffed me gently on his way out.

"You should write him a thank-you note," my mother said. She leaned close. "We broke in the mattress for you."

"Oh, gross, Mummy! I was gone an *hour*." I shot a look at the bed. They'd done it without even putting down a mattress pad. I would die if someone had heard them. "Thanks a *lot*."

"What can I say? He's nineteen." She laughed. "Don't take it so seriously. How was the lecture? Very important?"

"Not really. Nothing but rules and stuff about earning grades that'll get you into Harvard."

"Well, you knew the academics were going to be rigorous."

"I'm fourteen. Do I have to think about college?"

"You could have gone to that hippie school in Vermont," she said.

"Everyone's so preppy, so . . . stiff," I said. I felt panicky and needed her to see it. "These are not my people. I hate it here. This was a mistake."

"Don't be a drama queen. You don't 'hate' it here. Anyway, what are you going to do, go to Taos High? Are *those* your 'people'? You'll make friends. Kelly said she'd take you over to the dining hall for dinner."

"God, I don't even know her."

"Well, she's super, and she thinks you're super." She stroked my arms and started to cry. "My baby, baby, baby." She pulled me against her. I could feel how hard her heart was pounding, or maybe that was both our hearts. "Big girl," she said. "You're out in the grown-up world now." She gripped me, we kissed, and she left, wishing Kelly a great year as she headed out. I felt how exhausted I was.

Later, in a nightgown, I opened my door, carrying my toothbrush and toothpaste. Miss Peters stopped me.

"Lights out."

I said, "But I have to brush my teeth."

"You should have done it earlier. Sorry."

"But it'll take less than a minute."

She stood in front of me. "You'll get used to the rules," she said. "Back in your room now." I threw my toothbrush down on my desk before banging shut my door.

*   *   *

I'd been gone about a month. It was like a year, learning so much: Every building had a name, and a lot of them had one name but were called another. Older kids referred to things like Mug Night that I had to decipher, and my mailbox had a combination, and the bus to New York left campus on some Fridays, but not all, and the weekend hours were slightly different in the two dining halls. I was supposed to try out for sports, wanted to audition for a play, and someone handed me a flyer about the literary magazine. My stomach attacks came weekly, and weekly I'd get special permissions signed by Miss Peters and walk in the dark to the infirmary, where I would explain to a nurse that I already knew Valium worked, please, please. I missed home, my mother's rumpled bed, Penelope's James Taylor music, which I didn't even like. I missed being me.

My mother phoned frequently. When I heard the thrum of the ringer, I waited until someone called my name. One night I sat in the booth with the glass door closed. People looked in as they raced by for the stairwell. I sat in the sturdy chair, feet up on the built-in shelf for phone books. My mother went over the Taos gossip I craved. There'd been a party by the river and someone had dared someone else to jump from the bridge. Lincoln's brother was getting married. Penelope refused to learn to drive.

"She's only twelve," I said.

"She's so difficult," said my mother. "She really misses you."

"Me, too."

"Do you remember Justin?"

"Sure." He had been my last crush, a cute seventeen-year-old on the periphery of my regular crowd. All summer my mother kept saying he was crazy about me. "Well, I've got something to tell you, Sue. He moved in."

"What?" Why would he do that, I was thinking, when I'd already gone away?

"He moved in because, uh, well, you're going to hear this from someone—because we're a couple now."

I set my feet on the floor.

Now that she'd told me, she got excited. "I had no idea he was a virgin. He seemed so experienced."

"What?"

"Wouldn't you agree that our house is better than his crazy family's house?"

I agreed, dazed and furious. "He was a virgin?"

"It wasn't my idea, Sue! He and Penny are really getting along. I hope you approve, darling."

We hung up, and I walked down the hall to Katy's room. She was studying, leaning against a bolster her mother had sent in a care package. I was a little drunk on Katy, my new friend. She wore Love's Baby Soft. I knew her favorite color, her best grade, which teacher she had a crush on.

I dropped onto her bed. "My mother just told me she's dating my boyfriend."

"What do you mean?"

I'd started a lot of my stories to her with "My mother . . ." "She said that he just moved into our house, and she took his virginity." Saying it out loud gave me an odd feeling in my body, like putting on another girl's jeans. Everything fit, but not in the right places. She probably wouldn't believe me.

"Your boyfriend?"

"Yeah. We went out last summer." I hadn't actually dated Justin, but the story felt more credible that way, conveyed what this felt like. "We never even broke up before I left."

"Your mother's too much," Katy said.

I wanted something more from her, but I wasn't sure what and had to settle for that.

I got a crush on a senior named Larry, and you could see him anywhere on campus, he was that tall. He had a deep voice and a rash of acne scars. In October he was in *The Importance of Being Earnest,* and I made Katy go backstage with me so I could tell him he was good. The next night I timed my tray return in the dining hall with his. "Hi," I said. "Remember how much I liked your performance?" I asked him to walk me to my dorm. I could make him say yes because I knew you could get boys to do anything. He showed me a shortcut, crossing through some woods, and I asked him about acting, but he wanted to talk about an upcoming football game.

When we got to my quad I started up the steps, turned around and found him eye to eye with me, mouth to mouth. "Okay, enough about football," I said. He cupped his giant hands around my face and leaned forward and kissed me. This wasn't getting a kiss; this was *kissing.* I pressed into him, but he wouldn't open his mouth. Anyway, I wanted him to leave so I could race upstairs and tell Katy. The next night I refilled my milk glass when he did, and he walked me back to my dorm, and we reenacted the scene, because that was the only way to get the kiss to happen again. Walk, steps, hands, mouth. This time his tongue went into my mouth and moved around, dry and pushy.

But the word *kiss* floated up, danced over his head and held my attention as he held my face. French kiss! Girls trooped up the concrete steps around us, lugging at the glass entry door. He made a joke I didn't get. I just wanted the kissing, more, more. He stayed another couple of minutes, and then I ran in to find Katy.

I sat in class with "kiss!" in my belly, such a jolt and a jump, such a good, at-last feeling. I answered questions but couldn't hear my own voice. That kiss was loud. Walking between classes, I thought the white chapel was whiter, and the lines of the arts center starker, and every single dot and speck of other students on the campus didn't know what I knew I'd call my mother after study hall.

When she answered I was so excited. (We didn't mention Justin ever. Easier.)

"Guess what? I had a French kiss!" My tummy jumped again, the words unlikely in my voice.

"That's great, love." Her television was on. She asked Penelope to turn it down, and I could picture the way her hand rose to catch Penny's attention. "Next time you're in the city I want you to call my gynecologist and get fitted for a diaphragm."

"Come on, Mummy. It was just two kisses."

"There will be more, and one day, you'll want to make love," she said. "Remember what your father did to me?" She told me she trusted that doctor. "You know he delivered Penelope at New York Hospital. You probably need a small diaphragm. Did you know I wear the smallest size there is? Who kissed you?"

"This senior."

"A *senior*. Good kisser? Teenaged boys can be such bad kissers."

"Yeah, he was kind of bad, I guess," I said.

"Well, cheer up," she said. "You won't have to kiss *him* forever. You'll find the good ones."

I went into Katy's room.

"My mother thinks I should get a diaphragm."

"*Why?*" Katy still hadn't been kissed. She looked like I'd said a bad word, which annoyed me.

"To be ready."

"She wants you to be ready to have sex? Your family. We can't even have sex here, you know. It's against the rules. Imagine if Peters busted you?"

I said, "I bet she's still a virgin," and we cracked up. "Larry's so big, he'd crush me if we made love." It didn't sound appealing.

"I can't believe you can talk about that stuff with your mom."

"Yeah, we tell each other everything."

"You know, though," said Katy. "You seem a little boy crazy. It's always all about boys with you."

"Oh, loosen up," I said, getting up from her bed. She never even tried with boys, and all you had to do was try. I went back to my room. I felt mad at her, and embarrassed. And really, really hungry for more kissing. I lay down, replaying the hands, mouth, tongue.

Larry broke up with me the next day in the student center. He said he didn't want a girlfriend. Wow. My first boyfriend, my first real boyfriend. I could kiss anyone.

I liked a boy in algebra named Hammond. I'd go over to Willetts House, the freshman boys' dorm, and hang out in the common room. He was kind of mysterious, always able to produce cigarettes or Bacardi. One morning after math Ham headed back to my quad with me. We were walking along, a fine mood, nothing serious, when he jerked me off the path. I stumbled, and he grabbed my arm and pulled me several paces into the grove of dense trees. "Hey," I said. "This isn't the way."

"Hold on a minute," he said. He pushed hard and sort of pulled me and pushed me until I was on my back on the ground.

"Come on," I said. I think I was laughing, whatever goofy joke, dumb act this was. "Ham, come on, let's go."

"No, wait." Ham dropped to his knees and threw one leg over me. Then he pinned down my wrists and shifted his legs until his knees pinned my shoulders. I still thought he was kidding, a stupid joke, a joke. I watched his hand, enormously close to my face, as he unzipped his jeans one-handed and pulled out his penis. Not a joke. He pressed it against my mouth. I felt a hot animal surge of NO, strange pulses zooming into my shoulders, and I bucked my chest and threw him off. I ran a few yards toward the path. Then I stopped, turned around and looked at him, and I said, "Coming?" because again, back in sunlight, standing upright, this was just a prank. He hadn't meant it. He brushed leaves off his jean jacket and walked me the rest of the way to the quad. We didn't talk. I was amazed by the way silence swallowed the episode and threatened the memory.

That night I started to tell a sympathetic teacher what had happened, but I couldn't make it come out the way I wanted, couldn't keep it awful. Already unraveling, the experience was bursting into fragments, rather than staying whole, and I didn't trust myself to get it right.

"I told the school about what you did," I said the next time I saw Ham.

"So?" he said. He walked away in a drove of boys. There were a million ways to feel lonely at this school.

I waited a few days to tell my mother. I knew her reaction would take over the situation, make everything giant. Mornings and evenings passed, the classroom, study-hall and dining-hall demands insistent, and the details grew murkier. By the time I told her, I couldn't remember the things I wanted to, and it sounded made-up to me.

She dove in. She wanted me to press charges against Ham, against the school, but I knew how my voice sounded in this world—attention-getting, overdone.

"Good God," she said. "Why did I ever allow you to go so far away from me?"

I went home to Taos for the summer. One day, driving through town with my mother, we stopped for a pedestrian and it turned out to be Justin crossing the street. We watched him. She put the car back into gear and said, "You know, I think I might take up with that boy again."

I wouldn't go for the bait. "Randall? *Michael?*" I sneered. She was sleeping with both.

"Don't be melodramatic, Susy. It doesn't suit you."

*   *   *

Sunday, August 31, 1980

    Randall physically assaulted my mother, beating her
over the head, hitting her in the face, and punching her
in the stomach where she is now hemorrhaging. He then
drove to ——————, stormed into Michael's office, threw
him to the ground and kicked his face in . . . I'm glad I'm
not there—*so* glad! I don't want to deal with that shit! . . .
Mummy . . . and Michael are intending to charge
Randall with assault and battery. All of them are *fuckers!*

    I was visiting my father on the Cape, without Penelope, when
I heard this account over the phone. Things seemed to happen
when I wasn't there, exciting and awful, and I couldn't know if
they were true, how much was true. I could picture my mother's
injured face, the look of movie makeup.

    Worried for my sister, for both of them, I told my father.

    "Gracious," he said. "Is she in hospital?"

    I didn't know.

    The next morning my father said that if he thought he could
win, he'd sue my mother for custody of Penelope.

    "Or perhaps a social worker to visit the house."

    My stomach flipped over. My mother and Penny. All of us. I
couldn't imagine Penny gone; I should make a case for our life in
Taos. It felt like my father wanted to break up my family, and my
loyalties careened.

    I called Taos several times over the next couple of days, but my
mother wouldn't calm herself and answer my specific questions as
I tried to pin down the event. "What happened?" I kept saying.
"What happened?" And she changed the subject. But it was settled.
It was the way we were going to talk about Randall from then on.

    Anyway, my father never sent a social worker.

*　*　*

I returned to school for the fourth form year. On occasional weekends I slept at my father's new apartment in New York, where he'd had all the doorjambs removed to make way for his wheelchair. I'd take Amtrak to Penn Station. Once, I started flirting with a man on the way down, and I agreed to meet him later in Washington Square. He said he was twenty-four and didn't mind that I was fifteen. "How do you feel about Italian food?" I lied to my father that I was meeting old classmates at the Regency. I got off the subway at West Fourth Street and walked to the edge of the park. The stranger pulled up in his car, and I didn't wonder if I should get in but opened the door and let him drive us. We had a bland meal, and he turned out to be a bland kisser, too, and I said I'd call him but knew I wouldn't.

My father introduced me to his new girlfriend, Isabel, who had already moved in. She had almond-shaped eyes and short dark hair in a blunt cut. In a couple of months, he married her, and I brought Katy down to the city for the small party, a ceremony performed in the living room by a judge between dinner and dessert.

Katy took me home on a long weekend to her old stone house in Pennsylvania, a state I'd never visited. I wasn't even sure where it was.

We took our stuff up to her bedroom, and she showed me around. The bathrooms with pink soaps, the shining piano and sheet music, the brightly lit kitchen island. We slumped in her family room, her cat warming my legs as we watched a Marx Brothers movie. Her mother came in from the kitchen and brought us brownies. Settled in the velvet sectional, I held a heavy brownie in one hand, its chocolate separating in chunks, my arm warmed by my best friend's arm. Then Katy's mother came back in and told me I had a call. She held out the receiver in the doorway between kitchen and family room. I got up and followed the cord back to the kitchen and then out into the hallway. This was about my mother, and I felt fright and weary intolerance. I remember the tone of voice but not the caller, the hurry and descriptions and my almost instant anger, a collapse in me.

My mother, who had been visiting New York, was in the hospital, and it was an emergency, very bad, very serious. I didn't want to listen. I wanted to stay with my friend. We had plans to go shopping by ourselves in Philadelphia. The caller said, "Your sister's in shock. You have to come." I didn't want to. "Daphne almost died."

"My mother's in the hospital," I told Katy and her mother when I hung up.

"Good Lord," her mother said, putting her hand to her mouth. "Is she all right?" Katy hugged me.

My mother and Penelope had been staying in our old apartment between tenants, getting it into shape. They'd been going to clubs, taking our old tables at the restaurants on Third. That afternoon Penelope had walked into the bedroom when the shades shouldn't have been drawn. Our mother was inert at the edge of her bed, suspended in the middle of some act she didn't seem to be completing. Penny rolled her over and saw that her leg was unlike a leg. It was riddled with pussed welts, and Penny ran to a neighbor, who called the ambulance.

"I guess my mother had been shooting cocaine into her thighs."

"How do you do that?" Katy said. "Isn't it a powder?"

"She mixed it with tap water. I guess she'd been doing it for a couple of weeks. She used the same needle, so she's got a really bad infection." This was so *stupid*. Katy's mother, her hand still over her mouth, was staring at me. "It's okay," I said. "It's just a dumb move. She's been in hospital a lot. She'll be fine."

I had to leave. I had to. Katy's mother went to get the train schedule, and Katy brought my bag down from her room. They drove me to the station.

"Are you sure you're going to be okay?" Katy's mother said. Yes, I said again and again. "Well, are you sure? Will there be anyone to stay with you?" That question hadn't occurred to me. "If you need to come back, just call, and I'll pick you up at the train." No. No, I wanted to get away, away from their stupid house and driveway and stupid homemade brownies. I wasn't a child.

I arrived back in the city and took the subway up to the hospital. Lenox Hill was three blocks from our apartment, personal, like our florist, our chemist, our liquor store. That's where she got her first flat of Demerol and the individually wrapped syringes. I walked down the wide corridor, scanning for the room number.

My mother smiled when she saw me. I tried to avoid breathing in the smell that filled the room. Penelope was crying, sitting in a chair next to the bed. She grabbed my wrist and said, "Susy, *Susy*." I put my arm around her.

"What did you do?" I said to my mother. I wanted to make her say it.

"Silly me," my mother said. She held up the sheet so I could see, and it was shocking. Her flesh was turned brown and green and gray and purple, puncture marks scattered up and down her leg. "It's septicemia," she said, a stagy thrill in its medical weight. "How's school?"

"You used *tap water*?"

A nurse came in. "We're going to get her right, girls," she said. "If your sister hadn't found her when she did. Another few hours, she would have been gone." She put her hand on Penelope's shoulder. "You saved her life."

"Jeannie's from Trinidad," my mother said, smiling at the nurse. "Her brother plays soccer."

I stayed with Penelope in the apartment, ordering hamburger platters from the Skyline. We slept in our mother's bed with the television on. The pillows smelled like tea rose and her unwashed nighties. When the infection was under control, she was going to come home. I took the train back to school in the middle of a weekday. The porter in the café car sold me a beer, although he knew he wasn't supposed to.

My favorite teacher was Mr. Cutler. I didn't care about the others anymore, or my grades. I was transferring to a smaller school in Colorado, a three-hour drive from Taos. My mother and I had decided that was the right thing because everything here was too Waspy, overcontrolled, not like us, and we needed to be closer together. She was sorry she'd fucked up. "I promise you, darling," she said.

Mr. Cutler was square-jawed and blue-eyed. He lived in Willetts House in one of the suites assigned to teachers. He coached boys' lacrosse, striding the campus with paternal dignity. "He's like an oak tree," I wrote in my diary. "A rooted part of the school's identity." He let me into an English elective listed for seniors. We read Bradbury and Donleavy, and then we wrote "life experience" stories. I titled one "To Her Doctor's Health." It was about a girl who has to give her mother injections of Demerol.

She pulled the cap off the needle keeping her eyes away from the gleaming thread of metal. Down the needle jammed through the rubber seal of the medicine bottle, and up it came again full of its own clear, cold blood. She looked down on her mother's thigh, blue and green and purple from countless injections.

Mr. Cutler told my adviser I was the best writer he'd had in ten years, which I told my mother. I sent her the story, and she loved it. "Aren't you lucky I make such good material?" she said. I sent my father the story, and he sent it back with a note: "I don't know why you thought I should read this. It doesn't seem to me much good or particularly original."

When Mr. Cutler's picture was in the student paper, I cut it out, taping it to my mirror. Everyone knew of my infatuation, and Katy would get me to blush when Mr. Cutler came into the dining hall. It was better than boys; nothing could happen. I certainly didn't want something to happen. It was enough to know that he liked my writing, that I could catch his attention with content. Maybe I could get him to think about the unbuttoned top button of my cardigan, but I wasn't interested in anything gross.

In the first week of June the school mood was bursting with every relaxed rule, and I went to find Mr. Cutler. I slipped away from a grounds cleanup and crossed the lawns, which were bubbling with mowers. The air smelled of gasoline and rainy earth, and I felt excited. Inside the peculiar quiet of Willetts House I followed a carpet runner to his suite. His door was open.

"I was wondering if you'd like to go to the IHOP with me?" I said.

"When?" he said.

"Now. Want to?"

Mr. Cutler stood right up, left his magazine on the couch and took his loden coat off a hook.

"Why not? Let's go," he said, backing me into the narrow hallway as he locked up, and then we went out to the faculty lot. Actually, I hadn't expected his acquiescence. I'd just wanted to remind him I was leaving, that he was going to miss me. I wanted to come out and say I'd miss him. Away from the bulletin boards and lacrosse gear, he was a man. He probably wanted to get me out of his private quarters, whatever it took, but I wouldn't have known that.

In the diner I ate pancakes, and he had coffee.

"I have to ask," he said. "That story you wrote? About the little girl and the injections? How do you know so much about that?"

I told him about my mother's back. I told him about our house in Barbados and my father's MS, my stomach pain and Valium. I told him about Daphne's recent time in the hospital. "My mother, yeah, she does drugs, but she's not always like that. She's very beautiful. She went out with Clint Eastwood."

Mr. Cutler's face had gradually changed from pleasant interest to gloom. He looked aged. "You're only fifteen," he said. "And you have so many stories to tell. I'm almost fifty, and I have none." I had no idea what he meant. It seemed like a strange thing for an adult to say, and I thought he wanted me to feel sorry for him. I felt tricked, like he had asked about me, but now we were going to talk about him.

First Time

"Losing your virginity" was a phrase all over our house, a companion as regular as another sister. This thing that had to happen. That would happen.

I spent the summer in Taos before I started junior year at the new boarding school. My mother had purchased a house in Ranchos. She was proud. She didn't explain the finances of it, just that the realtor was *wonderful,* and her man at the bank was a brick. The house sat on the west side of a small plaza, presided over by a tiny church. We had a scruffy yard in the back with one crooked apricot tree and a clothesline we used to dry towels. There were a few other houses, also adobe. I don't remember any of us knowing the neighbors or looking inside the church.

* * *

"It's Sue's sixteenth birthday!" my mother said into the phone. "We're going to our bar, our fave." A few miles toward town, the place had live music and made good tequila sunrises, heavy on the cassis, which swamped out the taste of alcohol. Kids got served if their parents brought them.

I had taken my driver's test in the morning and had the scrap of paper, the temporary notice, until the plastic one with the photo came. I was eager to be behind the wheel. In the morning, our mother was taking us to Colorado, and I hoped she'd let me do some of the driving. Penelope didn't want to go to boarding school, but my mother said the education would be good and, besides, she'd have me. Duffels and boxes sat in the hallway, waiting to be loaded into the car.

All three of us filled the bathroom. My mother and I were still in our John Kloss Lily of France underwires with the front closure. "It looks better to a man when you open your bra from the front," she once told me. Our nipples showed through the sheer fabric, hers larger than mine and darker. She dusted blush on the bridge of Penelope's nose. We put on lacy sweaters and tailored pants. In my room I applied lip gloss with a little gold brush my mother had given me. She came in with my presents.

"First this," she said. We sat down on the bed, and I unwrapped a slim silver Montblanc fountain pen. She plucked it from its case and balanced it between her fingers. "Marvelous weight, isn't it? This is the finest pen ever made. It's for your writing."

"I love it. Thank you."

"I know you."

She handed me the next gift, a blank book.

"For your diary."

"Thank you."

"And, because you're sixteen." Her eyes teared up. "My baby." She opened her palm, where the folded white packet was nesting.

"Oh," I said.

"Your own gram. I cut it. It's fabulous," she said. She gripped my wrist. "Please, please, darling, don't ever do someone else's coke. You never know what it's cut with. Promise?"

"I promise."

She spooned up a hit and held it steady for me, then snorted two hits herself. We tasted the metallic trickle in our throats at the same time, sniffed together to keep our noses from running. I imagined I could already feel the coke's electric command in me. She wiped her nostrils quickly, a gesture of hers I'd been trying to develop. She refolded the sno-seal and popped it in my purse. For a birthday treat I got to wear her shoes, thin red straps around my ankles, ungainly height. She put on her white cowboy hat, and we drove in a hurry to the bar so we could catch the first set. We liked the band. I liked the drummer, Theo, who smiled at me whenever I sat near the platform.

When my mother walked in, an alert rippled through the room. "Enter laughing," she used to joke, but she actually did it, and Penelope and I could see it worked. We surveyed the crowded dance floor. Theo was playing on the stage, and I felt the twitch run through me, the nervous current of sexual prowess and coke-fueled buzz. Wasn't I beautiful and sexy? My hair fell in shiny ringlets, my skin was the "best in the family," my mother said, and I had that great ass. Penelope pushed between chairs and flopped down at a table an annoying distance from the stage.

"I want to sit closer," I said. "It's my birthday." I pulled on her arm, but she wouldn't move. I kicked out a chair and sat.

Over the music my mother yelled, "You want him, Sue?" She was pointing at Theo. She made a thumbs-up. "I'll get him for you. A birthday present." Then she went to the bathroom. I never liked it in there, women packed in tight, the narrow countertop loaded with wads of cash. People were always checking their Kleenex for blood.

The waitress set down napkin squares and took my order for

three tequila sunrises. My mother came back wired. She tucked herself into the chair. "Okay, I've got great news." She wiped each nostril quickly. "I just ran into that waitress in the bathroom, she works here on Sundays? And she told me that Theo fancies you. He thinks you're gorgeous."

After a couple of hours, she let me drive the car home. My sister in the passenger seat was cranky with being up too late. My high-strung anticipation had sagged, the brightness off the night. I drove slowly because you were supposed to pay extra attention if you'd had a drink. My mother was going to explain to Theo how tonight was special for me, my sixteenth birthday, my very last night before starting a new school, and she'd bring him back to our house.

"I'll get him to give me a lift. You watch, darling. I'll make it happen."

"Mum," I said. "I don't want to go to bed with him."

"No, of course not," she said. "But don't you want him to come over for a drink? An hour alone with him on your last night? Wouldn't you like that? Take Penelope home, get her to bed and wait for us."

My sister was happy to close her door, and I tidied up the living room, tossing clothes into my mother's room, clearing plates and glasses back to the kitchen. Theo fancied me. I looked around my room as if he were in it. I sat down, I lay down, I sat up, I stood up, unable to decide how I should be when he arrived. The poster of the Degas ballerinas was embarrassing. I checked the name of the drummer on my Police album.

She did bring Theo in. I was asleep, propped up in the corner of the couch. When I woke, I could hear them talking in her bedroom. I went and got into my bed, shutting my door. I didn't want to be seen slow with sleep and out of it. I woke up fully and listened as the murmuring changed to a higher register, as the sounds quickened. She fucked him. I listened to his boots on the terra-cotta tile when he passed my door. He started up his truck that had carried her home, the tires circling out of our little plaza and onto the blacktop.

In the morning I wouldn't talk to her. She pointed out I'd been asleep when they came in. "I assumed you couldn't have cared that much," she said.

I couldn't stand the mire of her arguments. Anything I answered would come back at me, and, anyway, wasn't she right? That I hadn't really cared about him. It was just a crush. He'd never kissed me or even called me. She had coaxed the crush along, which maybe made it hers more than mine. I dropped the subject of Theo.

I said, "It was *my* sixteenth birthday, and I had to hear you fucking in the next room."

She was icy. "Well, I'm sorry you couldn't lose your virginity on your special birthday, Susy."

"Couldn't you at least have closed your door all the way?" I said.

"The world," she said, "does not revolve around you."

The next morning, sunny and purposeful, we hurried our belongings into the rear of the hatchback. Penelope claimed shotgun. My mother, who loved the next new thing, was in a grand mood, hugging us and humming, eager to get going. We sang songs from musicals on the drive to Colorado Springs, and when we left the interstate, we got giddier and giddier with the adventure of decoding local directions. The street names seemed ridiculous to us. We were having such fun.

We dropped Penelope off at her freshman social and then found my dorm. It was tiny, a converted house, six bedrooms. In the distance mountains soared against the sky, but we didn't know what they were called. After I put my bags and stereo in my single, we went to meet my sister. We held hands, trailing the narrow paths. We could smell hay in the breeze and the tangy scent of pine needles. You could cross the whole campus in under five minutes, the adobe buildings and hacienda-style library adorable and soothing after my other school's Ivy League glaze. There were no mammoth structures to honor alumni, no grandeur to impress parents; the gym wasn't in good repair, and some of the grass was yellowed where the sprinklers didn't reach, but I felt I could learn where everything was, that I could be in charge.

"Maybe I should stay another day," my mother said.

"You should go," I said. "Go back home." I realized that my mother had gone from boarding school to my father to us. After she left us tonight, she would be living without an audience. As far as I knew, she would sleep, cut coke, drink, do coke, meet friends for drinks and fight with men. She had no job, no business, though she had a lot of friends who counted on her advice about depression or bad relationships or debt. She read books about Watergate and went to the movies and enjoyed bad TV about Princess Di. When she did have a job—"He wants me to copyedit his manuscript!" "I'm going to sell art!"—it was forgotten after a few weeks. She had never lived alone.

She stopped the man as he crossed our path.

"Are you on the faculty? I'm Daphne, and this is my daughter Susy. She's a new fifth-former."

"Junior," I said. We shook hands.

"Dr. Crawford," he said. "I teach English."

She made some doctor joke about the care the students needed, medicinal needs, and then, what had he written his dissertation on? While he was talking she whispered to me, showing him he was worth a secret. She whispered, "Redhead." She didn't like redheads, one of her violent and inexplicable tastes; except now she acted as if this were an asset.

When he'd moved on she said, "The doctor already has a real crush on you."

"Mum, God." I knew by now this wasn't true, but her saying it reminded me of possibility, a particular outcome.

"Didn't you notice? He couldn't stop smiling at you. He adores you."

"He was being nice," I said. "It's the first day. Can't anything be normal with you?" I started to pull away but she held my sleeve.

"Trust me," she said. "The world is about sex."

I signed up for Dr. Crawford's History of Satire and Shakespeare and his honors poetry elective. Two years of an eastern boarding school (and my father) had given me a sophisticated education, and I could flip literary allusions back at him. I read what he mentioned in passing and amassed notes if he let drop where he'd earned his BA or that he used to teach college. He lived off campus, which meant he didn't have regular dorm duties, and he wasn't findable. I never knew where I'd run into him, which loaded my walks with expectation. He looked older to me than I knew he was, his beard brushed through with gray, comforting, and he dressed in a cliché of prep-school style—brown loafers and a softened corduroy sports coat. English teachers were so easy. Everything was right there between Catherine and Heathcliff or splashing at the edges of Keats. I could give my precocious perspective on courtly love in Chaucer or on Hemingway's stoic lust. I alone picked up on the bawdy innuendo in those Early English poems, and he noticed.

I settled into teen obsession, fueled by his appropriate obstacles. My dorm-mate Jane became my closest friend, patient with me and happy to talk about all the cute boys. Dr. Crawford wouldn't let me hang around alone too long, often didn't notice me in the dining hall. I was dying to see his house but didn't get to until the night his wife made chili for all his advisees, had us over in a noisy herd. It annoyed me to be one of everybody. A couple of us snuck a look in their medicine cabinet, which contained Tums and nail polish remover and antibiotics, nothing my mother would have bothered to snatch. Dr. Crawford did invite me for homemade pizza a couple of times, inviting Penelope, too. She sat in the back of his car, and in the front seat I referred to things I knew she wouldn't understand.

Dr. Crawford's wife taught part-time at the school, and I grew familiar with the hours she was certain to be around and let my friends know I liked it better when she wasn't. Susanna's famous crush, her mighty crush. Nothing happened except silences made fraught by my imagination and, once, accidental coat sleeve against sleeve in the lunch line. Except for Jane, my friends and sister were bored to death by the subject of Dr. Crawford, and they teased me. Even Dr. Crawford teased me, imitating my nervous stammer. The crush was everybody's joke.

But something changed. When my mother, on the phone, asked for news, at first I had babbled about the crush. She asked, and I wanted to tell all the little ins and outs of being obsessed with somebody. Then, for reasons I couldn't identify, I started to keep it to myself. I sacrificed my desire to plumb Dr. Crawford's every move. Instead, I colored in the boys, made up kisses, detailed who-said-whats, the politics she valued.

"I *like* Mrs. Crawford," Penelope said one day, staring me down.

"So do I!" I insisted.

"Please don't make me go to dinner there anymore," and she wouldn't let me talk about him.

My friends started to worry. "You're going to mess up your life," said Pete Spooner, who wanted to go out with me.

"Don't be melodramatic," I told him. My stomach tightened with glory.

* * *

One day Dr. Crawford called me back as my classmates left. I felt deliciously singled out, mine the only student voice in the last forty minutes as we'd traded rapid-fire theory. I'd been reading his copy of Northrop Frye, extra credit.

"Listen, Susy. You have a crush on me, right?"

The pleasure slipped, and I felt caught, a thief with contraband.

"I'm very flattered. You're a tremendous girl, maybe even the most interesting girl I've ever known, but this is a little out of hand, and it's making me uncomfortable." My face was burning. "I love my wife very much." I nodded. "We have an incredibly strong marriage. Twelve and a half years." This was more than I wanted to know, more, I suspected, than he should be saying.

"Aren't you going out with Spooner anyway?" he said.

"Him. Sort of. Not seriously. He's not my boyfriend."

"Well, you should have boyfriends. Don't you like Pete?"

I seized his gaze and said, "He's a good kisser." Dr. Crawford raised an eyebrow. "We've made out. But his hands are always clammy, Dr. Crawford. And there's a way he's always too nervous."

He laughed. "Sounds like high school. Exactly what you should be doing. Have boyfriends, Susy. Have lots of them. If you want, you can tell me about them, and I'll help decode the mysteries of the adolescent male for you. And you can call me Wyatt. At least, when we're alone like this."

Penelope and I went home to Taos for the winter break. My mother asked about Wyatt, and I couldn't resist her face, open, soft, hungry and focused on me. I knew a lot about him by now, and she was the best at interpreting such details.

"This isn't healthy," she said afterward. "Should I be concerned?"

"No," I said. "God, he's twice my age."

"Lincoln's back for the holiday," she said. "I ran into his brother yesterday at the post office."

I'd kissed Lincoln a year earlier. I should remember that kiss, so long predicted and desired. But as soon as it happened, it mattered less than wanting it, and then Lincoln mattered less. Still, when he entered the Christmas party my second night back, his laugh made me turn, and in spite of my junior-year indifference I felt a homecoming.

"Babe!" he said, and pulled me close with a large, sloppy arm around my shoulder. I wanted to be cool, but the habit of craving his attention was too strong, and I threw my arms around him. He wasn't sarcastic anymore and didn't recite manic *Monty Python* sketches with the other guys. He was calm and kind, and, anyway, we'd already done all that making out, so there wouldn't be anything weird or tense. This was what you did on Christmas break. You welcomed the embrace of your old friends, and everyone wanted kissing, any kissing.

He'd forgotten his bong. "We're going over to Harrison's later," he said. "You want to come, babe? You're not still uptight about all that, are you? Daphne told me you'd mellowed out. You want to ride along while I stop over at my mom's to get my stuff?"

I had to act like I didn't know it was an excuse. We ended up alone, as we both wanted it, managing to lose the other kids.

We knocked around on the couch until our clothes were off, one piece at a time, a blanket over us. Lincoln naked. Would this be how Wyatt would kiss, how Wyatt undressed? I kept making it clear, have me, have this, you can have it. I slid half a hip under him and tried to bring his erection against me. I wasn't scared.

"Losing your virginity is serious business, babe," he said, and he wouldn't do it. He made me look him in the eye. "You're a kid."

I stayed until 3 a.m. and crept inside my house when he dropped me off, disappointed, my skin roughed from stubble.

In the morning I brought coffee to my mother's bed. "Well, I slept with him," I said. The lie blossomed. With the friendly bruises emerging on my neck from Lincoln's mouth, I elaborated. I crawled in next to her and made the night specific—his belt buckle got caught on my sweater, the television was on in the next room.

"How many times did he come?" she asked.

"I don't know." I thought she'd see through me now. "Three."

"What'd his come taste like?"

"No blow jobs," I said.

I made everything up, except the fact of being with him. I described the new me and fed her feverish interest. Underneath the charge that came with creativity was the regret I'd never get to lose my virginity with her again.

She was pleased. "You had your diaphragm?"

"No, we used condoms."

"Don't you hate condoms?" she said. My sleepy sister padded in and got under the covers on the other side of my mother, who said, "Guess what Sue did last night?"

Later I sat in the living room writing in my diary with fanatical precision—at 7:15, at 9:20, we got in the car at 2:50—amazed that my mother had believed me. I watched the ink string along the paper in thin wet ribbons. In a little while we were going out with Penelope to celebrate the big event, chateaubriand and champagne, just the three of us. I could hear Billy Joel's record from her room and the stream of my mother's voice as she talked on the phone in hers. The windows showed blue evening on the snow outside, and my blood was charged by recent arousal. I was exactly in the place I liked best, and I wished Wyatt could see me.

My mother walked through, delivering plates to the kitchen. "We should light a fire." She came back and sat close to me on the couch. She was grave, and my heart tightened. Had she phoned Lincoln to check?

"Listen, darling. You can't just go jumping into bed with anyone who asks you. I know Lincoln's special, and I always knew he'd be your first, but you have to behave like a lady. Otherwise you'll get a reputation." I stared at her. She went to her room, forgetting the fire, and I picked up my diary and struck the same notes of indignation any teenager would.

After dark we ran into Randall at the Stakeout, all of us dressed up, and we told him my news, my mother and I relating bits in turn, the pieces sliding together neatly. She played two fingers along my cheek and gazed at me. "Can you believe it?" The story flowed from Lincoln's couch to his car, to my bed, to my mother's bed, through the snowy afternoon and dressing for dinner. Time kept catching it all up, friends at the restaurant invited to hear, and the news kept getting augmented. It sounded better each time, event mastered by invention. I imagined how I'd tell Wyatt. Losing my virginity felt done.

Counterfeit

My English teacher kissed me in January. This followed weeks of strain as we walked gingerly around Susanna's crush. Naming it had made us feel we ruled its power and separating for the vacation had made us feel we deserved more of each other.

In our first private conversation after I returned I told Wyatt my Lincoln history, the saga of my infatuation, what a *girl* I'd been. Studying his minutest reaction, I inched up on the details, giving him more poetry than I had my mother.

"What I Did on My Christmas Vacation," I said. Wyatt always laughed when I was arch, enjoyed my show. "I wanted to tell you," I said and emphasized "you," aching to have him know how often I thought about him. The tension was getting tighter, I knew I wasn't crazy. He liked to make me blush, alluding to Lincoln in code during class. I scattered the names of other boys in front of him. I sat on the damp bench at the pool, watching him coach. I spent more and more time with him, rather than less, daring the crush to intensify. I followed after him, talking constantly in case silence broke our spell. Should I read more Swift? Would he let me see his dissertation? Tell me again the first lines of *Don Juan*. What does Shakespeare mean by "counterfeit" in act I, scene iv, of *As You Like It*? Here's the extra-credit paper I wrote, just for fun, on Rosalind and the uses of "counterfeit."

One late gray afternoon, shortly before dinner, I brushed my hair and went to his office. I tapped on the door, pushing it open. I liked what luscious appeal he must see in the doorway.

I said, "You going to dinner?" I stepped into the room, and he sprang up, yanked me against the wall and shoved the door shut.

"You're the sexiest girl I've ever . . . ," he said. I felt sorry for his wife. He gripped my shoulders and kissed me. "Susy, Susy," he said in a disappearing whisper.

At first I thought, "Oh my God, he shouldn't do this, he's the teacher. This will change everything. We're going to get in trouble." And then he pressed his hand against my hip, and we kissed another time and another. I let the kissing take over. How quickly that happened. By the time he opened his office door a minute later things were set. This would never not have happened, and since it had already happened it might as well keep happening, and it was going to. I matched his quick stride on the way to the dining hall, our silence an abrupt contrast to our usual way, and sexier for it. I kept an eye out, hoping we'd run into my sister, who would divine my triumph and joy.

We didn't get much time alone, and sometimes he forced me to stay away from him, deflect attention. "Better cool it for a bit," he'd say. But the attraction blazed between us. I felt strong and happy, had so much to write in my diary. Wyatt loved me.

A few weeks later we were driving on an invented errand. ("Just tell your dorm mother I said you have to come with me," he'd said. "Make up a reason." I'd told her he was taking me to the city library for independent study.)

Wyatt asked, "What sort of things turn you on?"

I laughed, but it was nerves, not delight. "I don't know."

"Of course you know—you think about sex. What do you think about?"

"You!" I said, loud and exaggerated. *Please* don't keep talking, I wished, but he was watching the road.

"What do you think of me *doing* to you?" I didn't answer, and he started to sound impatient. "I want to make you happy. I want to know what you like."

"Yes, well . . ."

"Susy, how long have you been having sex?"

"Since December—one month."

Wyatt was surprised. "So recently? Was that your first time? I thought—you act so confident, so aggressive. I was sure—I'm amazed. You appear very experienced."

"I've seen a lot."

"How did your mother react when you told her about Lincoln?"

"She was pleased for me." I mean, that was true, but she'd been pleased by a lie. I said, "Wyatt, I'm lying." He looked over at me. "I did spend the night with that guy in Taos . . . but, and—I'm still a virgin. I let my mother believe otherwise because I was sick of her asking."

"I see," he said. He let a long silence go by. "Why did you deceive me like that? I thought you trusted me." Oh, God, I tumbled, grabbed.

"I was afraid you would, would—"

"Would be scared off by your virginity?" I nodded. "I'm glad you told me." He sounded organized. "It's important that I know before we make love. I *want* to make love to you, and I would like to be *the one*." When he emphasized his words, he squeezed my hand. He found the turnoff he was looking for and pulled up beside a trailhead. We didn't get out of the car. He tugged down the zipper of my jumpsuit, and the cold air hit my skin, and then he covered my breasts with his hands. One warm hand on each breast. We sat like that, my exposed skin getting colder, and I looked down at his scalp resting on my chest. It hit me: I was *in* it. I'd really done it, made this come true—we were together. A wretched feeling came over me, a silent gong beating. I thought it was anticipation.

In another week he took me to his house. His wife was out. As we drove in the clear, white February sun, he kept glancing at me. He reached across the seat and touched my leg. "You do have your birth control, right?" The diaphragm was already in. I'd practiced until I could insert it with a quick gesture, like buttoning a coat. How different the words *birth control* sounded when he said them instead of my mother. "When he says them," I wrote, "they smolder." I had turned in the fraudulent permission slip in order to leave school grounds.

He parked in front of his house, and we got out. I was trying to concentrate on the normal things: you get out of a car, you shut the door. The door thumped in the hollow winter air. Had anyone heard? He hurried me along the flagstones, directing me with a hand on my neck to his front door, which opened onto the huge smell of him, yet mixed with her, too, the rest of his life. He pulled the drapes shut across the picture window in the living room. My body started to shiver with eerie nerves, and I couldn't stop. This was going to be it. In a small minute this gap of time would close, and I'd be having sex.

From a closet Wyatt pulled out a towel, which he spread on the carpet, then a sheet on top of that. "Take off your clothes." His voice was warm, firm. He was natural with instruction. Naked, I watched him undress, this big man whose sports jacket I studied in class, stripped to skin and shoulders, pelvis, hair.

As we made love, I looked around at his living room, wondering which things he'd chosen and which had been purchased and arranged by his wife. He'd prepared me for blood, for pain. There was none. I hardly felt him, and the intercourse was brief, a bland interruption of my fantasies.

I pushed that off. Nothing mattered but the finally getting, the finally having, the me wanted by him, the me here on his floor. He came, and then he tugged at the sheet and covered us. The scent of real sex rose up with the sheet, the smell of semen mixed with spermicide, the childhood smell of coming to my mother's bedside after a bad dream. My mother's smell was so pronounced it was if she had climbed in between us.

"Let's do it again," he said. He was panting, and sweat showed beneath the hair on his chest.

"I can't," I said. "You can only do it one time with a diaphragm. Then I have to wait six hours and take it out, refill it and put it in again." I'd read the pamphlet a hundred times. He gave me a look, which for years I thought was of disappointment, but one day I realized how foolish I must have sounded, and young, and how he made a decision, looking at me, to keep me that way.

I'd seen his body once already, sort of, as I walked into the echoing indoor pool after faculty swim. He was in a bathing suit, holding his towel by his side. I had made small talk. "God, I wanted to look at you," I said months later, as we wandered over every memory. This was the inventory of our affair, all we had. "Didn't I know it!" he said. "I felt *raped*." He was smiling, teasing, and we drifted on from the word *rape*. I didn't note his way of making it my engine that revved us.

In a few minutes Wyatt jumped up, again at the closet, and he produced the vacuum cleaner. As he unlaced its cord, he gestured at me to get my clothes back on. Still naked, he bundled the sheet with the towel and vacuumed thoroughly. "In case any of your hair is in the carpet," he yelled over the motor. It finally stopped. "Go and wash up."

After I was through in the bathroom he came in and peered at the floor, at the white porcelain of the sink's edge. He tore off some toilet paper and wiped at the rim of the drain in the bathtub. "It wouldn't be wet at this time of day," he said.

When his wife came home he made dinner for the three of us. I wanted her to adore me, a reflex, the way hungry me wanted that out of everybody. I asked questions about the pottery class she taught. I wondered if it showed, the flush from sex on my skin. Would she recognize his mood as postcoital, as something that belonged to her? She asked the most regular questions about school, and I answered, feeling the ache inside my thighs, the sore back from efforts on the floor. We all joked at the headmaster's expense.

Driving me home afterward, Wyatt said, "You can't write about this in your diary, you know. I can't risk any of the girls in the dorm finding it. You are in complete control of this secret. You can't tell your sister, or your mother. If you tell, I lose my job."

No, I wouldn't tell. Just promise me more, I thought. More.

"Okay," I said, pulling back from the words I had already started to gather for description. "Okay." My words would stay unwritten. The blank page would be our cover.

Playful then, he said, "What *do* you write about me in your diary?"

"About what you say in class, stuff like that." I was flirting. I wrote everything. I taped in scraps he left in my mailbox with the bits of Byron on them, but I didn't want him to know. It seemed girlish. I'd already betrayed him. I'd written down the first kiss, the time he said, "What we need is a weekend, so we can fuck each other raw," and when he'd said a few days later, "If we're still together when you're twenty-five, I'll give you a baby." I didn't want to lose any of it.

"Can I read it?" he said. He knew I'd tell him yes in spite of myself. "Only two people in the whole world know about this, Susy. Anyone else is just guessing, and they can't accuse us based on a guess."

"Good night," he said when I got out. "My *lover*."

I walked into the common room right behind the Domino's deliveryman, and girls were gathering around the coffee table.

"You want to chip in?" someone asked. "Hurry."

"No, thanks. I've eaten." I wanted to be alone with the full-length mirror in the bathroom. I wanted to wipe up the warm spermicidal jelly that was oozing out of me. The kids were excited about Hawaiian pizza while I had watched Wyatt sauté mushrooms in a cast-iron skillet with sliced onions and pour them over grilled steak. He had shaved the meat into thin slices, revealing its red center, and laid some on my plate, some on his wife's, then some on his own.

In the bathroom I took off everything and stared in the mirror. Wyatt had made love to me, and his touch had changed what I looked at. My breasts were fuller, my hips relaxed. This is the mouth that he covered. These are the breasts he stroked. I had no one to tell but myself.

Lying aroused us. We pretended to run into each other in downtown bookstores, where he bought me used copies of William Blake and Elizabeth Bishop, Helen Vendler, Robert Coover, Bettelheim on dreams, lots of Byron from somebody else's academic life. I gave him *The Good Soldier,* one of my mother's favorites, and he bought another copy, so we could read aloud to each other in his office on Fridays, alternating chapters. "*This* is the saddest story," he would whisper to me in the dining hall, smirking with our mutual deception. He bought me *Lolita,* a fat, white paper-back. He thought this showed off his sense of irony, his private lecture on postmodernism. It was postmodern for him, modern Humbert, to buy *Lolita* for me, to watch me read it. Postmodern to call me "Su, Susy, Su. Zah. Nuh."

"The fire of your loins," I toasted, one naked elbow rubbing dry on his old living room rug.

"I'm going to give you the best education anyone has ever had," he said. I believed that's what I was getting. I knew A. N. Wilson and *The Faerie Queene.* We parked at campsites emptied by winter. I knew Turgenev and Swinburne. We went to motels he picked or spent snowy Saturdays on his rug while his wife attended her book club. She returned once just as I finished lacing my second boot. We hadn't heard her car. We talked for days about the close call. He taught me the terms *strophe, terza rima* and *anadiplosis.* I knew twenty of the Shakespeare sonnets by heart. We discussed mimesis.

I started to let my mother do all the talking when she phoned. I was afraid she would catch the change in me, hear something in my voice that broadcast my adventure. I had to be careful now, even though Wyatt and I had only managed sex three times in six weeks. She was calling about spring break. Penelope had been invited to a classmate's house, and my mother wanted to take me to Mexico.

"Just us, darling. I'm going to take us to an absolutely magical little town. You'll love it."

I didn't like the idea of leaving Wyatt, felt it like a wound, but I couldn't give that as a reason, couldn't object to anything about the trip.

* * *

In Oaxaca we shared the hotel room, our dropped clothes and drying bathing suits in the bathroom, our single bottle of conditioner. She pulled lip gloss from her bag when she saw I needed it. I worried I'd talk in my sleep. In a way, I wanted to so that I could have some theatrical means of revealing the affair without violating Wyatt's rules. No, she mustn't find out. He'd get fired, I'd lose him. But what if she asked the right questions? I imagined her at night over my bed, drawing out with fairy fingers the untold and the held back, until she got the word, the name, the private sin.

"Don't you want any?" she'd ask, the tiny spoon quivering in her fingers outside the restaurant. Coke made her shake a little. You had to stare to see it. Her palms were coated in chilly sweat.

"We're in a foreign country," I said. "Please, Mum."

"Oh, pooh," she said. "I don't need your disapproval right now." Why did she get to have everything out in the open? It made me furious, longing for consequences.

We traveled down the coast by plane and bus. The unpaved roads were hell on her back, and now and then she yelped with pain, but no one paid her attention. On the bus we noticed the same things—those sandals, the sad little boy, the our-lady-of-something behind the steering wheel—in the hotels we noticed the same things. We sang "The Way We Were" and "You Don't Bring Me Flowers," breaking down with laughter before the second verse. In our usual holiday habit, we never parted, and I couldn't think about my affair.

At night she fell asleep fast, a Lethean stupor in which her face relaxed. Sitting up next to her, I read Kurt Vonnegut and Fitzgerald stories. Her lips were clenched together, and the hole in her nose gurgled when she inhaled, whistled when she exhaled. She needed to have a wall built to replace the ruined cartilage. "Like a bathtub plug," she'd said. I could picture her worn septum, the ragged tissue. The sound nauseated me, and I hated her sleep, the way it left me so alone.

In the last town, Puerto Escondido, we ate red snapper for dinner. "Have you ever tasted anything this fresh?" she said. For breakfast we had eggs with chorizo and corn tortillas. *"Café con leche,"* she ordered, her Spanish overdone first thing in the morning. But she began the day, opened it for us. She apologized to me for doing so much coke and said she'd stop. She whispered about the tiny sum the waiter earned, underlining our privilege. Our money gave us celebrity—we were the rock stars, the ones the Mexicans wanted to be, she said. "That maid earns six dollars a week." She left ten-dollar tips.

There were no museums here or shops. We planted Coke bottles in the sand to keep them cool. We propped ourselves up on our elbows and watched the surfers. We lay on our stomachs, one of us dozing, the other reading "naughty bits" aloud from some paperback. We passed the book between us. Have you ever done that? Have you ever done this? I told her about making out with Pete Spooner, how it freaked me out when he came in my hand. I tried to think of things sixteen-year-olds might say about boys. Intimate now and obsessed with Wyatt's moves and muscles, I tried to know less than I did. I body-surfed in the shallows as she asked the teenage boys about their boards, about the best wave. Every hour or so, she pushed up from her towel with an elaborate sigh.

"I'm going inside to cool off a bit," she said, and headed toward the exterior staircase that led up to our floor. Her heels sank in the sand, exaggerating the swing of her hips. As soon as she reached the path she straightened up and almost skipped. I lay on my back and listened to her feet. I heard the door of our room open with the key, then the screen slap shut. I could predict how long she'd be gone because I knew what she was doing exactly. I tested my accuracy, running the scene in my head to coincide with her return. She unzipped her wash bag, pulled out the snoseal and unfolded it. She tapped the edge of the paper with a finger, herding the coke into a pile. Then she dipped in a Bic pen cap (her wash bag was filled with them but no pens). She never measured, and a hit had no specific size. She was probably up to a gram a day.

I lay on my towel, wanting to call Wyatt. I'd tell him I hated watching her think she was sly and cute. I missed him so badly. When she returned to the beach, innocence pasted on her face, I said I was going to find a phone.

"I want to call my father," I lied. "I'll be back for lunch."

"You'll be gone all that time?"

"I want to walk around."

"It's just fishermen and schoolchildren. Absolutely no one else."

"I'm not looking to *meet* anybody."

"Don't get snotty with me, miss."

"Sorry."

I went through the town to the one store with the tin Pepsi sign over the door. Its colors were gone. I placed a collect call from the pay phone, Wyatt's extremely memorized phone number a happiness in itself. The phone in his house rang, my presence manifested in a bell, a vibration. No one answered. I followed the street back to the hotel, feeding my craving for Wyatt with an imaginary conversation. I returned to our spot on the beach, where my mother had left our book and my towel.

That night we remained at our table after dinner. No matter how angry I could get, how fed up, how smug with knowing better, she was still mine, as intimate and regular to me as my own fingernails or throat clearing, and my irritation washed away. We pushed our chairs back and walked past little fires on the beach until the few lights of the hotel were behind the bend of the coast.

"The men will get up early and fish," she said. "And their snapper will be our dinner tomorrow." We held hands. We never walked together without touching, arms linked, shoulders bumping or fingers entwined. Her mouth was always close enough to my head to whisper. I inhaled the warm and the dark from the ocean.

"Good night, sea, good night, sky," she said. "Go on, Sue." My grandmother Patsy had started this with me when I was three.

"Good night, sand. Good night, shells," I said. "Good night, snapper we're going to eat tomorrow."

We ambled back and climbed the stairs to our room. I flopped onto our double bed, my mother's voice endless—about money, men, her sister, her mother. She was worried about Penelope's marks, what did I think, was boarding school the right place for her, would I help her study? The fan picked up speed when she flipped the switch, a chill over my acute sunburn. She asked about my call to my father as she took off her choker of amber beads.

"I never got him."

"Isn't that odd?" she said. "I thought he didn't go out. That it made him too tired. Shouldn't someone have been there to answer?" She was right. Confined to his wheelchair with the MS, my father needed Isabel's constant care and a live-in nurse. I'd forgotten to follow through on the lie, to build up its walls.

"He goes out," I said. "Sometimes I take him to the park."

"Often? You need moisturizer."

"Maybe once a week. If the weather is good. The last time, I pushed his chair up to a bench in the shade, and we watched all the dogs." This made me smile, thinking of the tentative start of intimacy with my father, new terms, a relationship between adults, and the creases around my smile stung with sunburn. "He's going to get a new chair he can control with his breath."

"Fascinating."

She lay down, and we faced each other, lying on our sides.

"Actually, it's nice, you know," I said. After long periods of no contact with him, I'd worked hard to get to know him again. His MS had eased up, even after he'd been predicted to die. I loved my stepmother. "Isabel's made it a lot easier to be with him these days. He's been telling me about his youth."

My mother snorted. "*I* was his youth."

"No, before that. Before he met you."

"What, when he was with Irene? And does he say horrible things about me?"

"No. The subject hardly comes up."

"The subject?" Something spiked in her voice, and I felt careful. "You make me sound like homework."

"I just meant not lately. Lately, we talk about when he lived in Europe. I didn't know he lived in Germany."

"He was so happy when you were born. He came to the hospital to take me home, and he arrived with a Victorian pram filled, completely filled, with lilies of the valley. He wanted you to remember their scent forever. He was so happy."

"I do remember the smell."

"Don't be ridiculous. You've heard the story, you've learned to associate it with the flower. You couldn't actually remember."

"I remember every birthday present he gave me." I started to list them—the antique rocker, the collected Dickens—and my mother rolled onto her back and looked at her arms.

"I'm already peeling."

"When you were in Payne Whitney he gave me a book about—"

"What does that mean? What the *fuck* does that mean?" She sat up and stared at me. "Payne Whitney, Payne Whitney, how long till I live that down?" She grabbed my ankle and twisted the sunburnt skin, yanking as she talked. "And who do you think got him to show up? I had to call him. He wouldn't have bothered otherwise. He didn't give a shit about you two. I had to organize everything. And you're so bloody grateful for his fucking *present*?"

I pulled my leg away. I picked up a hairbrush, turned it over and over, and said softly, "At least the drugs he takes are medicine."

"Bitch. Look at me when you speak to me, you little. Melo-dramatic. Bitch. Are we going to talk again about poor Susy's childhood because her mother did drugs? Jesus, *get over it*. I sup-pose you're about to tell me he's the better fucking *parent*?" She grabbed the brush from my hand and smashed it against the bed-side table. The noise was tremendous, everything suddenly crash-ing and screaming. "You think he's such hot shit? Where was he at your eighth-grade graduation? Where was he when I moved to Taos? He didn't even protest. Some parent! Some parent who makes fun of what you read and makes you feel stupid for the boarding school you pick. Let me tell you something: Who do you think *gave* me my first coke, my mother?"

It was too tempting, almost a gift. I said, "That seems to be the family tradition." I wanted to be icy, instead of scared. Even as I tried to think what it would take to calm her down, I let a little dangerous rage seep out. She wrenched my arm, which burned under her grip. She jerked up my chin. Her breath was metallic and rank with the synthetic in the coke.

She screamed, "Get the fuck out of here and go to your daddy, you little bitch," and I jammed myself against the wicker head-board, sizing up the distance to the bathroom, the closet, the front door. She looked like she'd hit me, and I could feel my body get-ting ready for it, ready to curl around her fist. Hit me, I dare you! I thought. I was angry—that I didn't have Wyatt to protect me, that I couldn't talk about him or call him; I was mad I'd come on the trip, fallen for it, and mad at all the things I'd done wrong. I was afraid that she'd use this—Susy loves Nat!—that she'd assign me some label and everyone in the family would think I was this way. The way Susy *is*. She bunched up my T-shirt in a fistful and dragged me off the bed and over to the door.

"GET OUT, GET OUT, YOU *LOUSY* LITTLE BITCH, YOU *UNGRATEFUL CUNT*!"

I didn't believe in the proportions of the fight, so frenzied, so fast. I wanted to smile. I wanted to skip to the part where we'd be together on the bed, taking apart the scene as if we'd watched it in a TV movie. She hurled open the door, pushed me onto the narrow landing, and I grabbed for the banister. She wouldn't actually shut the door, no. But she did, and I descended the stairs, looking back a couple of times. I looked up when I'd reached the bottom, the closed door and her raging voice. I went toward the water, and the sand made me stagger and slow down. I could hear her screaming until I got close to the waves.

I wanted something to happen to her. Something to happen to me. Make her sorry. Make *her* scared. I walked up the beach a ways, then turned up a pitted alley and emerged on the town's one street. In the mornings chickens and bicycles and dogs picked their way around the ruts in the road, but now every window was shuttered, chairs abandoned, laundry pulled in. There wasn't even a bar for the solace of gathered voices.

"What, no sister?" said a man, an English accent coming out of the dark. We had met him the day before. He'd veered off his course on the beach to talk to us, and we pretended to be sisters. In the sun he was charming and older and carefree, his white shirt open. He told us he lived here, and it was a sexy eccentricity. At night, though, when he came up to me in his unbuttoned shirt and landed his hands on my shoulders, he seemed broken and much too old. His hands moved to my collarbones, and I thought he was hiding out in an empty town. He pointed across the road at a balcony. "Mine," he said. "Want to see?" I went, curious what I could make happen.

His apartment was almost bare and smelled of faint mildew. He turned on the lamp near his pillow, which showed books and newspapers piled beside the bed, a single glass on his table. He opened the skinny balcony doors for me, and I stepped out for the better air, but I couldn't see the ocean or anything else. He moved up behind me and circled his hands around my waist, pressing my pelvis into the iron rail. I didn't want to be there, but I was there, still intrigued in spite of myself about my power over him. I faced him, looked past at the old table fan. He tried to kiss me.

"I should go, I think."

"No," he said. "I don't think so." He kept his hands on my waist, as if he were about to lift me. I thought I was probably stronger than he was. "Do you like tequila?"

"Not really," I said.

"Wait just a minute." He let go of me and went over to the sink, where he ran a dishcloth under the tap. He came back and sponged off the back of my neck.

"Does that feel good?" Grains of sand dragged against my sunburn.

"No."

He led me over to the bed, where I lay down, my shoulder blades aware of the single sheet and the thin pallet. He put his knee between my legs, hovering over me. His kiss was weary and stank of beer.

"I've got to get back," I said, getting up. I could have sex with him, I saw that. He'd be Number Two. I'd lost my virginity to Wyatt two months earlier, and already I could have number two. I thought about the trappings of this story, how it could be told once I got back to my mother. I liked the edge in it, the dangerous window of risk and bad idea.

But this was a mistake, his small, tatty room, his dirty glass and the T-shirt hanging over the back of his chair. I wanted to get out.

"Sorry," I said.

"I should walk you down," he said. "Otherwise people will think I've paid for you."

"But I don't look like a hooker."

"It doesn't matter what you look like," he said. "But whom you are with."

I was glad to be out in the open. We went down the stairs, me first, and he sang in Spanish, which I didn't understand. I felt he'd probably been drunk all day and was stupid because of it, and that I didn't matter to him anyway, the way stoned people ignored everything.

When I came back to the hotel room, my mother was asleep, making her noises. I pulled my T-shirt over my tender shoulders, rubbed on some lotion and got into my side of the bed. The sheet was almost too much to stand on the sunburn.

In the morning she wouldn't look at me. I waited my turn while she was in the shower, and I came out of the bathroom to find she'd already gone down to breakfast. When she left the open-air dining room, I went in and ate. We spent the next three days like that. She didn't ask me where I went, and maybe that's why I can't remember what I did with my time except go off to another beach, away from her, my halfhearted daily pursuit of adventure. But I remember her three days, the hour she woke each day and the muslin shirt she wore over the bikini top she tied in a bow at the nape of her neck.

Whenever Mexico came up, my mother remembered "that divine older man who was *very* interested in you." Our broken time didn't exist, our fight erased. My suggestion of it made her nod as she would at the radio, heedless, indifferent. The three days in which she didn't see her sixteen-year-old daughter in a southern Mexico town cobbled of barbed wire and dog shit and public showers—"That's absurd." *Our* trip to Mexico: We walked around the plazas in Oaxaca, she fed me my first forkful of *mole*. She remembered the bright taste of lime in our beer. She reminded me about her pain, that constant, the bus ride that hurt her back for the last hours into that southern town, close enough to Guatemala that soldiers were a possibility, and wouldn't that have been thrilling, to see soldiers?

* * *

If she knew, I thought, his wife would hate me. But she didn't know, and I came often to her house, settled into their couch against her afghan, leaving my stray hairs on the corduroy upholstery. She cut up cheddar and set the butcher-block board in front of us all on the small chest they used for a coffee table. They drank wine, and she made ginger tea for me, or black currant, sweet and vaporous. I let it get cold, watching that wineglass in her hand. I didn't want tea. I wanted her to go, to be called off to answer the phone, to decide to go downstairs and fold laundry, and she always did eventually because our united wish was so forceful in compelling her from the room. Before she reached the bottom landing, Wyatt crossed with a quick, silent tread and got near enough for our knees to touch. He stood over me, cupping his hand beneath the chunky glass goblet. He gave me the deep gaze, the beseeching hungry need. "You've changed me," he whispered. "You own me." My body was bristling for any sound from the stairs, any drag of carpet to say she was coming back to us. When we'd been too quiet too many minutes, he would talk in a bright, gamey voice about my dorm's old plumbing or the fate of the swim team or the rehearsals for *As You Like It*. I was starring in it, and I was really good, getting private tutorials from Wyatt on Renaissance history, the Elizabethan court, the tradition of trouser roles, the complex meaning of archaic English. Knowledge was power.

"My Rosalind," he whispered, so inaudible only the initial parting of his lips for "My" made sound, his tongue lingering on the *l*. It turned me on, and I spread my knees a bit. I had two desires—to draw him closer, and to give him what he wanted to see. I couldn't distinguish one from the other. Wyatt stepped away, a stern look to forbid the behavior, and I felt wounded. I waited until he took me home and we were in the car, belted and driving down the grade of his little mountain. Then I put his hand between my legs.

What did grown-ups say to each other? How did they make things work? I was dying to ask him what his wife said about me. Didn't she wonder why he drove me forty-five minutes there, taking an hour and a half away from home on a Friday night? I felt superior to her because of what I knew.

Wyatt said they had a good marriage. The years they had amassed, four times anything my parents had yet managed, spoke to me of real marriage. The duration must mean an effort on both their parts, real love. It didn't occur to me his dedicated interest in his sixteen-year-old student meant something else about marriage, something he wasn't letting me in on that was also important. I came as the welcome daughter, the friendly pet.

As a couple they would sometimes take me to the movies, Wyatt between us. He held his wife's hand in his lap, and his other, unseen fingers applied warm pressure to the thigh of my jeans. During class, I sat in the first row and mouthed dirty things to him the other kids couldn't see while he tried to map out Blake's debt to Dante on the blackboard. "God, we shouldn't do this," he always said after class. "What have you done to me?"

His wife told him she was concerned about our relationship. He said yes, I do have strong feelings for Susy, but nothing inappropriate has happened. I think you should back off, she said. He said, Actually, I'm in love with her, and though I've done nothing about it, I cannot guarantee that at some date further on I won't want to act on those feelings.

I was so scared as Wyatt reported this to me, and astonished and baffled. I was so scared when he told me she wanted to talk to me. Adulthood was rushing at me.

The next time I came over, she and I sat at the kitchen table. Wyatt went out to the garage, another of his studies, overrun by more books.

"We both care about him a lot, don't we?" she said. She took a comforting tone with me, a therapist's tone. She put her hand on my sleeve. "I've talked everything over with Wyatt," she said. "And it's all fine. I don't want to get in the way of your relationship with Wyatt. Whatever I feel or other people feel—it's our problem."

"Thank you," I said, recognizing Wyatt's logic. I felt solemn. She was kind to me. They both were. "Other people I don't care about. You I care about."

"I know, and that's what makes you so special."

Special.

Wyatt planned to play opera for me that evening. He called me upstairs, and his wife stayed in the kitchen. He stood by the stereo, inspecting one side of an LP.

"Beethoven's only opera," he said. "Sit down and let me teach you about *Fidelio*." He explained Florestan's woe, imprisoned, longing for his lover, the way the music built its ecstasy, the heat it gathered. "Here, now listen, here's the climax." With Florestan's feverish "*Mein engel, Leonoren,*" Wyatt mumbled, "*Oh, God,*" and burst across the room to me (how many times we treaded the same lines, scenes replayed because we couldn't move forward). The kiss was rough, a performance to the Beethoven, and I was embarrassed for him. I didn't like him this way and was frightened his wife would come upstairs. In the final "*freiheits*" Wyatt worked his pelvis against me and put his mouth to my ear. "*Mein engel,*" he whispered. "I'm going to lend this to you. I want you to listen to it in your room and think of my cock when you hear '*freiheit.*' *Mein engel.*"

My mother could say "cock" with aplomb, even grace. She could make it funny or poetic. But Wyatt sounded like he'd only read it. I had given him the nerve to speak it, I knew. But he didn't know how to handle such a word, and I wished I could tell my mother of his rare awkward moment.

*   *   *

My mother phoned him at home one evening. I happened to be there. He adopted his manicured voice of classroom experience, smoothly, swiftly getting through the call. We laced our fingers in scheming knots as I pressed my head to his, ear to the receiver. I could hear her vocal darting, her efforts to get him closer, friendlier. "Surely you've noticed her crush has gotten out of hand, haven't you?" She was too late. My mother—able to see through restaurant walls into the bathrooms, able to divine a police officer's family history—didn't know about us! She would never, never know what I knew about Wyatt. "What are his hands like?" she'd say to me, hearing of a Scott, Brian, Kevin. I made stuff up, and she couldn't tell!

I wanted to tell her I'd lost my virginity, a desire as keen as longing for her hug. I wanted to talk it to pieces, benefit from her approval and experience, or let Penelope in on it, with the promise not to breathe a word to Mummy; or even just tell one other girl, Jane, upstairs. But Wyatt had made me promise that I understood what a professional secret was, its fuel, its land mine, its radiating force. "If you're as mature as I think you are," he said, "you won't disappoint me." I swore to him I was equipped for it.

When he told me he couldn't help it, that he would not help it, I believed him. "You have more power over me than anyone in the world," he told me. It made me smug, and I believed him. "You are the smartest student ever to understand me," he said, and I believed him. "You," he said, and I believed him. After the others had cleared out of the classroom with their binders and soccer shoes and clatter of zippers and snaps, I'd come around to his side of the desk and let him brush his arm against my breast as I leaned over to inspect some open page of the Norton anthology. I wrote in the diary how the spot he brushed burned hot under my shirt for hours. Behind the dangerously ajar office door, we pressed into each other up against the filing cabinets. We stood behind his car, our heads visible and nodding, practicing a false animation, while our hands touched with naughty selfishness. We laughed at the word *boyfriend,* and I used it for the boys in clumps around the campus, the slouched lazy profiles, skateboards and Walkmen, jackets carelessly open in the coldest weather. Stupid. We grew pompous and sloppy. We walked everywhere together, and still no one stopped us.

Wyatt concocted a "Mind of the South" trip to New Orleans for the mini-term, Twain, Tennessee Williams, etc. Some of my friends were going scuba diving in Baja. Some kids were learning printmaking, that sort of thing. We sat together on the airplane, observing each other at the everyday beyond the campus edge, the boundaries of our circumstance. The other teacher supervised the rest of the kids.

The first morning Wyatt announced, "Those who wish to visit the French Quarter, sign up with Mr. Ulrich. Those of you interested in Walker Percy will go with me." We went to his hotel room and made love, then lay awhile on the bed, no hurry. He ran his hand over my hip and said, "'This was not counterfeit! There is too great testimony in your complexion that it was a passion of earnest.'" He could quote Shakespeare in any situation. We went out and found curious things to eat, grinned at what we knew was a stunning deceit. No one knew us here, except that one group sent miles away, and he grabbed me in the street in a way he never could, kissing the breath out of me.

I was asleep in my dorm room on a Saturday morning, a bright morning, which I knew through my eyelids because I hated to close the curtains on my small single. The window looked out across the campus and monitored the driveway that fed from the town so that I could know the instant Wyatt's yellow car got to school. I typed my papers for his class, sitting by this window, waiting for yellow. When he was late, I couldn't stop checking. This morning he'd be in the dining hall at breakfast, a time of day I never got to see him, when he was usually at home eating his married breakfast, however that went. He had campus duty this weekend, and he'd be here all day, where I lived, signing permission slips, unlocking the gym, organizing bleacher cleanup. After dinner hours he was going to drive a vanful of kids to the movies. He'd already asked me what I wanted to see.

Someone was knocking, I was turning over, and there was Wyatt opening my door. I looked at the tower of his body as he grinned with one foot over the threshold. I wasn't supposed to have boys in my room ever. He knew that.

"Good morning," he said in the tone that sounded like "I want to fuck you."

I sat up under my covers. He was seeing me in my bed, as close to domestic congress as we'd come.

"Give me your diary," he said.

"Why?"

"I'll keep it safe for you, at my house, while she's here."

My mother was coming later in the week for a parent day.

"She won't read my diary," I said. He gave me an are-you-crazy look. "*I'll* hide it," I said.

"She'll find it." Then he said, "You'll show her."

No. No, no. He had been schooling me in secrets, how to treat them right, where to keep them, why to hide them. "You can't be careless, Susy." For three months I had told nobody about the affair, an intolerable hardship. I was in love, we were lovers! He wanted to know everything about me! Wyatt had told me to join the Disciplinary Committee, become ethically unimpeachable, an arbiter of behavior. He suggested I apply for a senior proctor position. "You'll be able to come and go as you please. Proctors can have cars. We can meet whenever we want." Responsibility, he taught me, granted immunity.

I got out of my twin bed and pulled the diary out from beneath a pile on my desk while he watched. He took it from my hand, letting his knuckles slide against a nipple, the sort of gesture we'd perfected. He pushed my book inside his briefcase. "I'll keep it in the garage," he said. "After she's gone, I'll give it back to you."

"I have the problem of my wife. I'm *married,* Susy. You don't have that problem," he said, but I was entitled to that problem, too. She was in my way when she answered the phone, in the way, maddening, when she canceled the visit to her sister because her sister was sick.

He had a study at home, a boxy office with a plywood door, teetering columns of books, unkempt stacks. The room seemed squashed by the weight of the rest of the upside-down house, the upstairs with its aging stereo, glass vases, small oil landscapes, front door, pressing down upon the office, upon the narrow, windowed bedroom, where I spent that whole weekend (finally, her trip to the sister), using my friend at Colorado College to write me a false letter of invitation. "All right, you can tell her, only her," he said. "We need her." Later he wanted us to have lunch with her so he could thank her. We'd act out some version of the couple we might have been.

"Why don't you stay naked the whole weekend?" he said. I didn't mind, and that felt precocious, the not minding. I went from room to room, opened their cabinets, carried things up and down the stairs. We had sex over and over again, racking up a record, until I was desperately sore, unfuckable. I didn't come, didn't bother to miss it, and Wyatt never asked. I brought glasses of wine up to the living room so we could lie on the floor and listen to *Lucia di Lammermoor* and *La Cenerentola*. In his bedroom, more books reached up to the ceiling. There was room for almost nothing else. Her pale yellow plastic bottle of moisturizer sat on the dresser, its scent an intimacy beyond my comprehension, and I didn't want it in my nose. I followed after him, taking breathfuls of the breeze he trailed, his aging sports jackets, sunburned arms, chalk dust on his collar and between the grooves of skin on the pads of his thumbs. The rooms had the yellow smell of old books, damp books, books crammed into dark, small spaces. The smell of paper was everywhere, what could go up in smoke at any time. Something was not right in that house. At the time I assumed it was me.

It had been almost a year. I was a senior. In some ways Wyatt and I were a real couple—we had our habits, in jokes, little fights. We had routines, a habit of innuendo and of postponing what we wanted, greedy consumption of it in the rare motel room. He had started to bring roast beef sandwiches, grapes in a bag, bottles of apple juice. The meat and bread were thick in our teeth after we made love. We ate naked on top of the bleachy motel sheets. We had poems and quotations that were *ours*. Exempt from the truth, we had started to think of ourselves as exempt from every oblig-ation or requirement, and I often returned to campus past curfew. And he was right about proctors—I was left alone.

One evening Wyatt pulled me aside at the salad bar and asked me to come to his classroom. "I'll be grading," he said. "Come see me." I defended myself to suspicious friends, those constant evenings. "It's extra help," I said if they noticed. I'd pretend to be anxious about my college applications, which, Wyatt assured me, would stand out because of his letter about me. He let me read it. "Never in the history of my professional life as an educator . . ."

I was supposed to look nonchalant as I walked over to his office. I always wanted to run. So what if I did?

"Sit down, Susy," he said. I pulled a chair across the linoleum, closer to his desk.

He stood before me, leaning back and clutching the desk's wooden edge, his large pale hands whitened at the knuckles. "My wife knows about you."

"I know. You told her we were in love."

"Not that. She knows we're lovers." My guilty, nasty success and my body and the taste of his saliva.

"How?"

"I just had to tell her. I've had a hell of a weekend, the longest weekend of my life. We hardly slept at all."

I should have been thinking about him, but I was thinking of her. Now she and I were a pair, a team, sharing the same lifting of the hips beneath him, and his heavy sleep, and the moment when we slid our palms over his shoulders and felt the raised freckles. Now we both knew we shared.

"I'm sorry," I said. I wanted to put my arms around him, but the classroom window faced the darkened campus, our scene spotlit.

"So now she knows."

"What are you going to do?" I was scared this meant the end, the closely held secret over, the smoke dissipated.

"I told her if she made me give you up I'd leave."

"Oh. Okay." Did this mean I was safe? I had no idea what it meant. He liked being married.

"We'll have to see what she says."

"When?"

"She's taking some time to think about it."

"Is she coming in tomorrow?"

"I think so. She has students."

I had pottery with her. There were just a few of us, and I liked her as a teacher. I could split her into two people. She was patient, described things well. It wouldn't be hard to see her, our Tuesday routine, in our smocks, the pegs where we all hung them.

What about the roast beef and the grapes, would we still have that? Now we could go to a restaurant.

"Don't worry," he said, sending me off to my dorm. "I won't let anything take you from me."

I thought, Now I know how animals feel. Threatened, fierce, terrified. I didn't know where to put these emotions. Wyatt seemed concerned with something else, and the idea of Mrs. Crawford kept asserting itself, the awful humiliation. I was not equipped for exposure.

I was roused at midnight by the girl whose room faced the phone booth. She came to my door and knocked, repeating "Phone," until I got out of bed. I tucked into the wooden cubby and lifted the receiver.

"Darling?" my mother said, her coo and whisper. She muffled something. I was brought awake with an uncomfortable knock in my heart.

"What happened?" I said.

"Darling? Don't worry. But I just got raped." Quickly, she said, "I'm okay, I'm okay. I don't want Penelope to know."

"You were raped?" She was visiting New York for a week.

"Oh, I don't want to tell you how, it would really scare you." She sounded like she might be giggling, or hiccupping. I couldn't tell, something slipping away, kept back from the call. I felt the panic of great geographical distance. Why wasn't she worse? Did she need help, police? Did she want me?

"I'm in shock," she said lightly. It was her cabdriver. She wouldn't tell me more, and she asked me questions about rehearsals and my grades, which I couldn't answer, except for "Fine." When she said her sweet, drifty good-night, I dialed Wyatt's house. Well, if his wife knows, she knows. At least I can call if I need him now.

Wyatt answered as if he was thinking about me, expecting me, and I told him about my mother. It was a relief for the drama to be about something besides our situation. I wasn't calling as his lover, but as his advisee.

"Get some sleep, Susy," Wyatt said. "Call her in the morning. Then let me know how she is."

Before breakfast I called her, a sour hole in my stomach, and my mother was hearty and had to be reminded why I was concerned.

"Oh, that," she said, as if the rape had happened months earlier. "Did you get the medallion number?"

"Why would I?"

"Wasn't it the cabdriver?"

"The cabdriver? It was some creep waiting in the foyer. He waited until the cab drove off."

As I returned to my dorm to pick up my books after breakfast Wyatt's wife was parking in the lot near the path. I was too near to change direction. She lifted a block of plastic-wrapped clay out of the passenger seat.

"Hi," I said. I had to talk to her. I had to see what had changed.

"Please, Susanna." She looked straight ahead, over my shoulder. "You've been fucking my husband."

I was surprised to hear her say "fucking." It wasn't welcome on our little campus, not from a teacher. It shut me up.

"Let's just not. Let's not do this." She hoisted the clay higher in her arms and stepped past me. She didn't slow or indicate I should follow, but she called back, "Sorry about your mother." This gave me a small satisfaction: they did talk about my problems. I watched her moving off toward the art building, her square-toed suede shoes and the leather handbag strap and her high-necked blouse. She wore the camel-colored spring coat that I had pushed past so many times in the winter, when I hung my parka in her front closet.

I had to tell someone. I ran into my dorm-mate Jane as she left the bathroom.

"Come in, Jane, come into my room. Close the door. I need to tell you something, but you have to promise, you have to swear, do you swear? I've been having an affair with Dr. Crawford." Words in air, words aloud. Words.

"You're having an affair? When did it start?"

"Ages ago. You know how I had that crush on him my first semester? We couldn't help it. He's in love with me. I was a virgin, I mean, I lost my virginity to him, and we're in love. His wife knows. It's like a Shakespearean comedy! But I can handle it. I can."

Jane shook her head. "Be careful." She had no appetite for my secret. I wanted her to beg for details. God, how I wanted to recount our every move and trick. "This can go really wrong," she said with unexpected weight. "You have to watch out."

But what should I watch out for? How could it be worse? Wasn't this the worst of it, the wife finding out, the flaming, tantrumming center of recklessness and rule breaking, the violation of rules and contracts? And I was fine.

"Do you think I'd get kicked out?" I said.

"You won't be kicked out," Jane said. "He's the one who should go."

I had a physical urge to throw my body in front of him, and I knew I mustn't tell anyone else. "Wyatt said they would never fire him. He's the only PhD on the faculty. Don't tell, okay?" I said as she left.

At the end of the week Wyatt told me, "She's decided I may continue our affair." Maybe she did tell him that, I have no idea, and I had every reason then to go along with his report. I brought my college applications over to their house on Saturdays and spread them over the living room floor, a stapler next to me, checklists. She made tea and read the newspaper at the kitchen table. He wore rag wool socks, which I avoided seeing, this one detail, finally, too much of who they were when I wasn't around.

Wyatt almost convinced me to go to college in Colorado Springs, to stay. Almost. He gave me the brochures, producing them from his briefcase after American Lit. "I drove in and picked these up for you." In the course guides, he'd circled the classes he thought I should take. "You can live in an apartment downtown," he said. "And I can visit you Thursday afternoons."

It was that "Thursday" that made me choose Boston. I loved him, but I meant to grow up. I wouldn't even stay the summer and went to France with Katy from my old school, shrugging off his grip. "Do you know what you're doing to us?" he said.

During my first college semester, Wyatt called all the time, quizzing me on my course syllabi. He asked where my professors had gone to university and ridiculed them and scolded me for not writing him more often. I started going out with Jason, and we had sex between classes and in the basement of the library, in my car. Good, fun sex, talking dirty sex, the opposite of on purpose. His body startled me, not wide and deliberate but tight, lean, quick, hard all the time, wanting me to come and making me come. Gleeful and obscene, we wanted to be loud in his dorm room, and afterward I would dart out in his towel to use the bathroom, flirt with the other boys I ran into in the hall before shutting Jason's door again, more sex. I was supposed to meet Wyatt in Colorado Springs for a secret weekend, but I canceled it, lying, and he knew I was lying, and I didn't care. He could hear me slipping off to a new life, nothing to do with him, and it infuriated him. He kept me on the phone at night—how I'd undone him, sacrificed him and jeopardized his very marriage for my selfish wishes, my craven need to feel special—until I stopped answering.

* * *

When the affair ended for good, after Wyatt's last harsh words and nasty blame, I decided to tell my mother. I regretted the barrier I had put between us to protect Wyatt. My mother liked that I was having so much sex with Jason, which gave us a lot to talk about—techniques, preferences, cocks, UTIs. But this! The affair! I would really impress her. The broken rules and flaunted drama. The day I told her, we stayed on the phone for two hours as she asked me insistent questions. How did it start? Did the wife ever know? Where did you do it? Was he a good lover? But I thought you told me all about the night you lost your virginity? Oh, you sneaky girl! Did Penelope know? Who ended it? What did you *say*?

I answered, letting relief spill out, letting her see my history's many angles. Her questions had warmth in them. We laughed at the ruses and close calls. She cried for me. "Oh, poor darling," she said. "If I'd known, I would have killed him." She said she thought she'd sue the school, and I felt alarm. "Do you want him to do this to someone else, Sue? Because he will. He probably already is." Vanity flamed up in me.

"Well . . . ," I said.

Then she changed her mind. "I could never put you through that. You'd have to testify, you know." We said good-bye and hung up.

Five minutes later, not more than ten, she called back. Her mood was unhinged, a mask dropped.

"You're making it up," she said. "I don't believe you."

I tried to object, and she cut me off, her voice a seething crack. "You *learned* how to lie from me, and now you think you can lie *to* me, and I won't know?" She spoke with incredulous contempt. "This never happened. You just *wanted* it so badly, you *wanted* some drama. How pathetic."

She hung up, the air gone still with the abrupt absence of her voice. You're making it up. You're making it up. I sat rattled and blinking on the edge of my bed, which felt like the world's edge. Had I made it up? I got down on the linoleum, reached under the bed and pulled out the box. I had every piece of paper, every letter of his, copied-down poems, directions, scraps torn out of notebooks, napkins from New Orleans, the Leontyne Price, the photo my mother arranged of the two of us at my graduation, snapped just a few months ago. She'd been standing right there, documenting the affair. I'd been so worried that it showed, as if she'd see his handprints obvious beneath my dress. On my shelf I had the books he'd presented to me, poetry and theory mostly, inscribed with his tight, controlled hand, quoting Shakespeare and Ford Madox Ford. He had used codes, the inscriptions private yet also innocuous.

I sat on the floor and sifted through the entirety of our affair. Other than my diaries, it was just poems, sonnets, comments in the margins of English papers. Wyatt had covered his tracks, although he hadn't resisted one explicitly pornographic letter. He had sent it to American Express in Paris. I'd read it once, sitting on a hotel bed, feeling sick and not ready. What if I showed her that? Would she believe that? Even with my meticulous diary pages open before me, I felt crazy, unnerved, as if my life had vanished. My eyes moved over words, but my mother could rewrite anything.

Parents' Weekend

Amy and I tidied up the room. We expected her parents and my mother for the first parents' weekend of college. We folded the extra blankets and stuffed them under the metal beds, hung things properly in the closet, swept. I picked my mother up at the train, and she flooded me with gossip and exclamation as we drove back to campus. That felt right, how we were us together. Even the pale twinge of dread felt right, something I mistook for the good kind of anticipation. I wanted to want her here. This is where I eat! This is where I have art history! She'd meet Jason and see his animal irresistibility. We parked near my dorm, and I tried to ignore her grimaces as she managed her body out of the car. I didn't want to ask about her back. We crossed the small green to the sixties building with the ugly name.

"What an ugly name," she said, reading the raised iron letters against the white bricks. When I opened the door for her, I smelled the dorm sweat beneath the piney deodorants and fruit shampoos, the latent odor of microwave popcorn that permeated the common furniture. She commented on all of it.

Amy was still in the room, her usual Saturday tennis lesson called off for Parents' Weekend. Her racket was on the bed. It looked like she was heading out to play anyway.

"This is my roommate Amy," I said. "Amy, this is my mother."

"I'm Daphne," my mother said, dropping her voice and slowing down her name. Amy shook her narrow hand.

"I'm Amy."

"You can call me Mummy. All my kids' friends do."

"Mine don't," I said.

"Penelope's do," said my mother. "Sue tells me you're from California, and she's told me how wonderful you are at tennis" (I'd said she took lessons) "and that you have your first serious boyfriend. How's that going?"

"Okay, I guess."

"What's his name?" She looked over at me, mouthing, "*Great* body."

Amy told her.

"How divine! A fabulous name! Have you slept together yet?"

Amy jerked back her head, an automatic "no" jumping out, but my mother's hex had sparked: she was gazing at Amy, and Amy relaxed and told her the details, more details than she'd told me.

My mother patted Amy's bare, tan knee. "The first thing we've got to do is get you on birth control. Susy, do you have a phone book? Look up Planned Parenthood."

"I could just go to campus health," Amy said. "It's free."

"I don't trust them," my mother said. "We'll go to Planned Parenthood. They're very good. That way you can get all the tests and a good fitting. You do want a diaphragm, right?"

Three minutes in the room, and she had managed her way up

against Amy's cervix. I could feel purpose leaving me, as I realized my mother would run the weekend. The activities planned by me or the college were obsolete.

Did my mother take her, using my car keys and letting Amy give directions while I waited back in the dorm? Did Amy drive her new Audi, my mother pulling out her checkbook at the clinic to pay for her "daughter"? It might have happened either way. I wonder if it happened at all. She and Amy went somewhere. I would have called Jason and had him come over for sex on my single bed. I'd distract myself, and that way he'd be there when Amy brought my mother back. We wouldn't have to traverse the campus, looking for him. Or did my mother just plan a rendezvous later in the day, offering Amy the hours meant for me?

In the afternoon, we reassembled in the dorm room. Jason was sitting on my bed, and my mother was reading a paper I'd written. "Brilliant, Sue. This is just brilliant." Amy's parents arrived, and Amy began the introductions.

" . . . Susanna, my roommate, her boyfriend, Jason, and this is her mom—"

"Daphne." She gave a short, strong smile, the way lots of parents did.

"So what do they have planned for us?" Amy's father said. He wore a gold watch, a white tennis shirt. All three of them wore tennis clothes. Her mother had the same socks as her daughter, the Peds with tufts of pale pink at the Achilles. For the first time, I registered Amy's remarkably obvious look of California, which I'd never noticed before. I was assessing her family for the conversation my mother, Jason and I would have later in the town's best restaurant.

"Amy and I went to Planned Parenthood," my mother announced. "Don't you think it's great that she wants to get her birth control together before she has sex with, with, what is it, Tim? Tom?"

"What, what?" her parents were saying at the same time, looking at Amy, at my mother, then back to their daughter.

Amy glared at me.

"Whoa," Jason said.

My mother started to talk fast, her rush of warm conversation—sexually active, what you'd expect from college, they *hadn't* imagined their daughter would stay a virgin.

"Let's go," Amy's father said, grabbing his daughter's arm and picking up her tennis gear. The three of them walked out.

"What are you doing?" I yelled.

"Come *on,* Susy! They have to face the fact that their daughter is an adult now."

Amy stayed away the whole weekend, and my mother forgot about her. We ate out, we went shopping. Jason said sweetly he saw what I meant, yeah, she was kind of nuts, and he let me scream about her right after she left early, after she got into the taxi she had to call to get to the train station because there was no way I was doing another thing for her. No matter how we started, we ended somewhere else, her viciously slammed door, the toxic fumes, my wilted finish.

Jason sat next to me where I ranted on the bed. Such hopeless effort in trying to speak the exact words that would explain her, stop her. How had she done it, blasted everything apart? I started sobbing, couldn't help myself as it turned to retching, the panic to purge her. "Get this to stop," I was screaming at him. "Don't let me feel this." He pulled me down the hall and pushed me into the shower and turned the water on my clothes. Finally, the hysteria of this situation overtook my mother's drama, and I felt silly and got out.

Amy never spoke to me again, and anything I knew about her after that first month I overheard on the phone, which was how

I learned she'd be moving out as soon as another spot opened elsewhere in the dorms. We lived together about nine weeks. One afternoon I came in, and everything of hers was gone, my half of the room turned into a whole. When my mother suggested that I push the twin beds together and make them up as a queen, I did.

Martin

My mother was visiting again, same dorm room, same year. I was skilled at forgetting her last cyclone so that I could have her come back, keep the luxury of her interest. There would be nice restaurants and presents and cash. I had picked her up from the airport. At a stoplight she noticed a vacant lot and a rug seller hanging rugs on the chain-link fence. She made me pull in. "That dorm room of yours," she said. She got out of the car, waving to the salesman. "You're Armenian, aren't you?" She picked the most expensive rug to make his day and had him hoist it into the trunk.

"I don't want a rug."

"Don't be silly."

"It needs to be vacuumed all the time. The dorm doesn't have a vacuum."

"Then we'll buy you a vacuum."

She had just met a new man, Wissam. He was a Palestinian

businessman and a real suitor, quite a bit older than she was. They had met on the beach in Barbados. He had a house there. "He's a recovering addict, too," she said. "We get it." His money relaxed her in a way that was actually nice to be around. She'd lost an edge of anxiety.

That night, as the rug shed pale tufts into the air, we sat around with my boyfriend, Jason, and Martin, this boy I knew from high school in Connecticut. My mother was aware—but Jason was not—that I had slept with Martin that summer when he visited New York. In the morning, after he'd left, my mother had asked how he was in bed, and we'd examined every detail.

But now he'd phoned my dorm—he was college touring— and wanted to come by and say hello, and I didn't want Jason to know about the sex, secrets my reflex. I was watching my mother for treachery. Coke produced a certain venomous laugh in her, intensified the British in her voice. Her mood had started to veer off course. She seemed eager to move on to the next installment.

"We need champagne!" she said. "Don't we? Martin, take me to get some champers!" He grinned, chosen, went and stood by the door. "Darling, give me the keys," she said, and plunged her hand into my bag. "We'll be just a minute."

They left, her clanging voice audible from the common room until the fire door banged shut. Then Jason and I had mad-dash sex to celebrate the relief of her departure. It was fun to clean up fast and toss the pillows back in place and pretend we'd never moved, and we prepared for the champagne and their return. In a long while the phone rang. Martin sounded tentative.

I said, "What's taking you guys so long?"

He said, "We're at your mother's hotel." She made a din in the background, calling instruction and giggling. He said, "We're, uh, we're fucking, and we can't come back just yet!"

My hand went cold. I threw the receiver back in its cradle.

"Fuck it," I said. "We're not waiting for them. Let's go. *Let's go!*"
I screamed.

"What is it? What?" Jason said.

"No," I said. Her laugh played in my ear, her drunken distortion, my lover strung between us and doing what she told him. I'd heard her shout, "She'll just have to wait for us!" I forced us out of the room, locked the door, and we left.

Years later I met Martin again, our lives in Paris coinciding, and we fell in love a little for a grown-up affair. He sent roses. He heated milk for *café au lait* in the mornings while I remained in bed feeling the gorgeous ignition of sex. But while we lingered over the red wine or tidied up his apartment in gestures of small domesticity, my mother was a shadow leaning low and long at our feet, and finally I asked him what happened.

"She wanted to get champagne," he said.

"I've changed my mind," I said. Martin's body was so fine under my hands. We made love instead.

Gambling

The guy was in my senior-year writing class, laughed the longest at the jokes I made to offset the sobriety on my pages. He took me out for the sort of date I'd had often. In his car, I teased him about his taste in music, and he teased me about the Cartier tank watch Patsy had given me for my twenty-first birthday. We would proceed from the restaurant to the movie, from the parking lot to my street, from invitation to sex on my fresh-sheeted bed in my one-bedroom apartment. But tonight I was derailed by his roommate, who appeared at the restaurant with friends and pulled a chair from a neighboring table to sit beside me and shake my hand.

"You!" he said. "I was supposed to meet you months ago. Your father told me to call you." He explained the unlikely connection of mutual friends.

"I wish you had," I said. I looked over at my date, his beaming pleasure. "Too late, I guess."

"Shit," Noah said, staring at me, and I was staring at him—the sophisticated Jewish lineage and deep-set dark eyes. The restaurant had turned loud because the belly dancer had started. We watched her flesh curving and rolling.

I leaned closer to Noah's ear. "I wish I knew how to do that. It makes me want to go to bed just looking at it, with anyone, straightaway." I'd knocked him off balance.

"You could take lessons."

"I could," I said. "I might."

But first I went to *Blue Velvet* and then home with my date, back to my cleaned bathroom and dusted bedside table, diaphragm case within easy reach. I had to give him the repertoire, because I was good at it, and I liked doing what I was good at.

A few weeks later (the writing-class guy by now sort of a boyfriend, but Noah, the roommate, all I thought about) my sister came to visit. I drew a deep breath at the train station as I watched her come up the platform. Her body always changed, part maturity, part effort, and she was stiletto tall, a vampish stunner with a short black skirt, a very white T-shirt for contrast under a fashionably slouchy black jacket. She still wore the gold letter on a chain from the Famous Lyricist. The Penelope she presented never matched my Penelope, the memory of her soft tummy, little hand, tangled hair from sleep.

The four of us went out to dinner, and Penelope shifted her body in her restaurant chair so Noah could look at her. "Susy's the one who always has relationships!" she said. I knew she looked beautiful, very beautiful, but I couldn't see it. My scrutiny took in each element but not the entirety. Her irises blazed blue with special lenses. She tossed back her expensive bangs, and the earrings that glinted in her long, glossy hair were made of some enormous stone for dazzle and imitation. She was wearing boots of smooth, unmarked leather that hugged her leg to the knee, boots I could never borrow because of having big calves. "You got the Jewish legs," my mother used to tell me. "Penelope has dancer's legs." I was wearing black tights and a houndstooth skirt, which had seemed stylish as I left the house, but her stockings, held around her thighs by some modern magic, cast a satin finish on her waxed legs, unassailable glamour.

Through dinner my sister cracked the unexpected remark, lanced the acute observation, and the men laughed hard with her mischief. It was her wit singeing the air as plates were cleared for dessert, my silence growing noticeable, huffy. I had my mother's instinct for the emotional hum in a room, but my sister with her gift for the brilliant allusion and tart pun sounded like our father.

After the dinner, she went to Noah's room while I followed my boyfriend to his. He put on *Born to Run,* as usual.

"You can't have him anyway," Penelope said the next day. We drove home. She smelled of Noah's shampoo. "So what does it matter?"

I complained to my mother, who said, "You don't have to have everything, you know, Sue. You're the one who's graduating college. You've got your own flat, a real relationship. You could give Penny a chance."

A chance? She was nineteen, living in our old apartment in the city. She'd become the curator of our childhood, the photo albums, kitchen things, Rizzoli art books. She'd shrugged off college to take drama classes where famous actors dropped in. She went to matinees with our mother when Daphne was in town. Her friends threw her birthday parties, flew her to France, bought her Fendi bags and flamboyant coats. When I was with her in the city, she'd storm the teeming huddle of cosmetics counters at Bloomingdale's, calling the sales staff by name. They'd give her double handfuls of samples, little zippered bags, cunning compacts. If they didn't, she'd lean over the glass countertop and make the most of her little-girl longing. "Don't you have *something* for me?" I could never look like that, move like that, pull any of it off, stuff I didn't even care about when I was in Boston, but after a day out with her I'd go into her bathroom and contemplate stealing her Chanel lipsticks, the thirty-dollar hair clips. We were better on the phone, away from her collections and trophies. Nor did I have to smell her smoke, and she didn't have to watch me disapprove as she lit up. She smoked a great deal, fond of couture lighters, heavy tokens of someone's affection, Cartier gold, Tiffany.

My mother and I talked a lot about Penelope, phone calls between Boston and Dubai, where she lived "on the compound."

"I'm so worried about her. She adores you, you know. You can help her."

That was the other Penelope, easier for me to understand but just as exhausting, the insomniac who couldn't fall asleep without the television loud for company, the one who called me at late hours and wept.

"What's wrong?" I'd say, soothing.

The list was long, a thousand ways to worry about the world. The shantytowns, the earthquake victims, the shoot-out at the fast-food place. When Cary Grant died, she sobbed for an hour. I was in the middle of writing my thesis and took a break to lie on the couch. Now my arm was tired, my ear was tired. I needed to understand Satan in *Paradise Lost,* what he wanted so badly. Our mother had cried like that when John Lennon died, her desperate sobs so uncontrolled when I came to the dorm phone that I was terrified of what she was about to tell me.

"Penelope, please. Can you calm down? You didn't know him."

"But now," Penelope gasped, "there will never *be* another Cary Grant movie, ever. And he was so wonderful! Wasn't he, Sue?"

My mother told strangers I was going to Oxford in the fall, which was true, and that I was nearly a Rhodes Scholar, which was not.

At my apartment before we left for the graduation ceremony she held out a slim box from my absent grandmother. I couldn't reach it before she was whipping it back, unlatching it and lifting out pearls. Aunt Irene and Penelope watched. My mother buffed them between her fingers.

"Susy gets pearls?"

"You must always wear them against your skin," my mother said. "Skin gives them their glow." She dangled them close so that I pulled back my head, trying to focus. She was already turning me by the shoulders. She got my hair up off my neck, planted my hand against the hair to hold it up and thread the strand under my elbow. I could feel the pearls slide across my neck and drop into their weight as her fingers worked the clasp. She turned me, surveyed me, and I still hadn't touched the present.

Because we had started out as a secret cheat, proud of our own crime, I didn't bother at first about Noah's gambling. He studied playwriting. He could quote long passages of Stoppard, Mamet. He knew musical theater history, and he noticed set design or architecture in unusual ways. I thought he was perfect for me, a record of my own education, the reward. After graduation he landed a tiny studio, and I camped out at Penelope's before I left for Oxford. My mother was around. I wouldn't let Noah sleep over, uneasy with their certain inspection, and we made love at his place in the humid afternoons, windows open, fan spinning, incessant noise of taxi doors and bus brakes. When I came home to change my mother asked what she always asked.

"What's he like in bed? Penelope said he—"

"Fine," I said, the single word, as short as possible.

"Does he like going down on you?"

"Please, Mummy."

"I'm just asking. It's important. Don't act like it's not important."

*   *   *

"She's going to make a pass at you," I warned Noah. "Because you're mine. Don't let her sit next to you. She's crazy." I felt like I was talking to myself. We sat on the crosstown bus on our way to meet my mother, Central Park fleeting past. This was their first meeting.

"Calm down," Noah said. "You're the one who's acting crazy."

We got off the bus and started down Lexington to the Skyline. I caught his sleeve and said, "Let me go alone." This had to be made to not happen. I thought of the first time she'd met Jason, my college boyfriend, the expensive Indian place she'd picked, inviting Aunt Irene and Penelope, too. She seated Jason next to her, me on her other side, and quite visibly she ran her hand over his leg. "This one's got a hungry look," she announced to the table, lechery slowing down her voice. "That's what you are, Jason: hungry."

"Noah, I'll say you were sick."

"No." He was annoyed, kept walking. "Relax, Susanna. Nothing terrible's going to happen."

We went in, and my mother jumped up from a booth and hugged me, the world on pause. Then she put her hand out to Noah, looking somber.

"Sit across from me, you two," she said. "I want to see how in love you are." When the waiter came she told Noah to order.

Then she exclaimed, "But you don't want a cheeseburger!"

"I do," Noah said. "That's what I get in coffee shops."

My mother looked up at the waiter. "I, however, shall have the moussaka, Yannis. *Efharisto.*"

I ordered a club sandwich.

"Tell me the name of your last play," she said. He did. "Good name. Has it been produced? We should get it produced. I'm very good at that sort of thing, I'm sure Sue's told you." She launched into the tale of the producing job, years ago, a large reliable salary, a limo to pick her up. She made it sound like a career, not just the six or eight weeks it had been. She told Noah that Judi Dench and Maggie Smith were friends, although they were actually Patsy's friends. She told about sitting behind Samuel Beckett once at the theater. "I touched his coat."

"What about Christopher Plummer?" I said, a little sour and adolescent.

"What about him?"

"When we went backstage?"

"When? In London?"

"No, here. He was in *Othello*."

She said, "You did?"

"No, *we* did, remember?" This drove me crazy, having to rehearse for her her own theater. When Iago made his entrance she had squeezed my hand. We were in the second or third row, close enough to return his gaze, should it land on us. I watched the sweat streak his makeup instead of hearing the Shakespeare. As soon as the bows ended, she tugged me toward an exit door that led backstage to Plummer's dressing room. She rapped on the door, said, "Chris?" She went in, and I was wondering if she'd known him in the sixties. "My daughter worships you. Sue, come on in, don't be shy. He's very nice." The actor looked tired, the buoyant stage life gone out of him. We shook hands. She told him how smashing he'd been in the play. She told him who her father was, waiting that tiny pause for his reaction. "There!" she said as we headed out to catch a cab. "He was brilliant, wasn't he? You shook his hand." It was easy in those moments to feel her triumph. Her force and thrust made things matter that otherwise would have just passed by.

Noah and I left the restaurant with Daphne, dropped her off at the apartment and walked on. We came to a movie theater, its show a few minutes from beginning. I didn't care what was playing. I needed to sit, regain the strength in my loose legs and calm my stomach.

"She's a riot," Noah said. "I don't see what you're so uptight about. She seems fine to me."

I couldn't explain. It *had* gone okay. Memory was a bully, shoving me into casting her as a fiend. "You're not fair to her," Penelope often said to me. "Mummy doesn't stand a chance with you."

Noah joked, "And how come she *didn't* make a pass at me? I'm insulted!"

"How was I?" my mother said when I called. "I'm better, right?"
"Yes."

"I'm really trying, Sue."

"I know." The prospect of being with her without drama or collision, without scandal and wasted energy, was tantalizing, melting on my tongue. I wanted it. A few days later we went to the Whitney, and she didn't talk about my sex life or hers. She talked about the art, sort of. "Calder lived right down the block from us on Sullivan Street." I felt myself ease up on her, release some of my vigilance. Let this be better. *Let this be perfect* was the unarticulated wish, the steady longing, the trap.

My father's doctor took me aside. The MS was worse. "He has about another year." I didn't understand at first what he was trying to say.

When I told this to Noah, we had to decide something about us.

"I'm not going to go to Oxford," I said. "This could be my last year with him."

Noah didn't say anything.

"Should we move in together?" I said. "Aren't you glad I'm staying?"

He sank into his unmade futon and fell asleep. I couldn't wake him. I sat on the chair and waited, thinking the nap wouldn't last, but it was dark when I left his place.

I loved Noah, fiercely, because that's the way I loved, convinced that my effort would make things be so, and he loved my ardent energy, my appetite for food and sex and friends. "You make things fun," he told me, but he would disappear to a backgammon club upstairs above Seventy-second Street. Over and over, he was at the club. "I'm going to the club," he said every afternoon, most evenings, and he left me behind like a classroom at the end of the day. I hated that I said, "Where were you?" when he came back to the studio three, four hours later than he'd told me, the cold Cuban food lined up on the kitchen counter. He made bets. He started to lie about betting, about losing, and when he lied his mouth went rigid and his lips didn't look connected at the corners. After he lost, his sweat had an acidic tinge. I was so used to lying, I forgave him, wanting him to know that I planned to overlook this.

Knowing Noah lied to me made me want to catch him, made me want the upper hand. I become obsessed with accuracy, exact details with which to trace his day. I said things like "Well, what time did you get on the subway?"

"What should I do?" I asked my aunt on the phone. She'd had a ten-year marriage, extraordinary. She was four or five years into another relationship. She was the one to go to in these matters.

"He may need help," she said. "But it doesn't have to be you, darling."

"I know when he lies."

"What do you *want*?"

"I want a real couch instead of a futon, and a tranquil relationship and time to write," I told her. "I want to make a real relationship work, not a series of them."

"Then you shall have it."

I liked hearing her say that, but I didn't believe it. I didn't believe I'd get what I longed for.

I walked down Broadway, my breath tight and fast. I sank in against a building across from the club. Its window was bright with fluorescents, and (I imagined) the air inside was used up by the stink of cigars in greasy ashtrays, atop those tin receptacles you found in lobbies. Noah was fixed in the same spot every time, visible from the street, same shoddy chair. He bent his head to the backgammon board. I didn't want to kiss him anymore. His partner assumed the same pose. They slumped, they rolled the dice, they waited.

Part of me felt vindicated. You lied! I had a right to my troubles. But part of me leapt with the cinematic adventure, the narrative train speeding along.

"I've caught you! I've watched you! In the *rain*, you should know, and it was cold. I stood there for two hours!"

"Why?" Noah asked me. "It's your problem, then, if you knew where I was. Why would you waste your time doing that?"

"Could we go to one of these?" I held out the list I'd made of Gam-Anon meetings.

"Don't you think you're overreacting?" he said. "Go by yourself."

I had started a job, a prized internship at a political magazine. My father knew the editor, invited him to drinks. I was the only intern who socialized with the editor. I stayed at my father's after the editor left, and we talked about the history of the magazine. I loved having a job, my desk phone, loved the toasted bagels in white deli paper, loved lunch, and flirting, and things in alphabetical order. Each week I ratcheted up the flirting with colleagues, taking comfort in success. I could make it go as far as I wanted.

"How awful," I said to Nick in the fact-checking department. He was telling me about his breakup. "But now you can order what you want on the Chinese menu, yes? And you got the apartment. Do you like it? Where is it? Will you take me?" I thought I was stealthy. And anyway it worked. Nick brought me to his building, and I grabbed the back of his shirt on the stairs and made him kiss me, threw myself into that kiss because Nick didn't gamble, didn't smell like panic, didn't talk about sports.

"Where'd you learn to kiss like that?" he said.

"It's not learned," I said through mouth, teeth, tongue. "Instinct."

His one-bedroom was hollowed out by the absence of the furniture his ex-girlfriend had taken. He took his time in the kitchen. A bottle cap hit the Formica, and I came in, and we ignored the beer, just great, hungry kissing that was filling up every little space in me. In the kitchen it was playful. In the living room we had to choose—sit, stand, lie down? And in the unlit hallway he pushed me into the wall, and I pushed him. By the time we were shoeless and standing next to his dark, unmade bed, our kissing was informed, familiar, pointing directly at fucking. Fine. I didn't *feel* unfaithful. I felt alive, inflamed. Later he walked me to the corner and hailed the cab, which hurried me home, damp air through the rolled-down window, breezing hair into my face as I thought up lies, satisfied they'd be good.

"Did Noah notice?" Penelope said on the phone the next morning. I was at my office desk, preparing for the moment Nick arrived. Think of the secret glances, the sudden conspiracy between us.

"How would Noah notice?" I said. "He came home after me, and this morning he was making notes on the sports page."

"So how was he? The fact-checker?"

I told her all about him. And the freelancer? How was he? His place was so close to the magazine I walked in the opposite direction and around the block and came at it from the other way. He kept a bottle of San Pellegrino by the bed, two glasses. In the copy department: that one lived in Hoboken, where the avenues on a Saturday afternoon seemed too wide to contain me safely. I felt exposed as I followed the directions from the PATH train, written in a copyeditor's regimented hand. His tiny room was stacked with books about anarchy. The window looked down a sunless air shaft dotted with pigeon shit. Everything reminded me I was here to go to bed with someone who was not the person lying to me. I took off my clothes, and the editor took off his, and Noah was at the club, holding off losing, betting bigger, then losing. Noah was at the club, at the club. I called up Jason from college. Dialing him I'd get turned on, our old voices, our understanding. He was the animal in me, the ready partner. Later I would use specifics: a drink at the Gramercy Tavern; the late aerobics class. Noah countered with his version of his evenings, similar belabored lies, and we settled into a kind of harmony, its own reality so compelling I wondered if I should marry him.

"How many is that now?" Penelope asked me at lunch. She could list everyone I'd kissed and slept with.

"Six?" I said.

"Eight, I think. Tell me when it gets to ten." I needed a record keeper. My numbers were pretty high.

"What about the gambling?" she said. "Has he admitted it yet?"

"No. He says he doesn't have a problem." We looked at each other. "Well, maybe it's not really a problem, maybe I do focus on it too much. Although it's annoying, about the money. Either he never has any or he has three grand in cash. I can't even try talking to him when a game's on."

"Don't they have meetings?"

"I tried that. No dice."

"Nice one," she said. "What are you going to do?"

But I had no plan. I only knew how to keep track. "Fuck him," I said.

"I think we should get married," I told Irene, pretending Noah was gambling less.

She said, "This is about your father, because he's sick. Don't do it." I had expected her to say that, so it was a comfort. "You're only twenty-two, Susy."

"Look at my mother. She was sixteen. I'm long past waiting."

"Darling, look. You know I'll be here for you."

"We can go to Bergdorf's and look at wedding dresses!" I said. "You know those private fittings, where they bring you the dress?"

"That's a small fortune."

"No, no, I don't want to buy the dress there. I just want the frilly pretend. Would you go with me?"

"Of course, my love," my aunt said. "Anything."

I took Noah out to dinner. It was a sticky, end-of-summer night, the French restaurant on a corner. We sat outside. Talk was difficult as traffic clattered past. My stomach in a knot, I wrote on a piece of paper "Will you marry me?" and pushed it across to him.

He looked less than surprised. "Yeah, sure."

I expected a different mood to infuse the evening, make the subway ride festive, bless our bed beneath the beleaguered air conditioner, but things stayed as they were.

"And you proposed!" my mother said at her place the next day. "My little bride. Let's get some champagne!" She skipped into the kitchen—her back okay—and opened the fridge. I knew this mood. It was the Big Everything frenzy, the Let's-Take-Over-Central-Park mood. She toasted Noah. "Now I *have* to like you. Only kidding, Sue."

I bought paperbacks on wedding planning and made appointments around the city to look at spaces, prissy, controlled rooms big enough for a hundred, for two hundred. Hotel ballrooms, restaurants you could take over, somebody's loft. Noah would meet me there, his shoulders forward, ready to turn everything down. We met with the caterer, turning the pages of his portfolio as he wrote down "marinated beef skewers" in a flying script that conveyed supreme busyness. In the evenings I listened to tapes sent to us by swing quintets.

Aunt Irene and I went to Bergdorf's, an appointed hour in the bridal department. We wouldn't buy anything, spend those many thousands of dollars, but I wanted the gesture of debutant entitlement, and my aunt and I giggled and trilled when the trim saleswoman left the private room for the thousand-dollar headpiece. I was standing on a platform, embraced by mirrors, beautiful white me everywhere and in the center, lots of my aunt behind me. How ferocious my desire was to be bride, to have everything be especially about me.

Daphne and Irene took me to Gino's to celebrate, the three of us in an easy knot in the small foyer, peeling off coats and bags. We kept holding celebrations, celebration drinks, celebration breakfasts, celebration strolls. Penelope got there. She stopped at the coat check counter, talked a few minutes intently, then very big laughter. We had a square table by the wall.

"You could never be faithful, Sue," my mother said. "You're not cut out for it."

"How long have you ever been faithful?" Penelope said.

"You're so young still," Irene said.

"Well, what about me?" my mother said. "I was young. Of course, I married a bastard. But if anyone can handle it, Sue can. She handles things."

"How come Susy gets to get married?"

The waiter, ancient and impatient, retrieved his pad from a back pocket. We each ordered *paglia e fieno al segreto* in a strong accent.

"You've already had six affairs," Penelope said.

My mother said, "You won't be happy in bed."

"There's more than sex," I said.

"What?" she demanded.

"He's very smart. No one else talks about *Paradise Lost* with me. We discuss things, theater, dance. I don't know. He's funny."

"He's funny? I never see him smile, let alone laugh. And your father was exceedingly smart, but did that make him a joy to be married to?"

"Noah reminds me of your father," Irene said. "He even looks like him."

"I know," I said. It was embarrassing, sort of obvious.

Irene said, "Noah gives Susy the intellectual validation she's always trying to get from Nat."

"I *guess* there's more than sex," Daphne said.

"Ah," Irene said, rolling her eyes at me. "Though he does adore Susy."

Irene never talked about sex, which gave her this sphinxlike presence in our midst. When my mother was in a bad mood she'd call Irene repressed. The manager paused to say hello, his hand on the back of my mother's chair. She arched to look up at him.

"Susy's engaged! Isn't it amazing! And you've known her since she was this big!" The manager and I looked blank. When I came to Gino's without my mother, no one knew me. He congratulated us in Italian and passed on to a table of well-dressed men.

"Well, here's to Noah," my mother said. "A good first husband."

"That's not very supportive," I said.

"There goes Sue sulking," she said. "Never mind, darling. You'll have a beautiful baby."

"Where are you going to get your dress?" Penelope said. "Vera Wang?"

"Yes, good," said my mother. "That's close to the apartment."
Penelope sat up straighter. "Can I come?"

Irene and I had agreed not to let on about our Bergdorf's date, sidestepping my mother's competitive streak, and I knew not to mention the trips to thrift shops with my stepmother, who wanted me to marry in something vintage.

"Kleinfeld, I think."

"*What* is *Klein*feld?"

"It's like an outlet. It's in Brooklyn."

"You *can't* be serious."

"I suppose Nat's not going to kick in," said Penelope. "As it were."

"I got married in a pink suit."

"We know."

One night I woke to the phone ringing. Noah and I had moved into a two-bedroom, but he wasn't there. He was at the club. It was Penelope, and she sounded careful.

"You have to wake up, Susy. I have to tell you something."

"Okay." I thought she needed to talk.

"Dr. Crawford got cancer, and he's going to die." Wyatt barely intruded anymore, an epic whose disaster had faded. Penelope said, "He's really sick."

"He's going to die?" No. No, no, no, not that piece of my life gone. First deep love, first of everything. He gave me Shakespeare. He had to stay.

Penelope had heard from old friends. The school was in an uproar. "I wanted to be the one to tell you, Sissy Su," she said. "Do you want me to come over?"

"No. Thank you." She could rally with the most giving comforts, but I wanted to lie on my back and project every memory of him onto the ceiling. The next day I wrote him a letter. I didn't want to console him, and I didn't want to say what other people said. Noah, who treated the subject as petty, thought I was making too much of it. I thought about the words a long time. "Dear Wyatt, Although I never planned to speak to you again, I cannot imagine a world without you in it." I resisted the impulse to tell him of my honors and successes. I spent a long time on the signature because I couldn't decide between much love, with love, your, yours, or just Susanna. I settled on love, Susanna, and it wasn't a lie. It felt scary to write his address down, as if my hand and pen would pull me to the stone walkway we used to hurry on. I just needed to say good-bye, but when he didn't answer me I was furious. Didn't he need to account for me, as he finished his life?

Wyatt had time to prepare the funeral, radon infecting him, his cancerous lungs on their long way out. When he died, not too many weeks later, he delivered his own eulogy, and his tape-recording instructed the mourners to go home afterward and read Plath. I heard from friends that everyone wondered where I was. "They were always so close," they'd said. "She was his favorite, wasn't she?"

Everyone said it was a terrible death. The house killed him, the pervasive toxin, the floor of his house, its dusty treachery muffled by the worn brown rug beneath us, hiding my errant hairs, her dropped contact lens, spatters of dried wine, a thin smear between our fucking and his death.

"We know where you'll buy Susy her ring," my mother told Noah. She didn't add that she and I had spent the morning in the Carnegie Hill antique jewelers, where we'd already instructed the owner ("I've known him for ages. He's always been in love with me") to sell this very ring to Noah when he came in, the Victorian setting, the pretty little diamond, the two sweet rubies. "Noah doesn't know your taste," my mother said. "I know your taste. Didn't I give you those?" She fingered my earring, a small blue pearl set in antique gold. She had me show it to the owner as she held back my hair. "And doesn't she have divine ears?"

"This, too," I said, holding up my wrist for him so he could see the thin simple gold bangle. She'd given me all the jewelry I loved best.

Noah was lying on the futon couch staring at a football game. I made myself not ask if he'd bet on the spread. I didn't want to fight that fight, nor have to see his threadbare sweatpants.

"There's something wrong with the toilet," he said, eyes on the TV. "You should check it out." I opened the bathroom door and saw a red velvet box sitting in the center of the closed toilet lid. My mother was right. Noah understood nothing of our ways.

Noah didn't stop gambling, and I didn't stop sleeping with other people. A couple of months before the wedding date I forfeited my thousand-dollar deposit on the dress and left him, and he said, as we surveyed our rugs and records, dishes, books, "You can keep that fucking ring I was forced to buy you." I hadn't planned to return it. When I looked at my hand I remembered leaning with my mother over the velvet trays, then having lunch together at the Russian Tea Room.

Going Straight

The man was visiting from London. Someone brought him along to our after-work drinks, introduced him around, and we faced each other at a table ringed with loud friends. The Englishman watched my general flirting, and I watched him watch. So far he'd made talk about airline comfort and the Japanese market. I turned to him.

"What is it you want in a woman?" I demanded, the crackle of abandoning good manners.

"Passion," he said, and then colored, as if he'd spoken in spite of himself. I was used to that.

Gordon returned to England, and I let the sliver of flirtation between us turn into expensive phone calls. When Patsy invited me to meet her in London, I gave notice at the magazine and went, but not for her. I went for the fresh start embodied by the man. I was almost delirious with hope.

I called Gordon from a sidewalk phone booth, knowing I'd wake him. I told him where to come get me and my suitcase, my breath in the mouthpiece. That first night we were proper, Gordon charmingly sleepy as he made up the guest bed with a white eiderdown. I let him slide past me in the doorway, let our clothes-against-clothes promise tomorrow. He was terribly tall.

How hard we fell, a thunder of the first nights that never stopped its din. The mad carnival of it: my second night in London, he took me out to a straitlaced dinner, and we flirted in every gesture, then tore at each other's hems and buttons in his front foyer; the next night he scored black-market seats to a hot West End show. We had great, unstoppable sex. Just look at us, we cackled, how well we work out, the shoulder and chest of him, span of hips, which he signed over to me right away. Has anyone ever felt this as much as we do? The third night, he brought home two tickets to Spain, for tomorrow! The sort of thing that would happen to Penelope. "I *never* take holidays," Gordon said warmly, wanting me to hear that this was "I've fallen in love with you," and I did hear it, and we went away for two weeks, Madrid and Granada, hotel rooms we assessed at once for how loud we could be making love. "Your first Beatles album, your favorite movie, your best kiss?" "*This* one." At the Reform Club his father confided to me tender stories of Gordon's boyhood and lost mother. They hadn't known me a month, and they told me everything. Gordon drove with confident speed through the nest of London streets, knowing the right restaurant for Sunday afternoons after sex; and wouldn't I like a skirt from Agnès B.? Wouldn't I like the jacket, too? Wool always hangs well. I changed my return ticket and changed it again, staying in London, expertly cared for.

"I made reservations," my mother said to me over the phone. "The restaurant is called Ménage à Trois!" She giggled. She was in town and, until today, I'd been dying for her to meet Gordon. I tried to ignore the push in her voice, as I was tired of jokes like this.

I said, "We'll pick you up at your hotel." Gordon and I were taking her to dinner. (Well, Gordon paid.) We collected her, and she was stoned on painkillers.

"The flight was hell on my back," she said. "God, you *are* tall."

She drank enough vodka before the food came that she never noticed the plates, never shut up. She'd been with Wissam for several years, more than anyone had expected her to last, traveling with him on business between the Middle East and London, New York and Barbados, redecorating his houses, buying copious amounts of gold jewelry duty-free. She said she hadn't touched coke in ages. She said they were talking about getting married. "The Arab and the Jew," she said. "Israel can't work it out, but we can."

She was supposed to be asking about us, to see I was in love.

The waiter cleared the plates, leaving a white expanse of tablecloth. My mother grabbed Gordon's cuffs and pulled his hands across to her. She stared at him.

"You must be *very* good in bed because sex is *so* important to Susy."

"Uh," Gordon said, snapping his hands back.

"She wouldn't have picked you otherwise."

"That's it, stop," I said. Heat rushed up my neck. I should have warned him, and I hadn't, hadn't gotten yet to that part of my life and the way my mother played her role. I wanted to escape to the bathroom, but I couldn't leave him with her. Although I didn't know him well, I felt his upright distress. All we had were our first heady and predictive weeks, and now this. I wanted a decorous English boyfriend. And privacy. What she'd said, that was a violation, wasn't it? She would joke away her behavior a few minutes later, and a few minutes later I wouldn't be positive things had gone as I remembered.

Gordon paid the bill as she fumbled around in her bag and took another pill. She tried to kiss him on the mouth as he put her in a cab.

"I certainly wasn't letting her in my car again!" Gordon was trying to be jolly, but we couldn't laugh. We returned to his house, and he held me, perplexed, as I cried with wordless rage. Then I wanted huge sex to shake her off and remind him this was still us. Don't look at her, look at me.

The next morning after Gordon left for work I picked up the phone. I needed witnesses beyond him, company. When I reached my sister, my aunt, my grandmother, I heard my mother's version of the evening, distributed early and absorbed: Bossy, uptight Susy ignored her, then packed her off in a cab, too rude to drive her because she couldn't *wait* to get home and fuck her (attractive) new man. She had already warned them: "Susy's going to lie about this."

He had the company move him to New York, for me I thought. Gordon was shy about giving me the news. I called Penelope first. She'd appreciate the romance.

"Wow," she said. "Do you think I'll ever have a boyfriend like that?"

I never wanted this feeling to go away, the high plain of Love. I'd force its longevity if I had to, stick to fidelity, keep recounting the first starry weeks! We never mentioned the Ménage à Trois dinner, and everyone knew not to talk about Daphne with me. I wasn't speaking to her. She left me a message, inviting us to her sudden wedding, but I wasn't interested.

It was work, though, that day, not to go.

Gordon and I moved into a Chelsea loft so enormous I was embarrassed with my friends but gleeful. I felt like a movie star, allowed to take up all that space in the city. Another magazine had hired me, a movie magazine, where I was an editor's assistant. I took messages from Warren Beatty and Billy Wilder. At home we had stemware, a custom sofa ordered. I waited for the phone company and the cable man. I waited for the man to install the air conditioner, pacing away the morning and then the whole afternoon on the bleached wood floors until the buzzer went. "It doesn't matter to them, does it, Susanna?" Gordon said. "If you miss a day, no one should mind. It's the sort of work anyone can do, isn't it?"

We gave crowded parties during which we didn't speak to each other but only to our guests, a married sort of thing to do. When my college boyfriend called me I said, "Sorry, Jason, no, not anymore. This is the real thing." I so much wanted a real thing. In the evenings Gordon stared out the window with its twenty-foot-high view sloping down the island. We had short dinners with my father and avoided talk of politics. I wished he'd stop saying the company paid for everything, his morning taxis, his rent. I wished he'd say "our rent." Why didn't I notice how often he had his back turned to me, that what I got of him was his back, his errands, his instructions? The eiderdown must lie like *this*.

"Must you bite your nails, Susanna?"

I got acrylic nails manicured over my own. Sometimes I went with my sister, meeting her at a corner place she liked on rainy evenings after work. She knew her manicurist by name.

"How's la dolce vita?" she'd say.

"I don't know, I can't tell. It's kind of flatter. Maybe that's the way a proper relationship is."

"I wouldn't know," she said. She launched into one of her look-what-the-new-guy-did-for-me tales. I was jealous of her carefree liaisons that had nothing but glitz and future to them, and she was jealous of my security.

"Mummy's coming," Penelope said. "She'll be here a week."

I felt the little stir. "So?"

"Why are you like this? You're so mean to Mummy."

"But I'm not!" I said. "I would see her, but when I do, when I do . . ." What? How could I set all this in front of my sister? The two of them had something else, a unity and barricade, and a complete futility washed over me.

"You never want her when you're happy," Penelope said. "You're so selfish."

I was waiting for the initial feeling to come back, the to-hell-with-everything-else feeling, the flying-to-Spain thrill, the hurry as he walked through the door, suit jacket half off the quicker to take me to bed. Instead, his decisive step throughout the loft, his concern at the coffeemaker, reminded me of the office. He locked his file cabinet and never spoke of his income, squirreled his mail away. His privacy insulted me. We still made love, which ended in his immediate silence and sleep. We both knew the love affair had shifted, deserved examination, but we were waiting for the custom-made Roman shades. He didn't like my shoes in the middle of the living room.

"Damn it, Susanna, at the end of the day, to come back to this."

He always left for work first, and I got home from the magazine before him. A year passed this way. One night, after we'd made love and our bodies were still connected by sweat, he said, "I don't love you."

"His heart rate hadn't even settled down yet!" I told Aunt Irene. We lay on her bed. She'd ordered me Indian food, put everything on a plate.

"Bastard," she said. She was pragmatic on the subject of love. She'd moved to New York from London several years earlier and

Daphne flirted with her new boyfriend when she came to town, but I don't know if that bothered Irene.

I was sobbing. "He said, 'I don't love you anymore.'" If I repeated his words, maybe I'd understand them and stop crying. "Why doesn't he? I've done everything right! I was never unfaithful, this whole year, not even once."

"You're not real with him," Irene said. "You invented the Susy you thought he wanted to see."

"That's a liability?" I said. I sat up. "I thought that was a present! I thought it was a brilliant, complicated achievement."

Gordon and I still had tickets to Mexico, and we still went. Had I been older I would have known that you don't do that to yourself, but I was sure passion could overcome our situation, his sequestered heart. I was *sure,* and when we arrived that afternoon it looked like I was right. We had a shaded cabana on the sand and unzipped our suitcases to retrieve the swimsuits we'd packed on top. We applied sunscreen, hands and lotion on skin and sweat, which turned into lovemaking, falling on the bed, the fan swimming above us, the door not even locked. Through the sex, through the coming, I was thinking, No, we won't break up. Every day we went scuba diving, and I watched Gordon underwater, his blue eyes even paler through his mask, and I reminded myself I was in love with him. At dinner we had nothing to say.

I moved to a studio on Christopher Street, and Gordon brought over a pillow and tossed it on my bed. He planned to sleep there, which meant he could, might, love me still, or again. A few days later, he phoned and asked me to dinner, and we walked to a central point from our apartments. I was dressed for having my clothes come off, one piece at a time, perfume on the pulse points between my legs. I rehearsed the outrageous phrase, the quick come-on and flirt, and walked into the restaurant exhilarated about the rest of the night, as if it were a first date.

"I thought you'd want this back," Gordon said, before I could say more than hello. He felt at his breast pocket and set a miniature silver clock on the table, an antique my mother had given me. When I'd given it to him, week two, he'd placed it among his cuff links and daily change so he could look at it every morning and night. "I thought you'd want to give it to someone else."

"Do you have someone else?" I demanded. I was seething, humiliated not to be wanted.

"Actually . . . ," he said. I thought, Get up and leave, Susanna, go. But I sat stuck to the leather banquette. I wanted one final trip to bed with him, the oblivion and release of breakup sex. He owed me. It would make a better story when I phoned Penelope: "In spite of everything!"

He took a swallow of his gin and tonic and said, "Shall we order?"

He paid for dinner, and I didn't thank him on purpose, trying to think up every little way to be rude. He walked me to the corner where he turned to face me, and for a second I saw him and what I'd never had access to. "I should tell you about Holly," he said.

She'd been to our parties. She'd asked how Gordon was in *bed*. And I'd told her, a tearful lunch with her when the breakup was imminent, days away, when I'd been fixated on what I was about to lose. Holly? I was supposed to be in that role, the late-arriving seductress, the snake of a friend. I shoved my fist into Gordon's chin, and from the sting in my knuckles I knew I'd hit him, but the punch was clumsy, not the way I would cast it in tomorrow's report.

When Gordon dumped me, I made the spontaneous lurch at a plane ticket to Barbados. I hadn't seen my mother since the infamous dinner, and the time off had given me some guilty delight, but my family believed in the extraordinary gesture—deliveries of gigantic gourmet fruit baskets, paying the cute guy's bar tab. It renewed us, and I counted on the effect, the flood of excitement to mend us. Daphne lived in her husband's giant house, with the pool, the staff, the wing for guests. Penelope visited her frequently. They also lived in Dubai, for his work.

I got a taxi from the airport, feeling worldly. In the driveway I eased the car door shut, then walked into the living room.

"Oh my God," said my mother as she came in from the kitchen, her hand jumping to her tan chest. Not speaking to her was how I had protected my fresh romance (she left me no choice, I told friends), but when I sank into her neck I felt crippled and empty for having made things that way.

"Is Gordon with you?"

"We broke up." Everything hurt, and I wanted her to soothe it. She smelled like white wine, coconut oil and that pharmacy smell from the crushed remnants left inside her pillboxes. She smelled like tea rose, Band-Aids, honey and coffee. I wanted to crumble and cry.

"Baby," she said, and put me in the guest room over the pool.

Easily, I told her everything. My mother's ability to read back-story like tea leaves was something people marveled at. I told her of the work hours Gordon kept, the dead mother, the friends he had, the deteriorating quality of our phone calls when he was away on business. Yes, how he was in bed, how I was in bed. Yes, my stubborn denials. Yes (a little carefully), how Aunt Irene had listened and helped. My mother was leaning back against my pillows, poking through my wash bag. Between my reports she held up eye cream and mascara to tell me what they would have cost in duty-free.

"Let's list five bad things about Gordon," she said. I shook my head. "Come on, let's do it. It will help you get over him."

"He was glad about Desert Storm."

"No!"

"I can't think of anything else. Everything was good. I always knew what was going to happen the next day. He was reliable."

"I want to clear up a few things," she said. Obviously, she was done with my part, which wounded me, but I could never not listen to her voice. "First, I am really, really sorry about that night I met Gordon, and because of that evening I will never touch another alcoholic drink again." Her eyes were hugely round, rims wet, the expression she used for absolute earnestness. I wanted to laugh. I wanted to hit her. "The pain of losing you for that year was too much to bear." When our eyes met, her insistent lock, we both started to cry. I sat down next to her, and she took up my hand and held it against her abdomen. I looked at the way each section of her face seemed to move on its own in isolated muscle groups. It was such a strange trait, as if she couldn't inhabit her whole face at one time. She could speak without moving her top lip, her bottom one sliding and shifting to compensate. "The other thing, well, I was very nervous. I was meeting the love of your life, and right away I didn't like him. I thought, if this is the man Susy's going to marry, I'm going to kill myself. She'll be unhappy the rest of her life."

"It didn't take that long," I said, inviting myself to cry harder.

"What are you thinking?" she said.

I was thinking that I hated to have failed and hated that she could predict me. "How could you have formed any opinion of Gordon that night? You were completely stoned."

"Watch it, miss." She was grave. "I. Am. Sorry." She let go of me, and her attention drifted, fingers back among my toiletries. "Did I tell you about my exam? You do your own breast exams, don't you?" She reached out, and I pulled away, stood up. "Well, do you know how to do them? Because I thought I did, but the last time I saw my doctor she found a lump here, and she *pushed*"—she caught my fingers anyway and pressed them into her breast—"and it really hurt. So I had the mammogram. I don't know the results yet."

"A lump? When was this?"

"And then she was feeling around in my ovaries, and said, 'What's this lump?' So that was a sonogram, too."

"Oh, God."

"I'm a mess."

It had taken an hour for me to want to get out, away from her tissue and organs, her foul breath and inquisitions. God damn it.

Sex with Everybody

I went to bed with everybody. I wanted the sex. When I told this to men, they look stunned. I imagined I mirrored their fantasies, my gift, I thought, being the ability to transpose our roles and divine what they wanted exactly. I had feisty, nervy dates I confuse now in the details. Unlikely propositions. Special situations. That dinner at Indochine? Was that the man who sent the car and knew the chef? Or was that the intermission pickup in the lobby of the theater? I said yes and yes and expected to go to bed on the first date. Otherwise I lost interest.

On a spring night (for instance), some man and I walked out of the tapas place with the siren of margaritas in our heads. It was late, and the garbage trucks were out. He had just started at the magazine, impressed by the proximity to movie stars and production gossip, and I'd told him to have dinner with me. Men liked that. I was voracious like Playboy bunnies and *Penthouse* letters.

On an empty street I pushed him into a doorway for superb kisses. Oh, I knew it, that my kisses were soft and hard and full, evidence of pleasure and intention, evidence I wanted, wanted him, wanted more. He slid his palm down the front of my pants, slipped his fingers inside me, then put them in his mouth. I thought he would come. I walked us to my apartment and helped his clothes off fast. He pushed me on the bed and knelt in front of me to lift up my camisole, but I rose, twisted us around, pushed at him instead. "And then she pushed me down . . ." I kicked away the sheets and climbed over him. I could picture me as he saw me. In the dark, my skin caught the nighttime light from outside the window. "I cannot believe this is happening," he said. I'd bought raspberries for us, for later, and in the morning put some in my mouth, then kissed him, pushing the fruit past his warm teeth. Raspberries scattered on the sheet like blood in snow. The sun through the window fell on the red. I wanted to look at it forever.

Sometimes I didn't make it to the first date. The deli owner turned over the Closed sign, and we had sex on the counter, my bare skin on butcher block. I seduced an Orthodox rabbi. I left a Paris restaurant with two brothers, and they put me in their car and drove me deep into a part of the city I didn't know. I took a uniformed air force cadet into the airplane lavatory, and he came on the front of my trousers. It was fun to stand in an elevator with a married colleague and burn up the space between us, and who in her twenty-five-year-old right mind would turn away from that? "Fuck me," I'd say, a slow whisper against his ear in the dark taxi. "I want you."

The blunt force of sex was useful, a purpose every morning as I dressed, an event every night, sex making the otherwise mundane interesting—crossing the street, buying cat food. Sex made me whole, I thought, as I lost my senses to the tempo, the elbows in the mattress, my hair all over the pillow, and my ass in the air. "Harder," I'd say, letting go, losing more. "Pull my hair." I knew what they liked to hear. I loved to get through a night this way, frantic, aroused, exhausted at once as I crossed the bridge from orgasm to sleep. I didn't realize how heavily the losing mattered. I thought I was great in bed.

But actually: The deli owner ripped my Dior panty hose, and at home I peeled them off and shoved them in the trash, angry about the $22 they would cost me again. The young rabbi sat up after the fumbled sex, clutching my pillow and saying, "I hope God forgives me," until I threw him out. I sprawled beneath one of the French boys, and the cross around his neck kept hitting me in the teeth. When I tilted my head I saw we were under a large, uncheerful crucifix. In the airplane bathroom I had to blot at the semen on my pants, hoping it would dry fast, because my boyfriend was meeting me at the gate.

I used to court oblivion, cancel everything, forget trouble. That was sex's delicious point, the glittering instruction of lust and its momentum. Do it. I didn't have a no in me, and a person needs a no, some way to halt what's going on and give herself a chance to choose.

A movie producer hired me to do development. I was supposed to find material for him to produce. "I love Preston Sturges too!" he shouted during the interview, which he conducted in his Mercedes roadster, speeding along back roads in the Hamptons, top down. "Who else do you like? This is just great!" He gave me a down payment for a car and moved me to Los Angeles. We had studio offices, and the pass I was issued to the lot never failed to feel pretend when I flashed it at the guard. A friend from the movie magazine, Steffie, had recently come to Hollywood, and we shared a bungalow in Santa Monica, the city of my mother's birth, where she'd been taken for walks by the nanny and adorned with gingham bows in her hair.

One day Steffie wanted to replace our mildewed shower curtain, but I wouldn't let her. It *had to* stay up, I *wouldn't* wait until she came back after work with a new one. I barred her from the bathroom, and my insistence frightened her. We fought, and after the fight had spun itself out, the morning ticking down toward the moment it wouldn't be worth it to get on the freeway, I unveiled: The married man from the New Year's Eve party, of whom she disapproved, was coming later, and he and I would need that closing act of midday adultery, the shower. She walked out, leaving the curtain.

The man showed up and crossed the threshold, door left wide for him. He yanked up my dress, found me bare, fucked me hard and then left. Neither of us said anything, which at the time seemed exciting—no sound in the back of the movie theater, wordless in the motel bathrooms—but really we just had nothing, absolutely nothing. I told Steffie later that he had canceled. Her bag of groceries stood unpacked between us on the kitchen table as I apologized. I was a virtuoso of the lie, and too busy at this to notice that someone might not want me for a friend, that someone might worry for me.

The producer fired me. I wasn't a good employee, and he wasn't a good boss, and I returned to New York and reclaimed my sublet studio on Christopher Street. I bumped into an acquaintance, Nathalie. We embraced on the street. "When did you get back!?" She looked great, those acres of holdable curls, her smoky purr, her lower lip. I'd had this lazy crush on her for ages because she broadcast sexual hunger. It was like having a crush on myself.

Nathalie had moved into a brownstone with her boyfriend, Max. "Come and see the place. Should we go out to dinner?" We picked a night and a restaurant in her neighborhood.

Outside the restaurant Nathalie faced Max, their bodies against each other, and when he saw me, they opened like the covers of a book to embrace me together. She wore a turtleneck in creamy wool. They sat me between them, joking about both wanting access. My head spun left to right. Max chose the wine, three bottles eventually.

I didn't think I was drunk. I thought the clench in us was the flirting. We got outside into the drowsy spring air and turned toward their house. I agreed to more wine; it meant I had permission to kiss her once we got there. We walked fast, so nothing would wear off.

In the narrow foyer Max hung each coat on its deliberate peg, as Nathalie led me by the hand to the living room. I waited for the excuse, coming any second, that would take us into the bedroom. I stayed close to her and didn't want to say much, afraid I'd reveal my nervousness. Max was talking, about the bookshelves. I didn't listen . . . And we redid the doors. We redid the walls . . . I didn't listen. I watched Nathalie's ass as she put a knee on her bed and reached for the lamp, pelvis shifting gently. Max had stopped talking, and how, *how* was this going to happen?

She sat up, pulled me between her knees and slipped her hands around my ass. As she straightened, I could feel her breasts trace a path up my body, rising up under my own. I was going to sink and die with lust. She bit at my blouse, her breath heating my nipple. Max sank into the bed and pulled me down between them. With my face turned toward hers, I could feel the moisture in her breath and Max's hand on my hip, and I accepted that he'd have to stay. He was the fee. They were both kissing me, which was confusing, two smells to the mouths, two textures to the tongues. I didn't know how to do this. They laughed and kissed each other and kissed me more. Max undressed us, raising Nathalie's arms, turtleneck yanked up, then tugging my skirt down my legs while Nathalie stroked her tongue over my mouth. They kept talking to each other. I tried to concentrate on my handfuls of Nathalie and on the sight of so many places on her to set my mouth. Max wanted to fuck me, and I wouldn't let him. If I just didn't look at him, kept him off to the side, I'd be able to push him right out of the story. So he fucked Nathalie, and she put her hand inside me, and I kissed her. But they had a rhythm, and I was cold. My knee started to ache, an awkward position alongside them, my limbs knocking into theirs, wrong moment, wrong gesture. It went on, it felt like, for hours. They inserted me into the sex scene they'd thought up and, I suddenly understood, played before. They didn't look for me, just reached, their hands laced together, trying to stroke some part of me. I was exhausted, and I waited on the bit of bed that was left until they'd finished.

I paid fierce attention to the bathroom towels, door handle, hot and cold taps. On my way out I fixed on the dead bolts and didn't look at Max. Nathalie still lay in the bed. He stepped into the dawn light in boxers and pointed me toward the best street to catch a cab. I wanted to be home to call my friends, to get home to the telling, the expert, ambitious words and the review of my performance. Great in bed.

Cherry Girl

I moved to Provincetown for the winter, into the house that had been my grandmother Nana's. My father's sister owned it and offered to let me write there. I was twenty-seven and had started a novel, which my mother knew was about her. She liked to refer to it cheerfully as *Mommie Dearest* or *She Came from Evil*. I drove up with my cat and laptop, ordered red pajamas from L.L.Bean. Wind pressed the windows of the house, noisy, announcing cold. The hulking clock ticked in the corner of the dining room, the table gleaming with someone else's labors. I called my sister to remind her of the oversized pink roses on the black hall carpet, the pantry that smelled of raisins, the squeak of the swinging kitchen door. We had mythologies about these things, sister inventions and ancient meanings. The master bathroom was unchanged, a monument to my grandmother, who'd been dead more than a decade. Penelope and I used to beg for baths there because the tub, set beneath a window facing the bay, was elevated on a pink-carpeted platform and corralled by a white wooden railing. We had envied the pink vanity its frilled muslin skirt, its sparkling decanters for perfume. The bottles still held yellow liquid, once Chanel No. 5 and Arpège, carnival amounts that smelled like dust and nothing.

I chose my grandfather's study for my apartment because of the massive desk, the bookcases built up to the ceiling, and filled with John O'Hara and Saul Bellow, the bed made from antique church pews with real mattress ticking, and because of a door that opened directly onto the deck. The soft sheets bought fifty years before at Bonwit's were still in the linen closet, and I made the bed and covered it with white chenille. The room was a good deal larger than the studio I'd relinquished on Christopher Street.

I was tired of lovers and bosses, and when an L.A. boyfriend visited I treated him shabbily, walking ahead on the beach, cheering on in-jokes with my new friends from the Fine Arts Work Center. I wanted the last lovemaking, the boyfriend a generous expert, but no more conversations, no future plans. "Leave me alone," I thought. "When he goes, I'll write," and I did.

But I didn't know how to be alone. For my breaks, I walked along the planks of the deck but got chilly fast and went back in. I would drift up and down the staircase, waiting for the phone to ring or the postman to come. Without the anchor of sex I was uneasy and missed the spontaneous reveries I'd had while making love, my mind loosed and wandering, falling on lost specifics, the taste of grass, the mosaic floor of a Paris bookshop. Being transported.

The town was crouched small for winter, and the writers and artists showed up to the same potlucks, the same bar, the one pool table. Some had paired off, and I'd already had the angry poet. Three months of that, listless sexual despondency and a novel I couldn't wrestle.

Then Christopher walked into a reading. He looked cold in

his denim jacket, and I beckoned him over and patted the seat of the empty folding chair. For many weeks after I met Christopher I told friends the same astonishing fact. "He doesn't lie." I used this as one might say, "He has brown hair, medium build." It was essential to who he was and the shocking draw to me, even before I knew it.

"I'm Susanna, what's your name, are you a writer, what are you working on, where are you from?" But I didn't hear the content of his answers, a fevered rushing in my ears.

How can you know when this will seize you, pull at you with unconscious imperative? *This man is the person you need* was hammering in me like a pulse, and we had not yet held a conversation. Christopher was not tall, not short, a little older than I was, wore glasses and a baseball cap from an Alaskan tackle store. He looked like he wanted to be unnoticed. His teeth were straight, eyes hazel with flecks of gold. While he spoke, I stared, thinking, *You are not my type. This doesn't make sense.* He was talking, I could see that, and I heard the warmth of his voice, how kind and rich it was. He smiled, and the lines around his eyes broke my heart and remade it. "Come to dinner tomorrow," I said.

The next night he arrived. I was in a dress, low cut to show the tops of my breasts, black tiny buttons glistening straight down the front. I'd made Marcella Hazan's spicy sausage and black-eyed peas that my stepmother had taught me to make. Christopher and I poured into each other, coaxing stories, going through beer, nervous as hell. You could feel this was big.

"I want children," I told him at dinner. "I'm twenty-seven, and I just thought you should know."

He didn't flinch, as if we had to discuss this. "I don't think I want them," he said. "Childhood is too difficult."

"Ha!" I said. "Listen, I know that. I know what not to do." Right away I told him of my vital struggle, my crucial failure of never quite getting shy of my mother. "You have to understand this about me," I said. "I am someone with a crazy mother." Then I laughed because words did nothing.

We watched *Double Indemnity*. How upright Fred MacMurray was, led astray in spite of himself, how superb and mean Barbara Stanwyck. We drank down a bottle of Glenfiddich and didn't feel a thing.

And then, when I had kept Christopher there so late, brought him to the fireplace in my grandfather's cheery study, when he was happy on the green rug against the chair, I made my pass. Christopher straightened up, put his palms on the floor and said no.

No? He brought my kiss to a definitive close, chapter over. I had no alternate route. I was giddy with him, unspooled that he was here when all day I'd been waiting and agitated, aware of this exotic, this nonfiction *love*.

All right then: I'd wait a few days, cook more, show up unexpectedly, wait maybe three days. But Christopher still wouldn't go to bed with me. He made me tapes, Hank Williams on heartbreak, Lucinda Williams on despair. He did not believe in sudden happiness, and I teased him. "Live a little." We drove to Wellfleet for a movie. He released information about himself with slow authority, not trusting me yet, pointing out that people didn't just *trust*. This drove me mad, and I was determined to show him that the reason he didn't want to go to bed with me was that he'd never had great sex. I would free him from his lifetime of wasted encounters and poor relationships. I would be the sex he had never dreamed of; I would *be* sex.

It took two weeks, a term I had never, ever waited. We walked on the dunes. He made us beef stew, with tarragon. In my kitchen we drank Lapsang tea, sharing our chapters over the blue-and-white oilcloth. Christopher was from Utah. "*Jack* Mormon," he was quick to say. His parents called each Sunday night, and soon I was on the extension, being shy with his mother and teasing him later that all three of them said, "My gosh." When I reeled off the stories of my mother, Christopher listened hard and then pushed aside the anecdotes and locations and asked me if she'd hurt me, helped me, guided me, scared me. He kept asking, steady company as I fumbled for the answers.

Finally, Christopher said yes. He was ready. We undressed with care and self-consciousness, and I lavished on him everything I'd been storing up. I wanted to take his breath away, force regret on him, even, that he'd made me wait. I kept a steady control over what we did, and he said, as I anticipated, "You are amazing."

In the lazy conversation after lovemaking, I told on myself. Christopher was earnest, and I banished irony and told him about the bad girl I had been up until a month ago. She lied, cheated on her boyfriends, thought only of sex, power, triumph, double-timed, triple-timed. I wanted to make it sound funny, loaded with family tradition.

"Poor honey," he said. His eyes were very close to mine, unwavering.

"Poor nothing," I said. "It was fun."

"You gave away so much. It sounds painful."

"Sex is the way of the world. Don't you always think first thing whenever you meet someone what they'd be like in bed?"

"I do not," he said. He looked worried, and I kissed him.

"I could always take care of myself."

"By cheating?"

"That helped."

"If you cheat on me . . . ," he said. "If you hurt me—"

Lucinda Williams sang, "But I can't get over the lines around your eyes." I had never loved so richly.

I promised to be honest. What a gesture, with its high-stakes hope. Other people did it? Christopher said so. I didn't actually understand, but he said cheating wrecked relationships, and I didn't want to wreck us, the meat of us not yet known.

"He doesn't want children," I told my mother, our phone calls ily, my moods dictating how much to reveal to her. Pull her in, send her back. Why could I never decide? Happiness made me feel invulnerable to her, and unhappiness made me helpless to resist her.

"Don't worry," she said. "If he loves you, he'll agree."

We drove down to New York and went for dinner at my father and stepmother's. In the elevator I remembered to say Nat had MS and couldn't move. "Don't offer to shake his hand." My father discussed the history of Brigham Young. The next day we met Penelope by Bethesda Fountain and walked in Central Park. She held me by the arm, controlling my balance. It wasn't something you'd have noticed if you weren't her sister, and I was glad when we parted. We had a date to meet my mother and her husband for drinks at the Carlyle, where they always took a suite. On our way I felt the warnings, but they were muted, because steady, clear-headed Christopher was with me. He gave things a sequential order, slowed down confusion. My mother behaved, reined in. Wissam told stale jokes about which she teased him. A formal waiter wheeled in a white-covered cart with the drinks and hors d'oeuvres. Daphne stroked my face and said, "I'm glad you're so happy. Just look at Sue. Isn't she happy?"

Afterward Christopher said, "I'm exhausted. Is she always like that?"

They said "catch and release," and Christopher leaned over and explained under the noise of conversation. They were talking about fishing. We sat around a plastic table on the concrete patio. Christopher was smiling and, with his sister, interrupting their father, who reported on the creek in central Utah where they'd grown up fishing. Christopher grew up getting into pickups and winding up canyons to park in tall dry grasses and wade into mud. I was ready should someone ask me more than the identifying enquiries. I had quieted in Salt Lake City with its lengthy store transactions, polite drivers of freshly washed SUVs, the comfort of money everywhere but without style. I couldn't join in, so I thought about the pale salad, the heap of dressing, the bowl of thin pressed wood. This was a fly-fishing family, which I did not understand bestowed on them a certain pedigree of sportsmanship, a code of behavior as right and decent as any in the sporting world. This family was honest *together*, ethically minded and schooled in sharing, protecting, offering help. It wasn't just the vocabulary of fishing I didn't understand, the act that didn't interest me, it was a way of being that made me hopeless. None of my talents mattered here. I itched to phone my mother—at the Carlyle, in Dubai, in Barbados?—and reveal this unknown America to her, which had always been here beyond the reach of our island and our airports, passport travel, good tables. I wanted someone to listen to me in my language.

Christopher and I had bedrooms on different floors. His parents made sure not to ask about the motels we'd stopped in on our road trip to Utah. We told them we were moving to Montana, and they didn't ask if we would live together. This confused me. "But they know we sleep together," I said. "They don't want to know," Christopher said. His mother's sewing table was set up at the end of my bed, which was covered by a quilt she'd made. I cannot be here, I thought, when I have lived in the Piazza San Marco with Bellinis, on trains through France, beneath wall-sized mirrors on Barbados estates, in seats ten rows from the stage at the Met. It wasn't money that had gotten me there (though it was) but the pursuit of center stage and the middle of things. In the Piazza San Marco, waiters watched, ready for your flicked hand. Men came and bent over the tiny table, their air kisses worth imitating later. On the train you'd meet a young man with his book. You'd give him an agitated shock to carry home.

Christopher's parents handed us the key to their small apartment in Sun Valley, and we drove north.

"They must be hoping this works out," he said. "They've never let me stay alone with a girlfriend."

We drove to Idaho, Christopher treading the grooves of childhood, me familiar with Hemingway legends. "And this river, and this river," Christopher said, pointing out ribbons of shiny water. The anglers were anonymous from the road.

"I'm rethinking," Christopher said. We put on our waders. "Maybe moving in so soon won't work." He wanted to be thoughtful, he said, take it slowly. He tied on my fly. All I heard was, Not you, and in a burst I wanted to walk off and interest someone else. "I want to fish, build my life around that," he'd told me a month earlier. "It makes me happy." I'd gone to a bookstore on Broadway, to look up Missoula, Montana, in a travel book at his suggestion. Missoula, I read, was a nicely sized university town with five rivers nearby, a paradise for outdoor enthusiasts. Writers lived there. My mother saw it mentioned in an airplane magazine. "Missoula's the new Taos," she said, pointing out that I was copying her. Christopher would be spending the summer at a writers' colony, but our plan was to live together after that, and I had volunteered to drive to Missoula first, set up a little. Now he didn't want me.

When I fell into the river my unwieldy pole flailed upward, and water rushed into my top-open waders, pinning me to the shallow river bottom. I was furious. A month ago I was ready to stop lying for good, to give everything of myself to this solid, loving, decent man, and now he was pulling away. How did I get here, dragged out to a meaningless place, and now you're rethinking? I was game! Christopher picked his way through the water to me as I lunged for the bank and pulled myself onto the grass, freezing and embarrassed.

* * *

Rosebud, Stillwater, Sweet Grass, Silver Bow. I drove through the Montana counties, my last day in the car, and said the names aloud, a pretty incantation. I'd been driving for days, alone except for the cat, and here I was, the Montana important to Christopher. We'd have separate apartments, okay? Please? The gleam deep in him was enough for me, a harbinger of something important, but I didn't know what. I loved the feeling of being told the truth, its simple direction. I was trying to make the best of it, staring out beyond the rim of the windshield at the blown fields and consuming sky. I had never felt more of an imposter, the New Yorker in new jeans, Jewish. I took the first Missoula exit off the freeway, one hand up to block the sun from my eyes. This was what the rest of the country looked like, the country Christopher grew up with—no, not the gaping fresh emptiness, not the butter-and-straw-colored expanses, but *this* at the bottom of the exit ramp: boxy restaurants strung together by parking lots, looming semis spattered with dirt, squat supermarkets, traffic lights swaying on black cables over the streets. The brief length of downtown ended abruptly at the former train depot, the town bordered by the track. No enclosure of subway tunnel, no elevated relief of the metro platforms on which I'd spent such vivid bits of my life. Paris at nineteen, I still had my *carte orange*. I had never looked at the naked rails. This will be the new way, I thought, rough and open, and I will be that way too.

The motel was named the Sweet Rest, the same fairy music as those counties, the name that looked placid on the page of the travel book in my hand in New York 2,422 miles behind. I pulled the car off a grim thoroughfare to park on a narrow strip of paving before the motel office. I'm game, I'm game. I had studied Christopher on our road trip. When we stopped at cafés, he'd go through the screen door, looking at some middle nothing, grab a stool at the counter and say, "I'd take a piece of that pie" and "What d'I owe you?" It was the right way, the indifference, the sliding beneath notice. That was the way people did it out here. With Christopher everything was the machine of the oiled world, just going along.

I left the cat with a crack in the window and walked into the office. I said, "Hey," while looking off to the side at a rack of chamber-of-commerce pamphlets (imposter, imposter). The man (let him go, do not ask about his leg, don't need to know about his family, his blues of the day) had me register and gave me a key attached to a plastic card. The room cost $147 for the week. Tomorrow I'd look for a place, but today I'd find a cash machine, name the neighborhoods, get something to eat. "It's my sister's cat," I said. "She'll be here tomorrow to pick it up."

I'd already lied, couldn't go more than a day. Tomorrow I'd start again.

The town was filled with bars. You could tell each decade from the signs, deco red neon, old-west-style horses and cowboys. What there was to do was beer and rivers. What there was to do was drive. The downtown parking spaces were huge, and when the light changed at the empty corner the people (who were *waiting*) walked across in no hurry. There wasn't a smell, a sound, a habit to remind me of myself. My headache lasted all day from the strong daylight undiffused by buildings or crowds. My face hurt from squinting. No one said "Susanna." At the Sweet Rest I looked up the synagogue in the phone book, but there wasn't one, and I wouldn't have known what to do had I gone.

I couldn't call Christopher easily. In the day he was writing in a cabin, lunch baskets left for him outside his door. During the dinner hour I got the colonists' busy signals. At a pay phone inside a bar entrance I called a friend in New York and cried when he answered.

"How long do I have to pretend this will work?" I said. The

receiver smelled of gasoline and cigarette ash. "Could I come back and stay on Elizabeth Street with you until the summer's over? Maybe I could get Christopher to move to New York then." When I said "Elizabeth Street" I thought I would throw up from longing. "You know what I'm looking at? A big store window that's layered with different-colored paints, and it's a huge cartoon of a grizzly bear in a crimson football helmet."

My friend was laughing, and I was crying.

"You have to give it more than a day," he said. "You're okay. You'll adjust." I imagined him with more friends at a restaurant that night, the quick story he got to make of me, and I was furious. I was furious at him, at Montana, at Christopher, at the lie in the name Sweet Rest, assigned to a paper-and-cardboard misery of a motel, bed weak in the center and sunken, bathroom walls stained, towels unable to absorb enough lousy water to matter. These towels couldn't do their single lousy job.

That night I wrote to Christopher, a long letter on the legal pad, words coming and coming, meant to stand in for me. I described, I listed, hopeful the hard word on the yellow page would place me here, make me part of it. I stamped the envelope and turned off my light. Women whined at each other in the back alley, and people flicked lighters, and they smoked beneath the slot of my bathroom window, my room infused with that and the garbled fume of gas and drying beer on warm gravel. In the middle of the night someone pounded on my door. "Gimme my food stamps, you bitch!"

I rented an apartment, the converted attic floor of an old house near the university, guys downstairs slamming doors, drawers, books, bottles. They started engines, they invited girls in, their voices rising with beer as they watched David Letterman. They were nice. Everyone was nice. A couple of them wanted to take

me to a hot spring. We drove a long ways, hiked in and took off
our clothes under moonlight, going silent when a moose picked
its way around the steaming water.

I expected the boys were hard under the water, which cheered
me up. I told Christopher we went. A carpenter wanted to take
me to dinner. I went, letting him think it was a date, told Christopher about it. "You're not jealous?" I asked. He said, "I trust you."
A woman at a bookstore took me for a walk up the mountain
with the college letter, a massive M in whitewashed cement. She
told me to say, "I walked up the M." But eastern still, with
seaboard lungs, I got only halfway and waited for her on a crude
bench as she reached the summit, then turned and came back
down the trail to get me. She invited me to a lesbian dance.
Beyond the carpenter and my neighbors, everyone seemed to be
a lesbian. I was desperate to be included.

"Cherry girl," someone called me, a hungry look on her lips.
"Meet another cherry girl." She pushed a woman into me at the
edge of the dance floor, who took my hand. She seemed young,
which made me feel more used to things, my two weeks here. She
whispered in her warped Australian accent that she was ready for
a first time. Oh, okay. Be my guest at my unready apartment with
its bed pushed beneath the eaves. Let orgasm make it home.

She came back with me, and I was making brittle jokes to seem
clever. I didn't need to try so hard. She liked being the novice,
mentioning her wonder at buffalo burgers and huckleberry milk-
shakes. She petted the cat. Had I slept with women before, she
asked, because she hadn't. She looked inside an open packing box
and took out a mixing bowl. "From Conran's," I said, which
allowed me an image of Broadway and Eighty-fourth Street.

As she was leaving a few hours later she grabbed me and
begged that I call her. "You will, won't you?" and I had sympathy
for the man put in this position, the way he wanted to peel off the
grip, dry off, never return. "If you don't, I'll call you. I'll call you

later. I'll stop by," she said, her last accented word taking a good long while, and then she left.

I sat down on the bed and started to write, summoning erotica. "Dear Christopher." The naked breast, the heat and wet between the thighs, an hour of going down on her. It sounded fake. I made her hair longer, made her smarter, and in the morning I phoned him to tell him, catching him at breakfast. I hoped he'd lose a whole day of work, distracted, heated, missing me and my brazen spirit.

"I went to bed with her," I said, my speech still a bit slow from the overused mouth, and he said, "Oh," but not in a turned-on way. I couldn't read him.

"How could you meet someone so fast?"

Did he forget where I came from, what I knew how to do? There was no such thing as waiting. I never needed to wait. I didn't know how not to meet someone, because every "Excuse me?" meant a willingness, every released button the aching awareness of my effect on people, that urgent agenda to show off in bed what just wasn't possible to show in the produce section or the bookstore. When we talked these colony weeks, pay phone to pay phone, I was play-suspicious, sorting through his news for the special name, the private encounter.

"Come on!" I'd say. "That poet? You mean you didn't kiss? Didn't you want to? She didn't try to kiss you?"

"Susanna, not everyone does that."

"Everyone flirts."

"No, they don't," he said. "You have to leave the door open, let them know they're welcome to come in. And my door is not open. I am yours."

I was taken aback by the candor, just like that, what he gave me. But my door had to stay open. If my door were closed I would have missed the invitation to the lesbian dance, missed the lechery of the downstairs boys, the hot-springs hard-ons and first dates, what added up to such precious inventory. Christopher didn't understand how the world worked, what mattered, the imprisoning gaze, the signals of availability, the purr under a coarse joke, knowing how to make a come-on out of the basic tools, how to turn a simple thing velvet and complex. My mother and I used to contemplate the men who knew nothing. "Thank God for us," she would say.

The cherry girl wanted to give me a leash, a right to her every hour, and I didn't want it, anxious to shake her off. She called, she came to my front door and pressed her face into the glass for a better look. "I'm working," I said, and didn't invite her in. Maybe I was meant to be the man, the sort who met need with idle cruelty. I wanted the quick flirt, the hot memory—the dark SoHo street, pulling what's-his-name back to the apartment, my body laid out across the bed, throat up, come on me. I wanted the material to spiff up and tell more than I wanted the mess and follow-up, the directions to the bathroom, just there on the left.

At the bookstore, my one place so far safe with routine, I hung around talking to the women who worked there. One told me she had a gun and always kept it loaded. "Why else have a gun?" she said. We were sitting on a bench outside the shop, watching a yellow color light up the M mountain. She took the gun back-packing, she said, gone for days, carrying what she needed on her shoulders. I looked up at the mountain, thinking, But who'd want to go into the woods anyway? The other woman at the store told me about her dog, the smart blue heeler. He was out in the truck; she took him everywhere. "An Australian breed, Susanna." They had the right to tease me, wanting more details of the cherry girl. I hadn't told the lesbians yet about Christopher, unready to give up my credibility and diminishing mystery. I needed these women and the consolation of my sexiness.

* * *

The day Christopher arrived was the day composed of waiting, hours of composing my face for the emotional reunion. I moved soap from sill to bathtub ledge and back, stood in front of the open refrigerator, cataloging what each item would mean to him, this brand of milk, what it meant about who I was in Missoula, Montana. I perched on the edge of the couch, facing the window, eyes locked on the speck of bridge that would become the first glimpse of his car. My eyes were burning and tired. I was tired of being here, wanted him here with whatever we were about to make of a relationship. I cared very much that I had hurt him, and that was something genuine and new. We'd have a place to be a couple, to have bank accounts and library cards, to make peace about the cherry girl. After we made love. I had tugged at the corners of the duvet and tilted the shade on the lamp, vacuumed near the bed so bare feet would feel only floor and rug. I took out the plastic garbage bag. My cat was dead, gone under the low-lying bed one day the week before, unwilling to be pulled out. I had to move the bed, and he was weak and asleep. I took him to the Yellow Pages vet, where he died in the night when he was supposed to be getting fluids. I had no one to hug me when I said he was dead. Three days as a waitress at the sweet-and-sour restaurant that called itself "Oriental," I was dressed in black sneakers and the T-shirt with the logo. I walked out of the vet's office, bleak and sobbing, shocked that the constant cat was gone completely.

This was where I lived, defined so far by alien curiosity, loneliness, now grief. Flirting hadn't changed it.

Choosing

Ⓦe married without a wedding. I married Christopher with-out anybody. In Montana you need neither witness nor official, just a third person to look at you both and say, "You're married." That's sort of how the proposal came, too.

We lived in an eight-sided log cabin by a creek. Christopher chopped wood for our stove. Black bears tore through our garbage at night. I was a waitress, we owned a blue heeler puppy, a breed I hadn't heard of before moving to Missoula. We had visited the pregnant mother, Sunday drives down the Bitterroot Valley. We didn't care about papers or talents, only that we'd decided to do this together and our landlord had said okay. We named her Ruby.

Ruby whipped us into joint action, united concern. We traded turns driving back to the cabin midday from work to unlatch the crate and follow after her in the driveway. At dinner we reported on her—and then she fell over! and then she chased a bee!—

glancing at her on her dog bed ($34, more than we allowed ourselves for anything), a tucked-in ball, no bigger than a melon. We enrolled in a dog-training class and let friends tease us that we were training for parenthood.

Ruby became increasingly difficult, and the trainer asked us not to come to class. In her ninth week, her tenth, she lunged for bigger dogs, ignored sharp jerks on her choke chain, bucked with a strength no puppy should have. At the sound of a command, she worked herself into fits as Christopher tried to hold her in his lap. She writhed hard, her eye vile, shit dropping on the floor. We were astonished. I would talk softly, and she'd sink her quarter-inch teeth into my forearm, scraping and biting as I tried to rid myself of her. In a snap, she was peaccable again, nosing the edges of her dish, happy tongue for the crumbs on the floor. Only a month of her, and we were wrenched with love, depleted by vigilance and worry.

"Look," the trainer said one afternoon after a private lesson we couldn't afford. "There are too many good dogs in the world to spend so much effort on a bad one." Ruby—agile, flop-eared, short-muzzled—had flipped into the air and seized the teacher's sleeve, shredding cloth and snorting. We watched from the porch as the teacher launched a tremendous kick to release our dog. She didn't think Valium would help, or training, or anything. The next day the fourteen-week-old puppy savaged Christopher's hand, puncturing skin, unable to give up, her own intention the transforming hypnotic.

We took her to a kennel so we could visit Christopher's parents for Thanksgiving. I didn't confess how good I felt, knowing someone else would be the one to open her cage for a few days. In Salt Lake we played Scrabble and did dishes, but driving home, the long gray hours, we knew we needed to decide.

"What do you want to do?"

"What do you want?" Neither of us could answer. I was thinking of the velvet spot beneath her jaw, even when she was fuming and fierce.

"We need to put her down," Christopher said.

"I know, I know."

We were both crying the same way, hope lost, betrayed by our own efforts.

He pulled into a rest station, where the bathroom echoed with doors, flushing, women in their dull moments. She was just a young puppy. I hunched over my knees, sitting on the toilet, one hand looking for reassurance against the cold wall of the stall. We hadn't even had her two months, but she wasn't any good, and we couldn't bear trying more.

I found Christopher by the snack machines. He looked timid.

"I know something that might cheer you up?" he said.

"What?"

"Do you want to get married?"

We liked to do things this way: pushed into some hole of privacy and hard sorrow, we would emerge with a decision, a start at something better. When Christopher's father fell from the tree he was pruning and severely injured his head, we returned from the solemn hospital vigil and decided to move in together. When he took a turn for the worse, we got the dog. We were drifting off from others, using our discrete griefs to build our life together. You could trust sorrow, straightforward and undiluted, and people left you alone. To us it was love.

The last half of the drive, hesitant and flirting, we fretted about the wedding, no mention of Ruby. Imagine when we tell our parents, imagine them meeting. But after the jokes, we didn't like it, especially my mother, of course, sorting painkillers on the bar, dropping the appalling remark to some uncle.

"When do you want to do this?"

"Soon. Why not?"

"Let's not tell anybody, and we'll get married right now."

Christopher scheduled the vet. I made him take her, but he couldn't stay in the room, came home in surrendered tears.

The relief of Ruby's death opened into a few quick plans, three days until we married. I asked at the florist's how much a bouquet might be ($14), ordered it for the Friday. I went to a vintage shop, Lucinda Williams on the speakers, and found a black dress from the forties ($27). At Planned Parenthood we had rubella tests ($12 each). We found gold bands in a pawnshop ($40 each), and then we couldn't spend any more. There was nothing else to do, no one to call, no effort except the effort of holding it in. So this was privacy, boundaries, selfhood.

Friday in the near dark of the ending day, I picked Christopher up after work, and we parked by the courthouse, which looked like a courthouse.

"Your mother's full maiden name here," the clerk said, just as she instructed all registrants, but I resented my mother's intrusion. We signed for our license ($42 noted on the handwritten receipt) and waited outside the judge's chambers as he finished with the juvenile DUI.

Fifteen minutes later the judge, with a weekend's good mood, sent married us out into the hall again, where I felt dizzy and had to sit down. I needed crackers from the vending machine ($1, in quarters). Then we drove in a snowstorm to a restaurant out of town, hurried through our steaks because the blizzard was getting worse and got back home to the cabin at the end of the driveway already choked with snow.

We gave ourselves one secretive day, feeding the woodstove and making love with unexpected reverence, and then I called my mother.

"How could you do this to your sister? You know she's been waiting to be your bridesmaid."

"I didn't *do* this to her."

Christopher looked up as he heard me, surprised. I wasn't, only redirected. I had wanted to tell her what getting married was like, what my getting married was like.

"Of course you did," my mother said. "You eloped, had a civil ceremony—this isn't like you. I know you," she hissed. "I know what you wanted, that Renaissance dress, a huge celebration with all your friends. But what the hell is this? This isn't you. This is Christopher."

I had to defend him, us, but she did know me, and she was right.

"Congratulations, then," she said. "If that's what you called for. I would put your sister on but she's way too upset right now."

Christopher and I were careful. We had adapted the pause for birth control in our lovemaking and assumed equal liability for its success. We shared the cost of spermicide, and he came with me to the cervical cap fitting. We understood the muffled threat of pregnancy, sex's invisible double.

Now I felt unwell in an unusual way. The body knew what it was. I went to Planned Parenthood for the free test, a redbrick building on a quiet sidewalk.

"Okay, so," the counselor started. "You are pregnant." I wanted her to back out of the room, never to be coming back in, to unsay this. There was no mistaking, no gauzy possibility. I was pregnant. "Is this your first pregnancy?"

My mother had had two children and five miscarriages, which became this map for me, a guide to expect the same. I was conceived, she always said, in an airplane bathroom between London and Paris. "And that was a short flight!" My mischievous parents stole into the loo. She described the faces of the passengers when she emerged and walked down the aisle. "Your father had only to look at me, and I'd get pregnant."

"How do you know?" I'd ask. "How could you tell that was me?"

"Because I always threw up the exact moment I conceived, and I did, before we landed."

"My mother could tell the second she conceived," I told friends; you have to understand the magic in my mother. She'd had three missed pregnancies before me and two between me and Penelope. I tried to calculate her uterine math, but I never quite understood it, and I gave up.

She was explicit about birth control. "An IUD," she told me when I was seven or eight. "That's what I use, and thank God." It was a piece of wire, she explained, pushed up inside her womb.

"How do you get it out?" I asked.

"There's a little string that hangs down that the doctor can pull on. But you don't have to get it out. It stays in a long, long time."

Was that the string, the glimpse of white cotton thread hanging between her legs sometimes, like a chain on a lightbulb?

"But the IUD is best if you've had a baby already. What you will use," she would say, "is a diaphragm."

When I was nine or so she took me to her OB in New York, to "get you checked," and she stood beside him as he inserted the pediatric speculum and opened me. She kept describing a discharge I'd had, that word, and I wanted to die—a man, the cold metal, her fake camaraderie. She said to him, "You know I have a tipped womb. I expect Susy has, too."

My first diaphragm came from a Taos clinic, which sat at the edge of a field in a battered trailer a few miles out of town. I didn't want to deal with Daphne's keen interest and her discussion with the doctor. I phoned her best friend of the week from a pay phone in the plaza and asked her to give me a ride.

"I'm going to get a diaphragm."

"Oh, you are. What does Daphne say about this?"

"I'd be grateful if this stayed between you and me." Although I was thirteen, I understood the wily uses of confidence.

"I see." She was quiet. Maybe she was wondering if it was legal to take someone else's thirteen-year-old.

"It's not like we're going across state lines," I said.

I didn't think of myself as cheating on my mother, although asking her friend gave me a thrill, which should have made it obvious.

The friend dropped me off to return in an hour. The grass was yellow under the tin steps. I came in nervous. The pamphlets on the walls were faded, and the doors didn't fit right in their frames. Would they report me or turn me away for being too young? They seemed used to secrets.

"Are you sexually active now, honey?"

I said, "Not yet." The nurse looked up. It wasn't the answer she was expecting. "I want to be ready." She gave a little smile of approval and marked something on her form, and I was glad I'd pleased her.

The exam cost $13, which stuck in my mind because it matched my age. The diaphragm and the tube of Ortho-Gynol were free. I used up that tube practicing over the next three years.

In senior year of college I missed a period and called my mother. She said, "What have you been using?"

"Diaphragm."

"Properly?"

"Yes."

She assessed the symptoms—"But why didn't you tell me earlier?"—and announced I was pregnant. This was an event: Susy's pregnant! We discussed the abortion that I'd be having. She'd never had one, so abortion didn't mean much to me, a word glimpsed on flyers posted around the women's studies building.

"Make an appointment straightaway for a test," she instructed, and I arranged to go in the following morning. I woke up with blood between my thighs, canceled the appointment, curled up around the cramps and called my mother.

"You've just had a miscarriage," she said. "Obviously, we have trouble carrying to term. Well, we dodged that bullet. Imagine Jason a daddy!" We thought up more ridiculous possibilities. "I can't believe my Sue, pregnant." We were prone to miscarriages, part of being a woman in my family, our bodies alike, our same elongated tailbones, our pair of tipped wombs.

She grew serious. "What if you can't have a baby?"

"I'm okay," I said. "You had miscarriages before you had us."

"True. You're such a brave, big girl."

On medical forms after that I always wrote "1" in the "spontaneous abortion" space, miscarriage. In time, I forgot that I'd never been actually examined after the bleeding. When the counselor in Missoula needed medical information, the truth, I couldn't distinguish between accurate history and cultivated report. I had to say I didn't know if I'd been pregnant before, and I was embarrassed to sound so unaware of my own body.

The counselor piled Xeroxed pamphlets into my hand, words in a feminine script font on their covers: options, choice, decision. I held them, frozen with shock: pregnant. "You have three options, and I'll go over them with you," she said in a voice monotonous with repetition. Have a baby, give up a baby, end "the pregnancy"—the use of "baby" came to a halt. Something had to be chosen. Something had to be decided. Pregnancy had its own timetable, and Christopher and I would have to compress our thinking and hurry.

I asked the counselor for the phone, banged my thigh on the desk that was too big for the room as I came around to sit in her chair. She left me. I dialed Christopher, fingers cold, thigh aching. I wanted him, but I felt so far away, that union wasn't possible.

The couple had been rearranged, not an "us," but an "I" and an "I." I carried a universe, the mineral fact.

"Will you meet me?" I said. "I need to talk to you." I wished I could wait. I knew it was difficult for him to leave work. This was the moment in our lives of thinnest privation, our demeaning jobs the sort without guarantees. Christopher worked inputting data at a law firm. I was still waiting tables. When we needed a day off, we risked heat and groceries, generic pet food, no-name laundry detergent. We'd lived in Missoula nearly two years, trying to write, and these were my first years without some kind of family money (my grandmother had paid for occasional therapy, my grandfather's trust provided my postcollege rents). Life was deliberate with the things I couldn't have. We never ate out, I didn't buy department-store mascara, and I found gloves and hats secondhand. We lived small like that, but Christopher had taught me to savor the discipline. We were making a conscious effort, and choosing could be its own strength. I had learned how to save up money, plan ahead for a movie. At the restaurant I did my duties and didn't use the phone. I had learned how to wait in a line, to let go of urban impatience. These sound like small things, but they were revelations.

In its bold crisis, pregnancy would be the exception. I would not wait, wouldn't have to. Its information thundered forward in my body, whether or not I spoke it, now, later, never, and I wanted to get in front of it.

Christopher came up the empty street, hands thrust down, shoulders up against the bite of the wind. It was March, the town wan and deadened, the granite buildings impassive. We came together at the corner. For one second, taking the last breaths before I told him, my cheek against his coat, I knew something about our relationship that he did not. When I told him, I would change us from then to now, the pregnant couple.

"I'm pregnant." I'm pregnant.

He held his sigh, complete stillness, and then he released it. "Are you going back to the cabin?" he said.

He didn't say the word *abortion,* the word my ear was shaped to hear. We knew each other's absolutes, but we hadn't anticipated how to make this decision, the one you get bullied into. No one does.

"Yes, I traded my shift."

"I have to finish up at the office, but we're going to think about this. We have a lot to think about." I tried to read him. He didn't reveal anything, squinting and fighting off cold weather. Two years of us—how ridiculous and slight, those months adding up to months and a dog, that was all. We still knew whose kitchenware was whose.

We agreed to three days, Christopher's suggestion. He could always put things into order, comfort us like that, the sort of man who cleaned up after dinner before turning on a movie. We would do this deliberately, and because of our effort and consideration the answer would present itself. First, we'd assume we were having the baby. The second day we'd say we were ending the pregnancy. On the last day we were to measure instinct, see which experience made the most emotional sense (adoption was beyond us). That's how we had decided to try again with another dog, decided to rent the cabin up the creek. We took our time, no one got overruled. We knew we could do that.

The first day my body seemed almost obscene in its scheme. It had me in its thrall, and I stood under the shower and looked at the familiar skin, beneath it someone unimagined. "I'm pregnant," I said, and water ran into my mouth. "Mother," I tried, an old word, freighted, invincible, her. "I'm going to have a baby," I said into the mirror, pretending I was telling my father and stepmother. What did I look like now that I contained someone else?

The next day, no baby: an abortion. The word had lost its dictionary decency; it was intimate, me, my guts and fluids. I'd only known "abortion" as a newspaper item, a legal term, but now I couldn't get a grip on the word, hard, empty. It disappeared when I reached for it, replaced at every opportunity. The handouts were vague on the "procedure." Even at the clinic, the act went nameless and separated itself from the reality. No one wanted to say it out loud. To turn unpregnant, I would have a procedure, its efficiency emphasized in a lavender pamphlet, along with its brief duration and prompt recovery, the easy access to sedatives. The act would propel my treacherous body on from this plot point, restore my uterus to its regular story. "Abortion," I said to Christopher at dinner, forcing him to put down his wine. "Abortion, abortion, abortion, abortion."

I turned stony and private, wished Christopher out of the house so I could wallow in this rich trick, this astonishment of my body turned by natural alchemy from body to home. We were supposed to spend this day thinking "abortion," but I kept thinking, absurdly, grandly, of the Renaissance paintings of the Annunciation, Mary with head lowered, showered by golden light, her clothes already draped around abundance. This accident of conception had cast an enchantment, and I was miraculous. I wanted Christopher to see this definition of me we hadn't known was there. The golden threads were everywhere. Look.

Christopher and I stayed in different parts of the house, made room, but a bleak space opened between us, sheets unwarmed in the bed, limbs not touching. We were waiting for this to be over. When the pregnancy dilemma was resolved, its temporary importance ended, we'd come back together, the recently married two of us. *We* would be in charge again of deciding our life.

The pregnancy hurried us forward, days ticking, growing, and we would have to decide. The accident had forced parenthood on us; we were already parents. The third morning, Christopher went to his office, I went to my restaurant. I wiped down two dozen salt shakers and the peppers. I was exhausted by the never letting up inside my head. I pulled the rug sweeper from its cubby and rolled it over the cold rice scattered on the carpet the night before. I went through the dining room with a soapy cloth, chillier from table to table, and swiped at seat backs and chair legs. The other girls on with me (we called each other "girls" because in Montana you couldn't stop the men from it anyway) did the same chores, folding napkins, tossing those too badly pilled, pulling the blue cheese and ranch dressings from the walk-in fridge and pouring them into metal tubs. The kitchen guys arrived by the back door, turning on the rock station, tying on bandannas and calling out their lewd jokes, tugging at us lewdly as we passed between fridge and dining room, arms loaded. Usually I liked the united activity and laid-back rush, all of us pursuing the same theatrical feat, the continuous motion of plate from kitchen to tray to table, the flirting out of boredom. Restaurant work went off seamlessly, a purposeful coordination that was almost sexy. You did what was asked of you, and you knew when it was time to stop.

But today the hostess station looked cramped and fussy. I hated the boys in the kitchen for being crude and stupid and hated the one waitress who showed up after the rest of us every morning.

"Hey, Susy-Q!" people said to me. "How's it going?"

These words were tin and spit. I wanted to say, "I'm deciding about having an abortion," but no one would welcome that word. I was caught in an appalling silence. An epic decision made in hiding. I couldn't even mention being pregnant—fatigued today and distressed and oddly achy—because all anyone knew how to respond to that was "Congratulations!" I hated Christopher that I was here in a restaurant in Montana. I hated hard, wanted out. Not me, I shouldn't be here. I should be home, real home, New York, upstairs over Eighty-first Street, on my mother's bed and spilling gallows humor over what was to be done, let's order something to cheer us up. I wanted a mother, but not Daphne's exaggeration and stage entrances. Not for this.

I counted out dollar bills for the bussers and kitchen, stuffed the rest in my back pocket, the soft cash that smelled of soy sauce and dish towel. Missoula looked thin to me, meaningless. I didn't belong here, and that afternoon, driving home from the lunch shift, $11 my total take, I had the clear impulse: the baby would fill this emptiness. The baby would be the reason I had moved here. I backed away from that thought. I knew that wasn't how to make a healthy decision. Christopher needed to not have a child. I didn't want to push him into a fatherhood he didn't want, couldn't handle. I didn't want to use a baby.

I managed the car down our rutted driveway and walked out into the field beside our house, which was dense with high winter grass. The frost crackled underfoot, pale afternoon sun on the stubbly earth. The creek was rushing. This wasn't me. I felt all gone, cracked in the false pioneer effort, revealed as the soft little me, wanting and wanting. When Christopher got back he plucked his bag from the backseat as usual and slammed the car door, heading to the house, but he changed course when he saw me and came out through the grass.

"What is it?" He was alarmed, as if something had happened to our dog.

"I want to have a baby." I hadn't touched these words once. When that dull counselor asked "What do you want?" I hadn't said a thing.

He dropped his bag to the ground and folded me into his arms. I knew we'd decided. We weren't having the baby, but I had to put my voice into it and lay claim. Christopher had done everything right, respected me, hadn't forced me to choose the abortion. I didn't feel forced. I knew the couple, in its early, shaky, thoughtful start, needed to not become parents. We needed the abortion. But I would have to shut down my own instinct in order to get through the thieving surgery. "I do, I'm sorry, I want to have a baby." Words like that have no accuracy until they're in your own mouth.

"You will, we will. Just not now," he said, and he held me, our shoulders shaking together. What? What? He surprised me, and a well of future opened inside me, all the possible futures for us, including a babyless possibility. Christopher in his three days had stepped toward the possibility of having children and, in a dance-like turn, I stepped back. A child didn't seem essential. I could let go of the wanting, air out the room, release my stern conviction that I had to be someone's good mother. I could wonder if I wanted children. Ambivalence arrived, made itself at home.

We had something to do. I made the clinic appointment and filled out their forms. "You're too early," the nurse informed me. She took a slow tone, the patience of condescension. "You'll have to wait."

"Not now?" My body had tricked me. It didn't seem bearable. "I'm really nauseous," I said. "And so tired. Is there anything I can do?"

"That will go away after the procedure." She gave me an appointment for my seventh week, ten days on. As soon as I was choosing abortion, no one would let me be pregnant.

In the waiting time I snapped Christopher off. I picked fights, looked for injury. If his boots were in my way, if he pulled too hard at the sheet in the night. I fought when he got out of the shower, before he reached his towel, about our grocery list, what he'd forgotten to pick up. The world shrank into mundane qualities. The $350 fee drummed against us, almost impossible to manage—how many restaurant shifts, cleared tables, day labors, matinees abandoned.

"We offer a mild sedative for the procedure," the counselor

said, uneasy with me in her small airless room because I couldn't stop crying. I didn't *want* to be crying, wanted to look like I believed in this idea.

"You can't *force* someone into parenthood," I said. The words came out too loud.

"Did someone force you?"

"No, not *me*. My husband."

I wanted her to know how much love was in this awful decision, that I loved him deeply, that love directed us both. What it felt like from the inside, I wanted her to know, was ghastly and complicated and different from the appearance. "You can't have a good family that way, and I want a good family."

She pushed back her chair to be closer to the door. "Should I go get someone?" she said.

She said "procedure" several more times. "What would you say your reasons are for choosing the procedure?" She stepped warily around each word, as if someone might burst in and stop us. Wasn't the clinic supposed to be comfortable, the one place where it was okay to be getting an abortion? I tried to offer this very young woman in her clogs what it meant to make decisions in a marriage, together, that it wasn't just you anymore. But I also knew—she worried the consent form on her desk, the line still empty where I was meant to sign—that I was supposed to assert *my* decision, to announce myself. The law handed me the right, and as a pregnant woman I should seize the moment. I had to look like I wanted this. I had to look grateful. And that, finally, was more than I could do. This wasn't my decision, or only mine. Another entity had revealed itself, a third force in our house: the couple.

March 30, 1995. I wouldn't let Christopher come in with me. Let him feel its hours by himself in the waiting room. He could be kept out, as the clinic had a tedious way of reminding me. They kept saying "what you want." I received the injection of Versed, and the room pulled away. The doctor loped in, didn't address me, stuck something up into me that hurt without relenting. The nurse held on to my hand and passed him equipment with her free hand. I tried to see what. "You're doing great," she kept saying, calm and familiar. She had experienced lots of women's abortions. They too must have done great. The doctor slapped his used gloves on a tray and left. The nurse swept me into the after-care room, recliners, paper cups of juice, other dozing women. One of them looked at me. "It *hurt*," I said. She nodded.

"You can go," someone said after she recorded my vital signs for the last time. I tidied my expression for Christopher as I went through the door that separated the surgery from the waiting room. I thought I wanted to punish him, but then I saw him and just wanted a hamburger. We drove to a restaurant, and he watched me eat. At home—opening our car doors together, together climbing the icy porch steps—I got into soft clothes and under the covers, wanting him gone but making him stay, desperate for him to do something for me, anything.

I grieved. Didn't want to be awake because I thought about it. The loss was unbearable, and I felt certain that every future thing I longed for would be lost. How would this resolve itself? At first each week was noticeable for how my body adapted to rude medical invasion and arrested hormones. A little bleeding, light cramps. "Call if you develop a fever," they'd said. "Otherwise, these things are normal, don't bother calling." Cramps, bleeding, depression. The counselor had doled out minimal information. "Use only pads for two weeks," she'd said, her hand stressing "only," as if I didn't understand maturity. "You stupid dumb bitch," I wanted to say. "I'm from New York." I was so angry. Angry that I had the abortion, and he didn't. He sat in a waiting room as my body was pried open, scraped out, emptied. Briefly, I'd assumed the most primal state, and I understood the meaning, angles, rigid rules of abortion in a way Christopher would never catch up to. The abortion became its own force in our marriage, beneath our routines. We didn't talk about it, its silence a polite agreement, but we had welcomed a mute chill, a hardness and ache. I saw that the two of us could be cleaved apart, that the couple wasn't unassailable, that married love was utterly different from what we'd been doing. We were no longer enclosed in our sweet pageant. In addition to the Provincetown romance, the move to Montana, the lost dog and the new dog, the both being writers, loving García Márquez and Alice Munro, etc.—now we were also what happened in Susanna's body.

The first period was normal, the second. I passed my hours in the restaurant, my body as altered to me now as it had been after losing my virginity. Something huge had claimed me. I refilled people's water glasses and said "coffee" and "you bet" with as much Montana in my voice as I could push. Did I sound like me? Was I still me? Christopher and I went to movies and drove to high spots up creeks and rivers for fishing. We used some money to buy me waders and a rod, and I learned knots for flies and cast poorly. I would glance upstream, Christopher in the better spot I didn't begrudge him, his hand, arm, shoulder all employed in something that made him whole. He looked himself standing in the river. Eventually I just stayed in the car reading *The New Yorker* with the door open, one leg hotter than the other in the sun.

Sex was different—a shadow over us, a presence intruding in our bedroom. We made love every day, but the sex had turned cautious, less oxygen to it. We knew what it could do to us. April 30, May 30.

June 30, July 30.

One day, on a drive through Yellowstone, on our way to Salt Lake City, Christopher said, "I'm ready to have that baby now."

He looked accomplished. This had been work for him.

I had wanted to hear those words for every one of the three

days we were deciding, the ten days before the abortion, for the five months that followed, so I forgot to be furious and collapsed into the relief. He wants it! The shadow is gone! We got out of the car, a canyon stretching before us, a lake below, yellowing sky, orange rock. The world looked edible, and we knocked against each other with shy adoration as we walked to an overlook and leaned against the guardrail. I surveyed the massive vista and thought, "Here is where we decided to have a baby." Before we arrived at his parents', we stopped at a bookstore, our decision a few hours old, and we bought a couple of pregnancy primers. Anyone could see me, there she was, carrying *What to Expect* up to the register, healthy with conviction and purpose. I wanted to be radiant and celebrated, but no one looked. In the car I held the books on my lap in their bag, and Christopher kept reaching for my bare arm, touching my bare knee to say again that we had set something in motion, the next ecstatic step.

But wait. Now you're ready? Viciousness filled me. My *body*. When my body was primed, you couldn't be ready, and together we shut it down. That baby, you're ready to have that baby? That baby's gone for good.

I felt my usefulness, the canny industry I held.

"What happened?" I said. We lay in his parents' guest room.

"I've thought about fatherhood. When you got pregnant I realized I'd never thought about being a father before. I just had a position. But through all that deciding about the abortion I began to realize what it all meant."

"So now you're sure?"

"Going through that process. Yes." He was so genuinely pleased he didn't hear the jab in my asking. In the last few months, as I clocked the intensity of my cramps and worried about uterine health and future chances, as sex shed its green romp and bliss,

Christopher had been across the room, the bed, the yard, compelled by a new identity. Gradually, he'd come to understand he could enjoy fatherhood.

"I'm not scared," he said. "Well, not as scared." He smiled, and his smile, lying down and in the dark, had been the first thing of the real him I had fallen for, and I loved him so much, my heart full with Christopher, instructing me in love, waiting for me.

"Okay," I said. "Let's wait till we're home."

But how little I wanted to make love to him, to embark on some magnificent enterprise. I took it on glumly. The thought kept coming back: I would still be pregnant if he'd realized a little faster. My March 30th baby was due in two months.

We were again careful, this time to become pregnant. Timing, diet, boxer shorts, we were going to start up whatever weird sorcery it took. And it worked.

I went to Planned Parenthood and suggested a post-abortion support group to them. I'd organize it, I said. No one would come, they said. Another clinic was reopening in town, rebuilt after arson had destroyed it. I went there and applied for a job as an abortion counselor. When I had my interview I was eight weeks and two days pregnant.

A few days before the job began, an old friend called from New York. She'd become a senior editor at a magazine, and she needed someone *now*, don't *worry* about the clips.

"Can you go to North Carolina on Monday and interview Melanie Griffith on location?"

Flies whacked themselves against the expanse of glass that faced our creek. Buzzing started and stopped. My friend wanted to cheer me up, remind me I was a writer and give me a distraction from the unrelenting focus on pregnancy. She expected the celebrity profile, its tepid revelations, making meaning out of the food ordered during the interview. I could go on location, a movie set, a distance from Montana. I'd interviewed movie stars at my old magazine, and I was reviewing movies for the Missoula paper. For my mother's birthday the year before I'd collected a hundred reviews and bound them at Kinko's. She told people I was a film critic, but in Montana I had learned to say that I wrote movie reviews sometimes.

"Shall I have our travel department call?" my friend said. Travel department, no one ever said that here. A paid-for flight, expensed meals. I missed that sort of validation, which was meaningless among rivers and low-wage hours and oil changes. I'd been imitating this rough, straightforward life for a good while, and maybe it had been enough. If I went, I'd miss the clinic training. Someone else would get my job. Plenty of people wanted to celebrate the new clinic after the notorious arson, which had left Planned Parenthood as the only place in town. My only "option."

I turned down Melanie Griffith and chose abortion work, which surprised Christopher and everyone who knew me. I'd never done anything of the sort. "Remember how crazy that counselor made me, her doubting, her tentative, automatic comfort?" I said to Christopher. "When I hesitated, she asked me if I was *ashamed*. She said, 'Are you ashamed?' suggesting the word, nothing to do with me or how I was feeling. She didn't even see me."

"I know," he said. "You need your own words."

The longing to pull my abortion back and undo its hurt had landed me here, which wasn't where I'd expected to go when I'd struck out for love and writing. No more New York, no more editors calling with assignments. I knew it.

"You're in danger," the executive director of the clinic told us. She had stepped into the conference room on our first morning to thank us and cheer us forward. The seven new counselors were dotted around the table. "But you're making it possible for women to live their lives." Birth control methods covered the plywood table. Today I would have been in a movie star's trailer, watching her eat her salad, adjusting my tape recorder. Instead, I was upright and attentive in a concrete building made to withstand bombing. In front of me, not coiffed golden curls and a pretty manicure but a middle-aged woman wearing sneakers, big glasses, nothing to hold back her coarse, gray hair. The rest of us were in our early twenties and our late twenties, reproductive danger on display. In the style of these gatherings, we went around the table with our names and the condensed histories of how we had come to be here.

"I want to hear you say why," the director said. "Because this isn't for everyone. You have to know why you're doing this."

The women had boyfriends, were single, had worked on rape-crisis hotlines, had been hoping the clinic would reopen. Some of us had had abortions, and said so. We were sexually active, biologically ripe. Danger was in all our bodies, barely contained. As the others spoke, I thought about wanting to get close and look at abortion straight on, to understand what had happened to me, in the space between the sex and the loss. I was looking for the absolute, the right, the good of the choice, because certainty had eluded me then, my counselor asking me was I "sure." Planned Parenthood had made me feel like I was one of a thousand careless girls doing something wrong. I wanted to know how someone makes an unbearable decision.

"I want to keep her company," I told the group. "Abortion is lonely."

We reviewed the biology of reproduction, the clockwork complexities of ovulation, the ratios of sperm to egg, the same lessons from seventh-grade sex ed. We sorted through the contraceptives on the table, passing diaphragms and condoms from hand to hand. We had lists of sexually transmitted infections, descriptions, symptoms, treatment "You have to be comfortable with all of this," our trainer said. Sex broadcast its power in a dozen directions.

The doctor appeared the second day to detail the exact methods of abortion, those he preferred, which were safest and when. He took us into the exam room, and we switched on the vacuum aspirator, passed around dilating rods and curettes. The third day the lab tech showed us a shelf of kitchen supplies, Pyrex dishes, strainers, for looking at the "products of conception." We learned how to run a pregnancy test, and we all handed over cups filled with pee, watching her release droplets on treated strips. I hadn't said anything yet. I didn't need to be the star. When my test turned out positive, though, I savored the change in the room, the buzz of excited girls, let them congratulate me, their touch on my arm and the small of my back.

After we shadowed the nurses through three or four counseling sessions, we began to counsel on our own, a sacred trust. Every situation of the world came up. Over the next months I counseled secretive teenagers, single mothers, grandmothers, professors, athletes and pro-lifers; a prosperous lawyer, a Catholic mother of four, a diabetic, a stripper, a quilter, a dog walker, an art student; kayakers, rock climbers, college students, high school students; women from Browning, Cut Bank, Anaconda, a girl from Idaho whose doctor told her abortion was illegal there; a girl raped by her stepfather, women deeply in love and women recently dumped, unfaithful wives, tender lovers, girls who didn't know what a cervix was, women accompanied by their mothers, or their boyfriends' mothers, or by the husband who sat listless in the waiting room as a squirming toddler ransacked the toy basket; and I counseled that fourteen-year-old who twisted a ragged Elmo doll between her fingers during her abortion. We allowed every reason—disinterest, fear, laziness and infidelity, burden and education and money, affairs and breakups. I described the surgery clearly. I used a straight, strong voice for the word *abortion* and gave it to her.

If I had started the job thinking there was a good abortion, a way to have something better than what I'd had, I saw that this was a terrible moment in any life. Each woman was suspended from her daily goings-on by a monumental decision, a choice that drained her as she made it. I listened to why she chose abortion, why she wanted it, why, why, why. I never asked the more slippery question: How do you make a decision that has no right outcome? I didn't even know how to form that question.

I tried to divorce myself from my baby. I felt impolite thinking of it when I needed to explain to a woman the gestational realities of ten weeks, to give her the information to help her decide. I was twelve or fourteen weeks myself, privately aware that we shared this half-full experience. And then I was more pregnant than my clients, and they rarely noticed, blinkered by the intensity of their emotions. Once, eight months along, I was leaning over my client during her abortion, catching up her hand in mine. My body pressed into the table, her arm buried against my abdomen. My baby gave one of its marine ripples, the rubbery, aquatic rollover. Had she felt it, this unnatural, alien hiccup? I was embarrassed, caught at something indecent.

In the exam room I would stand beside the bed and narrate the doctor's gestures, passing a quiet volley of information between us for the client's sake. I helped guide her hips to the precarious edge of the table as the doctor adjusted his head lamp. In the deliberately dim light, I unwrapped the sterile pack and filled a cup with Betadine, dropped a needle among the instruments and readied the cannula he'd need once her cervix was dilated. I could tell from his rustling and metallic sounds when to say, "He's just starting to dilate your cervix" or "Remember, we talked about how you might feel a tugging sensation." I prepared her for the aspirator, its motor as abrasive as street machinery. A fine rim of sweat beaded at her hairline. I stood by her head beside the table. This was how her lover must have seen her, features blurred with intimacy. On the other side of the bed, low in a chair, the lover took up her hand, kissed it and held it to his cheek. I wished I had known Christopher well enough to share that moment. I wished I'd been able to ask him, "Help me."

Come back in two weeks, we told them, and we'll check that you've healed. That your body has healed. Be gentle on yourself, I thought. Stay off your feet for a day, be gentle, but I knew this was the last stop. Only a few came back, and when they did, two weeks beyond their ended pregnancies, they were entirely different, no longer crying or picking at the shredded skin around their fingernails. They came in busy from the parking lot, crossed their legs in the waiting room, riffled the magazines, and when their names were called, they sprang up and followed the nurse.

This is what I'll tell my sons, when they ask, when I tell them about our abortion: We made a decision to be better parents, and that was what it took. Nothing yet in our lives had given us to understand the sacrifice of love, the efforts of parenthood, the heart flung open with generosity. The abortion was our preface, the beginning of who you would need and who you would know.

The False Daughter

My mother made her first visit to Montana soon after I moved, while I was still living in the converted attic. I baked an apple cake as I waited through the drizzly afternoon until it was time to go to the airport. Her imminent presence was always a thrill, how she would pretty the drab world. I wanted to impress her that I'd baked for her, and I'd planned a party for the following night so she could meet my friends. She quizzed me as we sliced a baguette. "Tell me who's coming, in order of importance." A friend of mine had a gallery show, and we went. My mother flooded the room with mention of big-deal auctions, the so-and-so collection. She bought two pieces. "I can't afford this," she whispered, "but I want her to like me." My friend was running the credit card, happiness on her face. She always had a soft spot for my mother after that.

Over the next four years, a scattering of visits.

One visit: She followed me into our cabin, saw Christopher was home and called me aside. She pulled an envelope from the muddle in her bag and lifted its flap. "It's two thousand dollars. Cash, Sue. Don't tell me you don't need it." She whispered, "You don't have to tell Christopher about it. It can be just your money." Christopher was of little use to my mother. He didn't lie, and he didn't flirt. He found her chattery and abrasive but tedious. Loudly, she said she had a present for him, too, and came at him, hand extended, something wrapped in a scarf. He drew out an antique silver napkin ring that had a *C* forged in it. The object was stupefying when you considered our life, and he didn't recognize its purpose. "It's a cock ring!" my mother said. She taunted us both for his frozen expression.

Once, my mother greeted me at the gate with an announcement. "I'm on Depakote. It stabilizes me." For a couple of days we had this easy time. The drug made her calm down and hold a conversation without twitching or eruption. Pieces of her soft self emerged, as she let go of that fretful need to make an impression on everyone. "If Depakote needs a spokesman," I joked, "I'll go on tour." But she "forgot" the pill for a few days. "Fuck Depakote," she said, as if she meant to be rude to it. She told us she'd taken a job, a position in Barbados, the church had begged her to take it. "I'm counseling teen drug users," she said, serious, suddenly in possession of church formality. "The kids know I've been through it. They know I'll call them on their bullshit, and they listen to me. I happen to be very good at it." When we were alone Christopher and I laughed and laughed.

One visit: I drove us down the Bitterroot Valley, heading for Kootenai Creek. I stuck to the business of driving as she spewed information about people I'd never met, talking-tos she'd given friends of Penelope's I'd never heard of. Her hands dipped in and out of her bag, window down, window up, radio loud, soft, loud, finger pointing at things across my line of vision.

"Please!" I said. "I'm trying to see the road."

She pushed my hair behind my ear. "You only have one good profile," she told me. "It's good it's the one visible to the passenger side, you clever thing."

How could a person respond to that? We had fifteen miles more to drive, but I veered off the narrow highway and parked at a trailhead. "Here we are," I lied. I had to get the door open, get out, and knew she wouldn't notice the forest service sign as we started to ascend the trail. We hiked in about ten minutes, which was all she had patience for.

One visit goes like this: She stole Tylenol and sunglasses at Target, producing them from her bag and pocket simultaneously with adolescent glee before we'd reached the car. She was waiting for remonstrance. I just got us in and started the engine. She told me to get over myself.

She had promised us an extravagant dinner. "Come on, you two, loosen up, stop being such puritans," as if we were playing at minimum wage. Money had always danced from her hands, an enchantment that at any moment could vanish, so why wait? The careless squander through my childhood, novelty notepads, cocaine, of course, tons of flowers—birds-of-paradise or three dozen irises. She knew our grandmother would buy our clothes, send emergency checks for the rent or the phone bill.

My mother pointed out the lamb chops, the crab cakes and salmon, the bottles running down the wine list. "Should we get a bottle?" Christopher and I were grim, not saying much. She didn't listen, or ask about the clinic. Conversation went nowhere. She was annoyed that I hadn't taken time off for her whole visit and annoyed I wouldn't choose the salmon. The menu looked like this: electricity bill, grocery bill, new jeans. I didn't mean to be irritating about money, and she was paying anyway, but Christopher and I had three jobs between us, a patchwork of schedules. We budgeted and thought things through. This was my first taste of ordinary, the repetition of freeway commutes and changing over to snow tires and the dish towel drying out over the faucet neck after dinner. She'd never taught me how to be part of everybody else.

Approaching, the waitress would have seen a lighthearted woman happy to be at dinner and two unpleasant companions. She flirted with the waitress—"And when did you move here, love? Which courses are you taking? What does Daddy do?"—then chose for all of us. "Rack of lamb for my ravishing daughter—very pink, right, Sue?" She wanted to please the waitress, have her return to the kitchen and point back at us, over there, table eight, the event of her week. She would tip hugely. When the girl left with the order, my mother leaned in and bitched, "Does she have to tell us *everything*? Like we care!" I felt Christopher prickling. I didn't want him to think I was anything like this, but I was forcing myself not to join her frenzy, and she knew it. She wanted a certain daughter of me, and I wanted a certain mother, our standoff.

After dessert, she asked for the bathroom and came back to the table saying she'd called a taxi. Always leaving by a different way than she arrived. Three hours ago we'd been collecting her. "I know you don't want to drive me home. Susy's mad at me for shoplifting."

Christopher and I relished the silence in our dark car, and Daphne went back to her hotel and picked herself up another daughter.

Maybe my mother stopped her for directions with a hand on an arm, then asked why she looked sad. Had she bought something from her, turning the transaction into the girl's boyfriend trouble, car payments, acne woes? I don't know. The next afternoon she brought the girl to the clinic and introduced her with urgent warmth to everyone. From my office I heard her voice in the waiting room, the sharp glassy thrill of it running down my spine. I found her surrounded, just like at camp or backstage after school plays. She had her arm around the girl's shoulders, and the girl—my height, curly brown hair, you'd confuse us from the back—looked perplexed but dazzled. She looked the way I used to look, wondering what was about to happen to her. My mother pointed out the clothes she'd bought for her. "She's a junior at the college, she just moved here last month, from Great Falls, she got her cat from the pound, same day she broke up with her boyfriend.

"We're going out to dinner," my mother said. "She's a vegetarian, but she *will* eat fish, won't you? And maybe I can get you to eat organic lamb? I know this place that has the most divine lamb." Her body was entirely turned toward the new girl, who hadn't existed in anyone's consciousness until my mother spun her into place.

"See you later," she said, not quite to me.

She left me, as she meant to, rejected and stung. One of the nurses said it was nice of her to help people. A friend asked me wasn't I supposed to go too? No, I said, I wasn't. I went home confounded and tried to figure out the behavior with Christopher, who didn't know where to begin.

In a shop a few weeks later, the clerk recognized me from the splurge of money Daphne had dropped buying me cashmere socks. I had come to return them, their baffling taint too much to surmount. They'd never be just serviceable things, warm feet.

"Your mother was so nice!" the clerk said, more than friendly, as if we could count on a common happiness. "She came back in the next day with your sister and got her this adorable robe." I experienced that buzz of being thrust out of my own life, the saw blade of my mother's invention getting close.

Many months later, I saw that girl downtown, that false sister, and we regarded each other with mute shame, as if we'd both been part of a porn movie. My mother's porn, what turned her on.

Labor

Who could resist my mother's pleasure? She wanted to take me shopping, "for the baby," and we were both in New York. There was so much I wanted—a painted white crib, a changing table to match, a very good stroller. Christopher and I couldn't afford these things, but with her husband's money my mother could, and she wanted to be the one who bought them.

"Oh, look! *Sweet!*" she cried a hundred times that day, holding up Swedish bibs, tiny moccasins, hats made to look like strawberry tops, striped rompers, jackets with bunny ears sewn to the hood, polka-dotted burp cloths, lace-trimmed bumpers for lining the Moses basket. She insisted: You must have the Moses basket, and this mobile, and the extra receiving blankets. "You need a chair." Oh, I did want a chair. I'd seen friends sitting serenely in those gliders, the matching upholstered footstools. I wanted it all.

"Well, I don't really *need* it."

"Silly billy, I *know* you don't need it, but wouldn't you like that? You're tired, it's the middle of the night, rocking your baby? Oh, my baby!" She was misty again. We both were.

"Okay." I would let her give me the chair. Why couldn't I just relax? Why did I always have to be so careful? We chose a white glider with a blue-and-white-striped cushion that reminded us both of Provincetown. I refused the stool, although I wanted it, but I didn't want to be thought greedy (I felt so greedy). The store would ship everything to Missoula—changing table, clothes and blankets, high-end stroller that could assume four different con-figurations. As she was handing over her credit card, she grabbed a musical pull toy that could be tied to the crib rail and topped the massive pile with it.

This was something we were supposed to be doing, a way we were supposed to behave. A pregnant woman and her mother, though I felt ten, rather than thirty, back-to-school shopping. She handed me the receipt, whispering that we shouldn't let her hus-band know how much she'd spent, and not old Penny either, who'd be jealous. We went to lunch and enjoyed the white table-cloth, the iced pats of butter and the catty remark about the waiter as he turned his back. Here indeed we knew how to behave, and for emphasis in a story she seized my hand. I jerked it back sharply. "Excuse me!" she said, hurt. She could be so genuinely wounded.

With pregnancy, the amassing fluids, my hands were too sore and swollen to be touched. I'd already explained that. I'd explained it three times, and I reminded her again. I set my hand back on the tablecloth, and we touched pinkies. I had a real rea-son for her not to touch me, a reason I could stick to.

Labor started Saturday before Thanksgiving. Christopher and I walked hand in hand down the middle of frozen streets in our neighborhood.

"Tomorrow we'll have a baby."

"Tomorrow we'll be parents."

We spoke softly, quieting ourselves. At home we ignored the phone.

The baby wasn't born Sunday, or Monday. We ran out of movies. We arrived at the hospital, and the labor wasn't fun anymore. It wasn't hallowed and sacred with intimate looks, the way we'd been promised by the birth-class coach. Without sleep for two days, I was incompetent. Christopher irritated me, but I wanted him close by. Monday night the doctor used a slender hook and broke my water, and for one minute labor became a warm, dreamy gush; then stark again, the cervical shards, broken glass up inside me.

Christopher slept upright in a chair with his feet on my bed. I had been in labor for fifty-seven hours. He gripped my hand, and I slept between contractions, fifteen seconds of the deepest sleep of my life.

I cannot do this. I want to leave this room, there's the door. Let someone else do it. But I can't get out of it, no movement but forward, but pushing, until it's over.

The world shudders, splits me open, crown of head, I cannot remember having any other purpose or people. I am blood and breath, this instant only, this single act. This boy.

I open my eyes, take in the new nurses and the baby warmer next to the bed. The room is transformed from when I knew it last, magic. The nurse lifts his shining body into the warmer and starts to rub his limbs. I try to reach, and my arm's weight appalls me, as if my body has been replaced by someone else's. I want the gap between us closed, the bleak, separate space corrected. The doctor delivers the placenta, which occurs to me vaguely. Christopher touches the baby's fingers, which are creased and blue. "Can I hold him?" I say, a few times.

In a long minute he is on my chest, the horizon of my gaze,

and the nurse lifts my blanket and tucks it over him. Christopher stands at the rim of us, barely important. I speak, "Hello. Daniel." Word, name, here. My eyes adjust to Daniel's and there is nothing left of the rest of my life, just tatters, crumbs, nothing but the delirious understanding: I am here for you.

In our private room daylight looked exotic. The shower pressure was strong, and I put on a fresh gown, grateful for the absence of snaps or buttons. Grateful for the smell of soap, for the clean sound of the word *Tuesday,* for the guy on public radio who played Elvis Costello. The nurse kept coming back to turn down the sheets or replenish the ice chips in the plastic pitcher, and I was positive I'd remember forever what she looked like. Christopher sat in a recliner, the baby propped against his raised knees. I crawled into the bed, not sure I wanted the baby on me, not sure how to. I'd call my family, my mother first, of course. This birth had made the world fuller, and I could be generous. I phoned Dubai, her voice the sound of the deepest home, and it made me choke.

"Mummy, I had a boy. His name is Daniel."

She called to her husband and cried, which pleased me. I was too tired to stay on long, but I couldn't sleep. We called my father, Aunt Irene, Christopher's mother, his brothers and sister. Other families did this, just like this.

I wanted to be the one to tell my sister. My mother had probably already phoned her, but that didn't matter today. I told Penelope it was a boy named Daniel.

She said, "Now you love someone more than me."

I rallied grim patience, which cost effort. I was hurt Penelope had nothing to ask about him, her own fragility our regular focus. This is not a regular day, I wanted to insist, but I also wanted to soothe her. "Of course I love him more than anyone."

Careful words. "He's my child. That doesn't change the way I love you." But I was tired, and Christopher was mouthing to me, "Hang up."

On Thanksgiving Day, we spent time leaving the hospital, a long time dressing Daniel. We tried to stay calm as our baby writhed on the bed and screamed. Christopher left me alone with him and went to the parking lot to secure the car seat. He was gone a long time and came back worn out. I wanted to stay. Please, another night, one more night. I didn't want to give up the sitz baths, the appearing food and the solicitous hands. A nurse handed me a clipboard and pointed to places for me to check and sign. Daniel slept on the bed, protected from his spastic limbs by a tight blanket around him. He looked strange because he hadn't existed two days earlier.

It had snowed and snowed, a historical feat. I trudged from our gate to the porch, carrying the baby, and Christopher followed with the stuff. The baby made noises in his guttural language. I felt I should understand him.

Two bags of groceries stood on the porch, an envelope tucked into one of them. I had to get the baby indoors, and Christopher hoisted the bags up and carried them to the kitchen. I set Daniel in the middle of our bed and came out into a room that didn't have Daniel in it. Christopher handed me the note, which was signed by our friend Sandra. "Dear Susanna and Christopher, Happy Thanksgiving and Welcome, Daniel!"

"Look what she's done," I said. It was the whole dinner, still hot beneath tinfoil and dishcloths. We could smell the pie. Christopher unpacked containers on the kitchen table, pulling out one thing after another. Stuffing, cranberry sauce. That should be it, I kept thinking. Salad, sweet potatoes. Sandra had whipped the cream.

"It's absolutely everything," Christopher said. "It's a whole turkey."

"What she did for us," I said.

He put food onto two plates, and we sat down and ate, crying. We didn't make another sound. I was so hungry.

I went from the hospital's safe luxury to listless fear. "What have we done?" Sometimes I said it aloud. Why couldn't I breathe? I felt resentful and hopeless. In the first weeks the baby shredded me with his hunger, his presence in the house a magnet of need. He was always sucking, my sloppy shirts undone, the odors of sweat and spit-up on my hands, on all the pillows. He had yet to smile, to be anything. His demand was inescapable, and I relinquished myself to his instruction. At four weeks old he lay on his back in the crib, his vision bobbing. The mattress was taut with a fitted sheet. There were no blankets, no plush bunnies with bows and treacherous ribbon ends. I reached my strange hand to turn the mobile on, my intentions already so motherly, my hand a mother's hand. I stood where my mother stood, hips pressed against the crib, low back muscles stretched with the overhead reach. My body was Daniel's mother—twisting, folding, wiping down, snapping, securing, dabbing at his skin with a washcloth that had become a mother's washcloth, what I remembered as a little rough at the corners of my mouth, her other hand gripping my chin. My life had narrowed to all the hands' activities.

This wasn't the mother I had wanted to be. I wanted to be patient and in love. But when I set the little piles of onesies into his yellow dresser drawers, I felt like Susy as she guided Penelope's foot into a sandal, and I wanted to scream. Even if Daniel was sleeping, I wanted to scream.

One night in those drab, perpetual nights I nursed the baby three times between 11:00 and 2:00 and after each time set him back in the crib, knowing it wouldn't work. Insanity in the futile gesture. Then I was asleep, clinging to it. Christopher pressed my shoulder, and I heard the shrieks, worse than claws on cold metal, and he said, "I'm sorry. I've been up with him. I think he just needs to eat."

"No, he doesn't," I shouted. "I've fed him!" I wanted Christopher to see I was doing what was required. I wanted the baby to thank me.

I pulled my sluggish body up and went to nurse, sitting in the white glider. I hated that word, *nurse*. And *sleep* and *night*. The hatred settled in my jaw. The baby fell asleep in a way that forced my elbow into an uncomfortable position. My tailbone ached. My ankles were cold. I thought about when I let Penelope have my complete set of Caran D'Ache markers in the flat tin box, and I wanted to scream. This weird sound started, moaning, choking. It was me, and Christopher came and lifted the baby out of my arms, which surged with freedom. My shoulder dropped, and my neck relaxed. Relieved and ashamed, I went to my bed, my smooth sheets, mine, and this wasn't the mother I had wanted to be.

When Christopher left for work, I saw the retreating help. I wouldn't be able to seal an envelope or have a glass of water, cemented into one chair by the nursing sessions. The day's momentum was defeated, just the hours until he got back. I talked to myself, narrating the monotony. My triceps ached from having my arm looped under the handle of the car seat, my hip bruised where it bumped at me. If Daniel fell asleep in the swing, I folded onesies and smoothed down the pile. A methodical beat as the swing swayed, baby propped up by blankets, go to sleep, go to sleep, take a nap, deliver me. Pacifiers dried on a dishtowel. I always had to pee. At night Christopher and I collapsed on the couch, keeping our voices low in case the baby stirred behind his door. We were always ready, a feeling of readiness about us even when there was nothing to do for him. The stroller parts were scattered across the living room floor in preassembled carnage, but there was no hurry as the stroller was useless in the welts and rises of snow. I didn't care about Christopher's day and didn't ask. We often mentioned Sandra's dinner.

Someone from work dropped by to see the baby and wanted to hold him. She brought him up close to her face.

"Don't you just talk to him constantly?" she asked. I felt insulted by her vigor and aware of my free arms.

"Talk to him? What would I say?"

"Just sweet nothings in his ear," she said. She had two kids. Later I tried to do it, raising him to my shoulder, putting my mouth against his head, and I couldn't think of a single nothing.

"I can't do this," I told Christopher. "I don't know how."

"You are doing it," he said. We were eating a white supper of sliced cheese and toast.

"I obsess that maybe he missed something from me today, something I was supposed to give him, that he needed, and that I didn't give him."

"Look at what you have given him. You nursed, you held him, you did everything all day."

"I did, but I'm so tired. I don't want to." Christopher didn't say anything. I wondered what he thought of me, then I didn't care. I said, "I haven't eaten an orange since the baby was born. I never have two hands free to peel it. That would be a good present to a new mother, to bring her a plate of orange sections."

"I'll peel an orange for you."

"All I want is to be alone." I started to cry, by now a frequent event, hourly punctuation. "What if he can tell?" I said. "He can tell I'm failing him."

"You're so hard on yourself, Susanna. He's fine." I didn't like Christopher saying I was hard on myself. I liked it better when he said I was strong and a hero and handled so much. And I liked the ensuing conversation, the brisk disclaimers and witty recountings, and then he always marveled that I'd turned out well.

But I haven't turned out well, I wanted to say. When I change the baby, I look at his penis and wonder what sort of man he'll be. What will his penis be like when he grows up? Would he be a good lover? *Who thinks that?* Dressing him, bathing him, my hands stalled on his skin. I checked. Was this touch okay? Did I touch him in a way that stole from him? I put an invisible barrier between Daniel and my hands so that he wouldn't feel me think those things. I didn't know the touch of love, a blank in me, only the touch of arousal and promise, of sex. Every day I had to stop, revise, train myself. I didn't tell Christopher about any of that.

Daniel was six weeks old, and it stopped snowing. He had enough of a centered gravity to settle in the Babybjörn's hammock. The Babybjörn was a serene dark blue with an orderly white stripe, and in rounds of isolated frustration I had learned to snap it up, toss one strap, snap a button, yank on the quilted flap and secure my son against me. I stumbled over the words *my son*. At the pediatrician's office, the nurse had called me Mom without looking at me. "Now if Mom can just hold his arms down." These *words* were eating my identity. I was a mother, which was strange. I had a boy. I lived in Montana, which was strange.

I zipped my parka over the baby in the carrier, re-creating the pregnant bloat. All day I had wiped my fingertip at the baby's eye, sopped up drool, heaved him between shoulder and the cradle of my arm, unsnapped the cup on one side of my bra, snapped it together again one-handed. I had paced through the rooms, the walls so lifeless. It was almost 10 a.m.

Warm, booted, laced, I left the house. The sidewalks were cobbled with hardened snow, and I was glad it was difficult to walk. It was something to do. I'd go to the bakery. It would cost precious money, but I'd be hailed by friends who hadn't seen him yet. I needed someone to see us. In public I was a better mother. I walked with my chin tucked over the baby's head, my hand returning again and again to set straight his knitted cap. In the middle of the bridge over the Clark Fork River, I stopped. I drew incomplete breaths from exertion and cold, rested my hands on the freezing rail. I looked down to the black water, white where bits of ice chunked along. The black-and-white of baby vision. His black-and-white mobile, his black-and-white board books, his weight against my chest when I read, his dense belly smaller than an octave spread under my hand. He could have seen the river, had he been facing out.

I'm going to throw him in, I thought. Unsnap the Babybjörn, upend the bunting, release a pillow from its case. His drop would end in seconds, and the swallowing river would take him. My power warmed me. I could do whatever I wanted, cold water, split seconds, and he had nothing but his wordless appeal, his dumb innate cleaving to my decision. I was hungry to shake awareness into him that because of *me* he was here, barely here and easy to undo.

For several seconds I quivered between excruciating impulse and action, petulance and responsibility. I moved my feet: move, go forward, walk into the next moment, which will be better than this one. I continued across the bridge and didn't look at the river. My hands craved the baby, and I cupped them around his body. I loved him. He was mine, and this was what it was like. This was how hard it was.

We didn't let my mother come at first. Before the birth, we believed we weren't going to want anyone at all, our solitary way, but three or four minutes after Daniel was born I wanted someone. I didn't even ask Christopher. I wanted a mother, and I asked his. We met her at the airport with our five-day-old son.

This hurt my mother's feelings, which Penelope told me. Aunt Irene and Patsy told me too. I was sorry, but I needed—the *baby* needed—help that helped. Two months later, I took Daniel and went to the airport to meet my mother. At the sight of her outline among the other travelers, I burst into laughter.

"Look at him!" I said, clutching her, Daniel between our chests. I felt proud, exhausted, shy, happy to have her witness all the things she knew in me and the new way that I was, too. I wanted her to see someone tall and strong. We shared the baby, my eye on her hands. She babbled in the car, and I knew she was nervous she'd fuck up and that I'd banish her. I didn't want to. I hated that air of inevitable doom.

"You know how we are," she said.

"Yes," I said. "But let's just see this time. Let's not make it happen that way."

"Okay!" she said.

"Okay!" I said. We both wanted it.

It was our most regular visit. I had a reason to leave her each day, didn't need to wait until she'd pushed me to enough. "He needs a nap," I'd say after an hour in her hotel room. "I'm going home to put him down."

Returning to work was going to make everything okay, easier. All I needed was a mutual conversation and the chance to pee. But I worked counseling women who wanted abortions, and they needed so very much. Had they always? Their underpants looked faded, their bras cheap. They left blood on the paper sheet when they hopped off the exam table, and after they left the room, I had to tear off the table paper and stuff it into the biohazard bag. The disposable disinfectant cloth looked like a diaper wipe. I didn't want to fill small paper bags with condoms and instructions. I was tired of accuracy, the way we had to chart our notes. "The patient has ruled out adoption," I wrote to indicate the clinic had told her about it. "And she chooses abortion because 'my boyfriend and I just broke up.'" I gave my client the contraception talk. Gingerly she picked up a demonstration diaphragm or cervical cap. Hurry up, I thought. Just pick one.

I said, "You have lots of options. What would you be comfortable with? It's important that you're comfortable."

I felt I was faking.

For two years I had called them by name, taken their hands firmly. I had loved this work. Be proud, I wanted to tell them, that you're getting through this. Feel courage, transformation. But I soured on their stories, disparaged their chances, predicted privately they'd return, pregnant again. At the end of the first session on my first day back, I was slumped and tired of anxiety and ambivalence—theirs, mine. I didn't want my next client, another freshman athlete who had no idea where to find her cervix, or another recently divorced middle-aged woman who knew she couldn't have a baby alone. During the session I started to glance at the sedate clock, read aloud faster through the consent form.

I assumed I needed more energy for my infant son, but when I was at home with him I had the same itch and yawn as I had in the counseling room, the same shortsighted irritation about the remaining hours until Christopher came home to salvage the afternoon.

My mother sent Daniel valentines and Easter cards, little letters and notes all the time. Each week she sent boxes of expensive toys, frivolous things. She sent large packages, pop-up books, cardigans, stuffed bunnies and a sheep in a fitted sweater. She picked out exquisite Petit Bateau clothes, and I'd lift them from their tissue paper, thinking of her in a small shop in Paris, telling the clerk about me, overdone French in *grandmère*. She phoned and asked about the baby. Then she'd push into the topic of sex and ask about me and Christopher. Had we resumed making love, how frequently, did things feel different down there, and did he notice? But all of this mattered less, I found. Daniel had diminished her. I could laugh. I could change the subject.

Every few months she visited. One day we sat in the sun on the front porch. Christopher tired fast around her, the fatigue of assessing a foreign city, and he was out. She wouldn't stop talking, and I was watching the baby as he started across the wooden planks, her voice percolating above us. Daniel was puzzled by his new crawl. He didn't like grit on his hands. I wanted her to soak up everything that announced him.

"Cher in security!" she was saying. "She had masses of people, the airport people, and security was a madhouse." She leaned forward and slid her hand around the back of his head, a slow and feathery touch, and my body went alert, some ancient signal reignited. Her fingers nipping at my body, my new breasts pliant in her hungry fingers, too much hunger in them. I hurried him to another part of the house where her hands could not reach.

When Daniel was about a year and a half old my mother brought her husband to Montana for his first visit. "Wissam's always wanted to see the West!" They came out of the Jetway, fussing with buckles and gloves.

"Oh, darling," she said as if she'd remembered something at the end of a conversation. "He's not doing well, and I forgot his medication when I packed. Me and my memory. We've got to get to a doctor. He can't go another day. Just anyone who can write a prescription."

Already, having two of them was a commotion. She didn't mention the baby.

At the baggage claim she asked about my obstetrician. Would he see my stepfather? In the car she pushed her head forward from the backseat. "Or your pediatrician. Who's your pediatrician? He'll do."

I said, "He can't see our pediatrician. Why don't I make him an appointment at the clinic?" I was proud to offer.

"Would it be this afternoon?" she said.

"Probably not," I said. "But tomorrow morning. I won't be able to see you though. I'll be in with clients all morning. I have to be there at six o'clock."

"How awful," she said. "Aren't you exhausted? Where are we having dinner? I'm dying to change. The man was so sweet on the phone. He gave us the room with the two sinks. He's going to drive me over to get our car in the morning." Her blur propelled us, and my stepfather and I didn't speak until we said good-bye at the B&B. I couldn't remember what I had planned for the rest of the visit.

The next day after abortions I ran into the doctor in the hallway.

"Hey, it was interesting meeting your mom," she said.

"She came with him?"

"Who?"

"I thought my stepfather was coming on his own." I had labeled his chart myself and propped it with the others for the receptionist.

"Your stepfather? I saw your mother." I was silent, and she tried to help. "*She* was the patient. She shouldn't play tennis with that history of her back, but we set her up with some painkillers, that should do it. I hope she feels better." She continued down the hall.

My mother lied straight off the plane, not even a beat, a hello, beforehand. She showed up for her husband's appointment and talked the receptionist into her new plan. She lied in the waiting room, in the hallway, limping heavily, in the consultation room, setting her bag on the empty chair her husband had not come to fill. In the clinic the lie had a judicious use. We kept the abortion doctor's name confidential. We arranged alibis for clients who couldn't let their parents know where they'd be that morning. Teenagers covered their bellies with oversized sweatshirts, and married women at home, waiting for their secret appointments, slept beside their husbands, no mention of their cramps or yeast infections. Here, in rooms of sorrow and trouble, of ordinary struggle, my mother got her way.

Her trip came down to getting drugs. I couldn't argue about it with her, because she believed she came for her grandchild. She believed her husband was out of his medicine. Her habit of procuring drugs was her way of being, as regular as using toilet paper in a bathroom stall. She didn't know that when she lied this way, blunt and obvious, I felt I didn't matter, nor did she catch the child's question: Why don't I?

"*Have* your drugs then!" I snarled at the answering machine, as it recorded her fourth message. All day it had been, "Call me. I want to talk to you. I bought Daniel something." Then slow and fierce: "Your stepfather's come all this way. How *dare* you treat him like this." Finally, she said, "Darling? We're renewing our vows. Won't you come to our wedding? You'll adore the man who's marrying us. We met him at breakfast."

"What the hell is going on?" Christopher said.

The baby was standing against the fridge where I had taped magazine photos of dogs, because he loved dogs. He tried to lick the pictures. I took a sponge to the tray of the high chair. In a few days, my mother would be sitting on a plane, holding the flight attendant back from her work, telling her, "My husband and I just got married in Montana! Did you know in Montana you don't need a witness?" Those were my lines.

Don't come back, I thought at the airport curb, concentrating on the handles of their luggage. Don't come back. From the back-seat I pulled her coat, sunglasses and the bear-motif shawl she had to buy at the hotel checkout. She was talking. I kept my mouth shut: Don't come back. I hugged my stepfather's sturdy, blameless body, which was somehow a relief. I was glad she had him. She hugged me too hard, trying to meet my eye. She meant to include our whole history, shake off her recent infraction. I couldn't look at her. Don't come back, don't ever, I kept thinking.

That night I was rocking Daniel to sleep in the glider when Christopher handed me the phone. He shrugged. A woman congratulated me on having a baby. She explained that she'd been sitting next to my mother on the plane. "We had such a great time! She told me all about you! She's so proud of you! I make artistic arrangements of dried and pressed flowers. Swags and wreaths, that kind of thing? Your mom gave me money to make one for you, a really nice one, so I wanted to find out what sort of flowers you liked. She gave me your address already, and I could get something to you by the end of the week."

"I don't want anything," I said.

"Well, your mother gave me quite a bit of money. She wanted you to have something special."

"I. Don't. Want. Anything."

"Oh? Uh, should I send her the money back?"

"Just keep it."

"She's going to be mad at me if she finds out you didn't get anything. Will you tell her you ordered a wreath?"

I looked at my son's face, his dark orange curls, shiny, relaxed mouth. How had she done this? I was talking to a stranger who had my phone number, who had a new relationship with that exciting woman from the plane, all that warm, excited babble, the startling and intimate details, the name-dropping of unlikely locales. The stranger already understood the usefulness of lying in our particular triangle.

"I have to go," I said. The woman had fallen for my mother and become a tentacle reaching for me. I hung up.

I spent many days thinking carefully about what I wanted to say. What I wanted. I was always calculating with my mother how to minimize her harm, her craziness. One calculation for another. This time I paid myself close attention.

"I know you got drugs from the clinic," I wrote. "I work there. Didn't you realize I'd know about it? I'm so tired of you lying to me.

"I love you, Mummy, and I want you in my life and in Daniel's life.

"When you stop using drugs and you stop lying, we can have a relationship."

Those were my terms. I braced for days as I opened the mailbox, nervous in my gut for the effective lashing.

She didn't answer, which wasn't like her. Had something happened to her? I was left hanging.

I found the board book at the library with the pretty pictures of the sweet bunnies. "I want to turn into a bird!" the baby bunny said. "If you do," the mother threatened, "I'll turn into a tree and you will build your nest in my branches."

"She's not threatening him," Christopher said when I told him I hated the book. "She's letting him know that he's safe enough to explore the world because she'll always be there for him." He was studying attachment theory, training to become a therapist.

"No," I said. "She's a bad mother bunny."

When people gave me copies of the popular book I got rid of them fast. I preferred the books with big, bold photos of baby faces or cubist illustrations of trucks.

I took baby Daniel to New York to visit my stepmother and father, now immobilized completely by MS. I described Daniel, pouring forth details I imagined would interest my father. My father said, "Uh-huh," and then asked if I'd read the week's *Book Review*.

"I don't have much time for reading right now."

"How can that be? I always did."

"Can I have a grilled cheese sandwich?" Daniel said. He was four, another afternoon, his new brother napping.

"I could cut up some apple," I said. Less work, less thinking. The apple was right there.

"I really, really want grilled cheese."

Grilled cheese sandwiches came from diners, from Howard Johnson's and the Skyline. They were like onion rings or rice pudding—they got made, and you paid for them. I had to call my friend Sandra and ask how to make one. She gave me astonished instructions—butter the bread on both sides, press down with the spatula. I set a skillet on the burner and sliced the cheese. I laid a piece of bread on the hot surface, then arranged the cheese, covered this with more bread. It felt like a lot of work. In fact, it was making me tired. I pressed, I flipped. The underside, incredibly, was browned and gave off the pretty smell of toasted butter. I set the sandwich on a plate, cut it into quarters and called Daniel to the table.

"How is it?"

"Good," he said with his calm, regular inspection. He was a steady boy. After he was in bed Christopher and I would say to each other, "How did we end up with him, the luck of him?"

"Can I taste it?"

"Here," he said. It tasted like a grilled cheese sandwich, miraculous.

* * *

"Mama?" Daniel's voice is outside the door, and Christopher jumps away from me. I've just come, lovemaking not at all finished. We don't have much opportunity for sex, parenthood wreaking its schedule and fatigue, but when we make love we are together. I am not the woman who lured men to bed in Provincetown, no longer the voracious show-off. It's taken years for me to choose my own course in sex, to make love without fury and performance. I talk to no one about our time in bed, because it's ours. I've learned how to lace desire to love, to be inside myself and revealed. Sometimes, still, that intimacy is too much, too risky and bare, and I lose my way, want to revert to the courtesan with her superb command. Then we pause, we wait, we begin again.

Christopher opens the door as I try to regulate my breathing, grabbing up some of the sheet.

"What is it?" He has always asked the children this way, not a mean way, but when they get out of bed again, and then again, he says, "What is it?" the question mark unstressed so they know this is no time to interest him.

"I need to hug Mama," our eight-year-old says, chin down, getting past Christopher like a cat and dashing to the undone bed. My skin still dreams, the orgasmic tremor on its surface. My son buries his head into my chest where I lie, and I put my arms up to hug him. Our closeness chases off the last hum. This is too close, my little boy, my sex, mother body, coming body, the returning little girl of me.

"Back to bed now," I say, and he goes. Bearing Daniel's fingerprints and loosed strands of hair, I will not resume lovemaking.

Another night: I'm holding my hand over my mouth. I'll stay quiet, my children at the edges, but the guttural sound escapes me, the defiance of orgasm. The doorknob agitates, Daniel's hand on

255

its other side. He must be confused by the lock, which he hardly ever encounters.

"Jesus, Daniel," Christopher says, something escaping him, too. That is not the normal way he talks to the boys.

"Why is Mama making those noises?" Daniel calls through the door. He has pressed his face into the crack, the hall light visible above his hair. "Is Mama all right?"

Christopher yanks on his robe and opens the door. He stands between Daniel's vision and me. He hustles Daniel back to bed, and I hear Daniel ask again, "What were those noises? Is Mama all right?" My heart breaks, my body hurries to collect itself. I know this moment, and I wonder, as sex is dawning in him without his knowing, if he feels sick. He and I sometimes dream the same things on the same nights. We are connected by the invisible paths that switchback between child and mother. I know, even if Daniel cannot, that he's not at our door accidentally, that he is waking up to a strong and important presence. The only words in my mind are my mother's. "It's a good thing, the best feeling in the world."

Christopher comes back. "He's okay."

"Thank you for going. I couldn't."

"I know."

"What did you tell him?" We don't lie to the boys. Yes, the shot hurts but just for a minute. We give them straight answers in terms they can handle. But now the straight answer knocks up against the sexual realm and another rule: Let them be children. We make careful distinctions between the sex they can under-stand—their own bodies, the making of babies—and the play and passion that belong to us.

"I told him we were goofing around."

"We were."

"Yeah."

I hear Daniel rustling his books, the lamp switch flicked, his comforter pulled this way and that. I put on my robe and go in to him. I draw his blinds on the dark windows and push aside some of the debris on his floor, the mess loaded with meaning for him.

"Can I snuggle?" I say. This is hard. I don't want to put my body next to his in case he feels more than his mother, its heat, the thumping heart, traces of his father. He is pleased and makes room. I tighten my robe and arrange it to cover my legs as I lie down. My breathing is normal, and the sex I was just having fades, its love remaining. Christopher, I can hear, is already sleeping.

Daniel sets his head closer to mine, and I take up his lovely hand. We're looking at the ceiling.

"Mama? Can I ask you something?"

"Yes?" I will know what to say, I think. As soon as the moment is here, I'll know.

"Why do you think there are so many conifers in Montana?"

That's what we talk about. And about the time we went to Greece; then baseball, then breakfast. I stay for half an hour, a special treat for bedtime, but other than that there is no marking this occasion.

It feels to me like raising granite, drinking a whole river—to know what to do. I've watched this scene before, its close-up on someone else. My son doesn't want to talk about my noises. That's my story. He heard a sound that reminded him, What will happen to me if something happens to her? I have come in to show him his mother. I haven't been transformed. I'm still his.

Ask

I always saved my mother's letters. I saved her birthday cards, scrawled notes, the small cards she sent with flowers. I thought when I'd amassed a significant collection, I'd examine it, a complete portrait assembled. I would trace her flights and distortions. I'd understand her self-absorbed parents, her first forlorn marriage, the rule of pain, her body's angry habitat. I'd answer why my mother was as she was. Many of her letters have my handwriting at the top, filling in the dates she often ignored. On a dozen hotel letterheads (the Carlyle, the Capital, the London Ritz, the Sheraton Jeddah), the letters swing from accusation to reminiscence, from scalding torment to apology, from indignation to pride in my movie reviews or new boyfriend. Her intensities burn up the page with little reference to any event beyond the writing itself as she details her itineraries or her trials with Penelope. Pet names for me litter the page—Squash Blossom, Mighty

Mouse, Bell-Like, Doodle Bunny—and the letters often turn nonsensical, nursery-rhyme musings. She is peculiar and passionate. When I was pregnant with Daniel she started the letters, "My Dear Double Baby." She sent a picture of herself and wrote on the back, "This is your Mum with a baby to show I don't drop them." She wanted to prove so much, conquer my resistance. Again and again, her longing for me overtakes the letter. Why, she wants to know, do I limit our calls, turn down her visits, reject her? Why can't things be as they were? This is the hardest thing for me to read, how much she wanted me, how distant I stayed. "Darling Susy," she wrote in a furious letter my first year out of college: "We need each other & the faster you realise it the better life will become."

Thinking I wanted evidence, explanation, I called Paul, my school friend's older brother, the one my mother seduced at my eighth-grade graduation. This was years later. I asked how he remembered that first day at the boarding school, and his focus was different, naturally, but in keeping with mine. Then I said, "She told me the two of you had sex on my dorm bed that day," and he said, no, not at all, that didn't happen. I called Martin, the long-ago romance from Paris, the boy my mother took from my college dorm, the one I'd stopped from telling me his version of that night. I said I was ready. My mother, he said, had instructed him that night to tell me they were in the middle of sex. No, they never slept together. Again, I heard an upending, a story quite different from what she always wanted me to think.

There's a way people sound plain when they tell the truth. There are no corners or hidden hurts. These men were at ease. I believed them. I knew what it felt like to be lied to, the grip in the belly, the physical notice of something amiss. That never came. They were at home in their stories.

*   *   *

"Let's have a real cocktail party," I told Christopher. "With candles, and I'll make plates of hors d'oeuvres." The children were old enough to need less of us for an evening and sit through a video. I invited ten friends. We all looked beautiful. We swayed on the floor, making quick jokes and drinking splendid martinis, as my grandmother Patsy had taught me to make them ("Drain the glass of its vermouth, then pour in the vodka"), the shred of dancing lemon peel or the olive soaking in the valley of the glass. I stood beside the table we used for a bar, pouring with huge, bold gestures. In sweat and pleasure, ribs aching, cheeks tight from laughter, I drank three. Just as the party ended, I knew I'd gone beyond where I should go, and the merry intensity gave way to some dark nasty cliff. I never could hold a drink ("Cheap date," my mother used to call me sweetly). I hunched over the table in the kitchen, lunging at air, which did nothing, as the front door closed repeatedly, the noise thinning in our house. "I think she'll be fine," I heard Christopher say. "I'll tell her you said good-bye."

It will pass, I'll throw up. But I didn't, and Christopher shepherded the boys to their beds. "Mama sends you kisses. She'll be in later." I never came, couldn't. Christopher returned to the kitchen, where I was supporting my leaden weight at the sink. He stood with me for two hours, as the spike in my head climbed higher, twisting, a tortured trip I'd never had all those years I was turning down drugs. I gripped Christopher's forearm without feeling him. Do something. The hours went on. He went to bed.

I tried to move to our bedroom, holding each stair with both hands on the precarious ascent, but I had to stop at the landing. On my knees in the hallway I got inside my mother that night, into her clutter and confusion, beat at by the terror of being unfooted. Who like that could parent a child? Who in that state could button someone's sweater, brush someone's hair, take someone to school, when she's slumped and sliding down the staircase trying to make it toward the goal of a single egg scrambled?

I had one concern: "Don't, don't let the children see this," I urged Christopher in the morning. I was mortified that I'd scare them and that Daniel, my first one, would be disgusted, realizing that the mother he thought was sound and straight was not. The villain mother, failing and collapsed, would ooze out of me.

"It's different," Christopher whispered, knowing what I was thinking. I slept the rest of the day, beating back shame.

When I was fifteen: I went to Greece with a school group. We sailed from island to island on a boat crewed by three men from New Zealand. "Dishy," my mother would have called them. I took their pictures. I wandered through ruins with a girlfriend, slept on deck as our boat bobbed against the docks. I made out with the crew, one at a time, comparing next-day notes with the girls. Each evening the new me in a Greek cotton dress entered the tinny discotheques, drank dangerous ouzo, climbed the town's ancient steps in the dark, one rough hand pulling me along, and the smell of sage and goats in the wind. We leaned against a stone wall, his hand under my skirt.

I returned to Taos, a pause between one boarding school and the next. I brought my mother an immense tin of olive oil, and bracelets and posters for my sister. It was hard to be back. After the bracing sea wind I had come to a stop, my suitcase open on the floor in my familiar bedroom. My clothes still smelled of the boat, and a salty stench had penetrated my watch strap. I toured Penelope through postcards and museum ticket stubs, keeping her on the couch. I wanted to call friends from the trip, but when I phoned they were out. I lay on my bed, flat and hopeless, and recited "Santorini, Mykonos, Kéa, Kythnos, Rhodos," but I left my door ajar so I could hear the goings-on in the house.

Later my mother burst through our front door and hurried into the kitchen, then raced back to the hall. "Sue? Darling?

Come out here!" I got up and went. Her hands behind her back, she said, "Close your eyes." I did. "Now open your mouth and *taste*." Her fingers, delicate insects. Salt and tang filled my mouth, and I burst into tears. "There!" she said. "Tastes like Greece, doesn't it?" It was feta, then oily, briny olives. The cheese was so dry it made me shiver. I opened my eyes. She held my shoulders to gaze at me, happy she'd made me happy. I loved her so much, her ecstasy and swooning joy, and kept saying, "Thank you."

"I know how much you loved it," she said. "I guarantee you'll go back one day." She had driven seventy miles to Santa Fe to find a specialty food shop. She led me by the hand into the kitchen where she had made me a salad of tomatoes, cucumber, feta and the olive oil from the can I'd carried through customs.

Six years earlier: One afternoon, nine years old and sick with something to grant me access to my mother's bed, I said, "Who's that?"

"Who's who?" my mother said, leaning over her bathroom sink, intimate with the mirror as she tweezed her eyebrows. She wore a blouse of the palest purple. My grandmother Nana was expected for tea.

"I saw someone," I said. Half a face around the doorway. I stared at the space, piercing the empty air with my recollection, the certain image of a large Afro moving off to the side. I looked, and it was just a spot made particular by my looking, nothing there. I needed her to believe me. "There's someone here," I said.

She trotted from the bathroom and said, "I'll go see," tossed her tweezers on the bed and whisked out, pulling the door closed. She didn't seem scared. In a state of rigid fear, I hurt with listening. I was listening for her. *If I slow down my heart I will know what's going on.* My legs, crossed under me, began to cramp.

She came back in, hand at her chest. "Quickly," she said, and she grabbed me and shut us both in her bathroom, turning the latch that had never turned. I was impressed. Her other hand was still at her shirtfront, fingers moving up her chest, flicks at the pearly buttons. "Be very still, love. He'll go away."

We stood in the bathtub, the cold off the porcelain shooting up my nightie, and she thrust up the aged, grumpy window that I couldn't remember ever having seen open. My grandmother was getting out of a cab, and my mother yelled, "Don't come up! Get the police!"

The police must have come, interviewing my mother elsewhere in the apartment, noting what she told them had disappeared. Back in the sickbed, I sat with Nana, her dry hands warm around mine, soft little pats. My elegant mother was with policemen. She had again lived through an extraordinary day.

My mother told me later the burglar had stolen the silver. "I let him take it," she said. "I let him do whatever he wanted so he wouldn't come in here and get you." She showed me how he'd forced open the antique sideboard to get at the silver (the drawer never sat right again). She'd led him to the other end of our apartment, all the way to my little bedroom. After that, she would often say into the phone, "I didn't want Sue to hear anything."

Coming into her room one day when she didn't expect me, I heard her say, "I let him rape me." She saw the look on my face, hung up and had me sit down.

"He *raped* you?"

"I didn't want you to know that part," she said. "I let him rape me. So he wouldn't come for you."

I still had the image in mind of her hand on her buttons, buttoning up. That's what it had meant. Everything crowded together in my head: the disappearing Afro, her calm and the closed door, me protected and paralyzed on the bed, the word *rape* and the way she said it as if it was a sexy word, her unbuttoned shirt, the looted silverware I'd never known we owned. And my favorite nightshirt was gone, a long lavender T-shirt with a decal of Clark Gable's face. "I had to tell the police about it," she said. "It was evidence. He used it to cover my face while—so I couldn't look at him." Later still, she returned the nightshirt to me and told me the police had found the man. "And how did they know?" she said. "Because *your* nightshirt was there in his apartment. It's because of you they caught him. Think of that."

I didn't make a choice to believe her, didn't know I could. She said, and I believed. I can't know what happened; I listened to what happened.

Go back another year: The maid's room in our apartment was tiny, and my single bed bisected the middle as if its head and foot kept the walls apart. I got to move in when I was eight, a special treat to leave my sister and have my own room. The bed divided the room—one section by the window could be reached by crossing over it, the floor covered with cast-off clothes and books. On the other side I had the door, dresser, bedside table and an orange clock that flipped each number over. The shag rug ate up dimes and earrings. The furniture was so tightly arranged that the edge of the door, opening or shutting, whispered against the bed, *shoosh*. Below the knob the lock had been painted and overpainted, and the door wouldn't latch fully. "This is really cramped," my mother would say, but I liked it. For the first time I had privacy. She wouldn't climb over the bed to get to the other side, so I could keep stuff there. After she came in for good night, I would crawl down the bed and reach for the light switch. I'd try to lie down before the room changed to dark. I knew it wasn't possible, but I liked these private games.

A few weeks after I moved we had our routine established: I went off to my room for bed, allowed to read until my mother appeared. She often forgot, distracted by putting Penelope to bed in her room or by a phone call or a boiling kettle. After fifteen minutes I began to thrill at the top of each page, race to its end before she came. On the nights she wasn't at home, I'd read coiled for action if I heard the elevator land, her singing, breathy voice as she brought someone through the front door. When she came into my room, she'd bend over me, planting two fists on either side of my pillow to support her babied back. We kissed on the lips, and she'd whisper, "I love you, love you, love you." *Shoosh* the door would almost shut on her way out, muffling her noises in the kitchen.

That night I waited, reading. She had a friend over. When I caught her sound I paced her progress through the apartment until she got to me.

"Still up, bad girl?" she said, a scold she didn't mean. "Time's up. Your sister's been asleep for ages." She tidied my covers and pulled the quilt to my chin. She lowered to give me my kiss, and her head blocked the overhead light. Then, with no prelude, she went into a seizure. She had convulsions, minutes and minutes of them; no, seconds. Her eyes stayed open the whole time. She was suspended in massive close-up, an earthquake. She collapsed, and her body forced the quilt around my arms, binding them against me. It pushed at my neck because her weight was on my chest and hips.

She was dead. I was scared there was a dead person on top of me. I squirmed and called, "Mummy! Mummy!" and made a space and was able to push her up and off, I don't know how. She tumbled back and crashed against the door, which shoved all the way closed. Her skull thudded against the wood, and her face was strange. I didn't want to look because I thought I had broken her neck. I wanted to get out, but her body blocked the door. What if I'm never able to open it? I was trapped. I remembered the friend across the apartment, but I couldn't make anything come out of my mouth. I'd lost my voice.

I got my foot between her body and the bed and used my weight to heave against her. I kept shoving, but she kept slipping back. There was only the tiniest second to grab at the doorknob and pull before she fell again, and I wasn't fast enough. I wanted her face to come back to life. I forced her aside a tiny bit and wedged myself through the door, which slammed shut after me. I was scared we wouldn't be able to open it again and rescue her. I ran to get the friend, and she started banging against the door. She yelled and pushed.

"Don't hurt her!" I shouted. The door would force at my mother's spine. This terrified me. The friend got in, stepping over my mother, and pulled her onto my bed so she could get her hands under her armpits. Then she dragged her back to her room.

I was shivering too hard to talk. The friend came back to the kitchen and poured brandy in a glass and handed it to me, telling me it would get me to stop shaking. I didn't think it would, but I drank it. It tasted like a sore throat and made my chest hot. She gave me some more and told me to go to bed. She said, "Your mother's fine."

I don't know if I ever told my mother. She may not know this happened to me.

Five years earlier: Provincetown, my two parents, me three years old. Upstairs in a white bathroom her arms reached for me, her rolled cuffs and her wrists wet as she slid her hands under my ticklish arms and lifted me over the porcelain wall of the tub. The breeze came through the dark window and touched the water streaming from my hair down my back. I was cold. She crouched (knees snap), she reached behind me and produced a towel. She talked in the best tiny song. She flicked her magic hands and the towel settled over my shoulders, cold gone, as she tightened it around me, binding my shoulders, arms, legs, and in the same move tugging me close, my head at her shoulder. Her arms hugged me around the outside of the towel, tightening further its snug grip, and she rubbed the water off, and it made me warm, and I was sleepy. How soft and good I felt. That was everything: the drying in her hands, the home in the towel, the sweet relief of her arms where I could stop the day. My body dropped against her, and she lifted the whole of me wrapped in the towel and carried me to my bed.

I stored this gesture of motherhood in my arms, so that without thinking about it I lift my children from the water and rub them warm with the towel. I bind them tight, hold them against me, whisper into their hair. I know this love. It's the single moment of parenting in which I'm certain I am doing the right thing, in which, without review, I yield to an instinct.

I am made by the remembering. The last crossing of the *Queen Mary* is my origin, although the name of that ship was the SS *Statendam,* and that wasn't its final voyage. It's how my mother put it. It's how I put it. She told me she made love in my high school dorm room, and I spent the year sleeping on a bed she'd christened with sex, her folly my foundation. I thought I liked eggs softly scrambled. One day as I stirred eggs in the pan for my sons, using a wooden spoon as my mother had taught me, it dawned on me that I didn't like soft eggs at all. She did. I liked them firm. I was thirty-eight years old, and it still took me days to believe that.

I'm all the ways she was right—about Charles Jourdan shoes and the splashy frivolity of cash; about *The Good Soldier*; that I'd return to Greece; that you downshift to second when turning a corner; that beauty matters; right about the delicious weight in a Montblanc pen; that Christopher would want children. She saw that writing was crucial to my life, and she was right that preserving the immediacy of pain is tricky. It isn't something you want to do.

I also stow her wrongs—the confusing slur, the fat syringes filled with Demerol, her lascivious way with "coccyx," the heedless pickups on the dance floor, her unchecked violence, the fortunes gone on cocaine, her casual report that any vibration can give you an orgasm, "for instance, Sue—that electric toothbrush you had? I used that." She was wrong that the lie broadens the world. I'm a liar's daughter so I doubt everything I'm told. I doubt myself. I tell the story of my own experience and wonder at the crazy details.

When my mother was dying, I didn't go. I ask every day, Is this right? Every day I consider and think and answer, It is. Like love or grief the decision is stitched into me. It is me, and it beats at me with a "Yes, but." I continue to ask, What kind of person doesn't go to her mother's deathbed? What will my sons understand of family from their mother, who didn't go? The questions cannot be answered in the way we ask and answer, seeking the solution, the collective understanding. They cannot be answered except by me. I chose to stay away from my mother, a choice someone makes because she has to. Not because I preferred home, couldn't afford the plane tickets, wouldn't forgive her. I didn't go because I couldn't. That's what had become of us.

For the two weeks after my mother's wreck I walked around saying, "She won't die." She never died.

"She won't die," I said, exhausted and cynical from her bad back and affairs, her injections, rapes, disappearances.

I said, "She won't die." My mother invented the waters, sky and terrain; she couldn't leave them.

My mother didn't die. She had had, finally, an ordinary disaster. Her car wreck and surgeries were grave. She recovered slowly in a sad, painful story, which includes details I'll never know. I have chosen not to know.

My sister stopped talking to me after that. News came to me second- and third-hand, and I didn't feel a right to more. Penelope had suspended her own life and spent two months in Barbados, while I stayed at home, dressed my children, took Daniel to school, comforted myself with their routine bedtimes. Penelope sat in some hard hospital chair and read get-well cards aloud to our mother, talked antibiotics with the nurse and made friends of other daughters at other bedsides. When our mother was released, my sister flew home. I wanted to call her, but I was ashamed, and I was afraid of her anger. It would be another year before we spoke.

Penelope agreed to see me, and I went to our old apartment. I had come to let her be angry. We hugged in the hall. As grown women we'd never been easy together, but we couldn't pass up this relief. Even the redolence of her perfume was a comfort. She showed me in, stalked to the mantel and lit a cigarette. Most of the furniture had been delivered one manic afternoon when we were young after our mother went on a spree. The upholstery had turned dingy from summer after summer in front of open windows. Living there, my sister probably didn't notice. She and her husband had added a dining table where they gave Sunday luncheons for twelve, she'd once told me, with lamb and wine and roasted potatoes.

"What would you like?" She sounded like a receptionist. She marched to the kitchen. I looked at her slim black trousers, snakeskin cowboy boots and the clean white shirt with the cuffs turned up once. A dozen gold bangles on her tan wrist. I was dressed, by habit, for my children, in roomy denim, washable cotton. I didn't want anything, didn't want the guest's debt, but I couldn't resist making her do something for me. I asked for water, and she poured San Pellegrino into a glass I didn't recognize. I noted out loud changes to the apartment.

"You got a new fridge."

"We've had that forever," she said. I didn't know which "we" she meant.

I followed her to the living room. She stood by the open window, cocking her head to blow smoke out. I sat down near her in one of two chairs. She looked different, altered by strain. The midday noise from Lexington Avenue made our silence a little less awkward, but not much. I took sips of the water, held the glass in my lap. Between us stood a handsome table our parents had brought over from England, its finish dulled with water marks, little nicks in its legs. She continued to stare out the window, and I waited.

Finally, she sat down. She looked at me for the first time. "I had to do *everything*." She smashed her cigarette out. "*You* did nothing."

"I know," I said. "Yes. You did." I forced myself to look at her eyes. "I made a mistake." I'd never said this out loud, and it surprised me to name another corner of the decision. I didn't mean I was sorry, because I was not sorry for me. I was miserable for us. I couldn't fathom her fear in the hospital. "I should have been with you," I said.

"Would you make the same choice again?" Her sarcasm cut me off: there was no question about the way Susy had *always* been. Then she asked more urgently, "Would you?"

I let a long time pass. I couldn't think "no" and couldn't think "yes," although I was waiting for one of them. Waiting again. How many times would I consider the decision? Penelope was inspecting my face as if to catch me in something. I hadn't come for forgiveness, but sitting in front of my sister I needed her to ask about my sorrows, too. She had hers, vigilant beside our mother's bed; Daphne had hers, more pain for an already ravaged body. And I had made an impossible decision, which unearthed the true calamity of being daughter to this mother.

"Penelope."

"Yeah, well."

"Thank you for—"

"*Don't* thank me. Don't *you*."

Our habit for years had been to ramble through afternoons. Decide on a movie. Go into department stores, browse makeup counters. After I had Daniel, then Jack, she'd meet us at the Natural History Museum, or walk through the park with me and the stroller, chatting expansively and answering her cell phone as I doled out Cheerios to the baby. It seemed mandatory today we should spend more hours together, but we had nothing to talk about except our mother, our corrupted center.

"Okay, I have to go," I said, hunting for a reason if she asked why, but she stood up to walk me to the door. We said good-bye. We had to hug because that's what we always did, but she made no characteristic quip. In the empty moment where the wisecrack would have been, I felt so lonely. My shirt would smell of her smoke and perfume later, and I'd still hate that. I went out to the hallway. Penelope stood holding our front door, ready to close it when I stepped onto the elevator.

New York streets weren't home to me anymore. In Missoula for ten years, I'd lost the native skill of seeking the tiny voids between pedestrians. I walked through the park to my father's apartment for dinner.

My stepmother perched on a stool beside the hospital bed, where my father lay with his shoulders elevated. He could move his head, had some range in his neck, and as I came into the room he lifted his chin at me, animal emphasis. "Look who's here!" We ate Isabel's perfect pork roast and braised cauliflower. She fed him a bite from her fork, then herself, and I sat in a chair with my plate on my lap. A straw stood at an angle in my father's glass of red wine.

"Tell us about Penelope," Isabel said.

"Yes, how did she look?" my father said. He hadn't seen her in years, and she didn't return his calls. One daughter went this way, the other that. My mother and Penelope used to ridicule me. "How can you bear him? He's so mean, so pretentious." They couldn't understand how I could forgive him. One day it occurred to me I had nothing to defend. I loved being with my father. Yes, he, too, had scared me in childhood, betrayed his duty. He could hurt my feelings, still exasperate me with his self-absorption, but we enjoyed each other. I no longer dreaded his disapproval or swallowed my opinions. We had our complications, but that's another story.

"She looked tired," I said. "She's worried about Daphne."

"Of course."

"Yes," I said. "Of course."

We talked of friends, joking in a shorthand of references. It felt good, the family I belonged in. Five days in New York, I'd gone to an Iranian movie, eaten some chic meals, met a friend's new baby. We talked about those things, about the boys' teachers, Christopher's work, Isabel's work, a play my father was translating from French. Isabel remembered a cashmere jacket she'd found for me in a thrift shop and left the room to get it from the closet.

Had I seen that article in the *TLS,* or those important Dutch drawings at the Frick? I had not. My father raised an eyebrow, and I raised mine back.

"I'll miss you, Sue," my father said. "Why do you live so far away?"

I pulled my chair close to the bed and set my head on his

chest. He pressed his chin against my hair, and he gave a soft growl as he did.

The next day I am to fly home. I'll arrive late, catch a ride from the inevitable acquaintance on the plane and greet the anxious dog at our front door. I'll brush my teeth, the bathroom windowsill cluttered with plastic animals. I'll slide into bed next to Christopher, welcome his kiss between my shoulder blades as he falls back asleep. In the morning, before light, first one boy then the other will climb into the bed, seeking our rituals. Jack will plant tiny kisses along my arm. I'll feel Daniel's mangy curls. We will batten down their flying limbs so as not to be jabbed too much. We will be laughing.